D1281994

RATIONAL ZEN

The Mind of Dōgen Zenji

TRANSLATED AND PRESENTED BY

THOMAS CLEARY

SHAMBHALA

Boston & London

1993

Shambhala Publications, Inc.
Horticultural Hall
300 Massachusetts Avenue
Boston, Massachusetts 02115

9 8 7 6 5 4 3 2 1

First Edition

Printed in the United States of America on acid-free paper ♾

Distributed in the United States by Random House, Inc., in Canada by Random
House of Canada Ltd

Library of Congress Cataloging-in-Publication Data

Cleary, Thomas F, 1949–
    Rational Zen, the mind of Dōgen Zenji/Thomas Cleary.—1st ed.
      p.   cm.
    Selected translation of the writings of Dōgen Zenji from Japanese.
    ISBN 0-87773-689-8 (acid free paper)
    1. Dōgen, 1200–1253. 2. Sōtōshū—Doctrines. I. Dōgen,
1200–1253. Selections. 1992. II. Title.
BQ9449.D657C44   1992   92-50126
294.3'927—dc20   CIP

CONTENTS

————

INTRODUCTION

Among the diverse roots of Japanese civilization, Buddhism is preeminent in providing an intellectual outlook that can transcend national cultures and sustain a genuine egalitarian global vision. This quality of Buddhism derives in part from its history as a spiritual culture absorbed by many different national and ethnic cultures and in part from the intrinsic nature of its philosophy. It is also the only universalistic thought ever widely accepted among the Japanese people.

The first and only major Buddhist work to be composed in the Japanese language is the colossal *Shōbōgenzō*, or *Treasury of Eyes of True Teaching*, composed by the brilliant thirteenth-century Zen master Dōgen Zenji. Neither the extraordinary literary quality nor the consummate metaphysical adroitness of this work has ever been surpassed in Japan; it stands on a par with the greatest of parallel literature throughout the world.

As a groundbreaking masterwork in what was for Buddhism a local and nonhieratic language, Dōgen's *Shōbōgenzō* was not only a landmark in Japanese and East Asian intellectual history; it also ranks in sophistication with similar achievements taking place at more or less the same time in Europe, West Asia, and Central Asia in the use of Catalan, Persian, and Tibetan languages to express the sacred knowledge of gnostic Christianity, Sufism, and Tantric Buddhism.

The critical influence of Zen Buddhism on Japanese culture has long been recognized in the West through the writings of the late D. T. Suzuki. Because his voluminous writings have had in turn so

1

much impact on Western ideas of Zen and Japanese culture, Suzuki's effect on Western attitudes was tremendous. The peculiar fact that his works disregard Dōgen Zenji, however, who was indisputably Japan's most intelligent and most articulate Zen master, has resulted in correspondingly distorted views of Zen and the Japanese culture and mentality.

This is not the first time Dōgen Zenji has been overlooked in Zen studies, in spite of the fact that his work is now recognized throughout the world for its extraordinary power of vision and expression. Dōgen's *Shōbōgenzō* was not published for five hundred years after his death, and for most of that time was not studied even in the Zen schools tracing their descent to his direct disciples.

During the eighteenth and nineteenth centuries, only members of the Sōtō schools of Zen read Dōgen; and most of them read very little of Dōgen's massive body of teachings. In the late nineteenth century, more than six hundred years after his passing, Dōgen was granted a *Daishi,* or "Great Master," title of honor by the Meiji emperor of Japan; and in the twentieth century his work became the subject of intense secular scrutiny, first in Japan, then throughout the world.

Nevertheless, while intellectuals worked to draw meanings from a difficult text with no historical transmission, Dōgen was virtually ignored in D. T. Suzuki's popular presentations of Zen and Japanese culture to mass Western audiences, which included a whole range of interests from philosophers and artists to religious and secular intellectuals involved in the soft sciences. Not until recently did there begin to develop widespread recognition of Dōgen's work, still perceived but dimly through linguistic and conceptual barriers.

Most of Dōgen's teaching is encapsulated in two works: the aforementioned *Shōbōgenzō (Treasury of Eyes of True Teaching)* and the *Eihei Kōroku (Universal Book of Eternal Peace).* The former work is a collection of essays, the latter mostly speeches and poems, with a few letters and essays. Many of the essays in *Shōbōgenzō* were also read in person by Dōgen to his circle; most of his speeches in *Eihei Kōroku,* collected by two of his most accomplished

2

successors, also appear to have been written down or outlined in notes by Dōgen himself.

There are numerous formal differences between the two masterworks of this great Zen teacher. *Shōbōgenzō* is bilingual, written in Japanese with an admixture of Chinese; *Eihei Kōroku* is recorded in Chinese, as was customary among learned Buddhists in Japan at that time. *Shōbōgenzō* is relatively prolix, like most literary Japanese, its main language; *Eihei Kōroku* is generally laconic, which is more typical of Chinese, especially Zen Chinese. *Shōbōgenzō* is more innovative in form, *Eihei Kōroku* is more traditional in form. *Shōbōgenzō* demonstrates Dōgen's virtuosity as a master of pan-Buddhism; *Eihei Kōroku* shows his mastery of Zen.

There are, naturally, more fundamental underlying similarities between these two works. First and foremost, they are one in their aim, which is to liberate and enlighten the whole mind. Second, in pursuit of this aim, both works are extremely intense in their presentation of ideas. Third, they are richly arrayed with quotations and allusions from pan-Buddhist and Zen lore. These three characteristics pervade both *Shōbōgenzō* and *Eihei Kōroku*.

All of the above factors in Dōgen's work combine to present special problems in translation. There is so much meaning in Dōgen's every turn of phrase that for the translator no practical alternative exists, in a host culture lacking the corresponding centuries of Buddhist background, but to provide parallel explanations in ordinary language. The translations contained in this volume are therefore analyzed and expounded in the annotations with reference to pan-Buddhist and Zen traditions.

With the exception of paragraphing, which did not exist in classical Japanese writing and has been introduced for the convenience of modern readers, the translations in this volume follow the original structure, content, and meaning of Dōgen's own writings and speeches, in order to enable the reader to accompany the mind of the Zen master as it soars through the skies of enlightenment.

In addition to the translations and explanations of Dōgen's works, translations of direct reference materials from source traditions are also included to assist the reader in practical corroboration of the principles elucidated in *Shōbōgenzō* and *Eihei Kōroku*.

ON ZEN BUDDHISM

Buddhism includes a wide variety of principles and practices, presented in a vast number of scriptures and treatises and organized into many different systems and schools. Overall, Zen Buddhism does not hold to a fixed system of philosophy and is not based on a particular text, but throughout its history it has employed and incorporated elements from Buddhist scriptures and schools when and as they have been useful. The absence of a standardized system, in spite of the existence of temporary local systems, is due to the Zen Buddhist emphasis on suiting the teaching to the specific needs of the learner.

The stress placed in Zen Buddhism on the specificity of instruction and adaptation of application according to the particular situation gave rise to a large and variegated body of teaching material, much of which would seem to contain a great deal of contradiction and controversy if it were laid side by side and regarded as representative of static doctrine rather than dynamic effect. Throughout the history of Zen Buddhist teaching, it has been the practice to select appropriate material from available didactic lore and then amplify or, when necessary, modify the use of the items selected in accord with the imperatives generated by current local conditions.

One of the main sources of Zen lore was the sayings and stories of the masters. These sayings and stories contain the patterns of Zen insights and techniques, so they were often used for the purpose of recollection and discussion. The Tang dynasty of China (618–906) and the era of the Five Dynasties following it (907–960) are usually considered the classical age of Zen; many simple statements of basic Zen attitudes and practices are to be found in the sayings of the teachers of those times.

Zen Buddhism lays great emphasis on understanding the mind

as the crucial pivot of all experience. The following statement by Huangbo (Ōbaku), one of the greatest of the Tang dynasty Zen masters, illustrates a rather typical Zen presentation of the doctrine of inherent enlightenment:

"All Buddhas and ordinary people are just one mind. . . . This mind is beyond all measurements, names, oppositions: this very being is it; as soon as you stir your mind you turn away from it."[1]

The "stirring of the mind" to which the Zen master refers is what scriptural Buddhist traditions calls the Buddha entering into other states of being, straying from inherent enlightenment. In Zen terms, a deluded conception of Buddhahood as a state to be acquired is not a suitable basis for attaining enlightenment. Huangbo's statement continues, "It's just that ordinary people cling to forms and seek outwardly. The more you see Buddhahood, the more you lose it. If you employ Buddha to seek Buddha, if you try to grasp mind by mind, you will never succeed all your life. You do not realize that if you cease thought and forget cogitation, Buddha will spontaneously appear."[2]

Huangbo also elaborates on how to become aware of the original mind: "Just recognize the original mind in perception and cognition, remembering that the original mind is not *in* perception and cognition, yet not apart from perception and cognition. Just don't produce views and opinions on top of perceptions and cognitions, don't stir thoughts on perceptions and cognitions, don't seek mind outside perception and cognition, don't abandon perception and cognition to grasp for truth. Not identifying, not rejecting, not dwelling, not sticking, you will be free in all ways, and everywhere is the site of enlightenment."[3]

It is often emphasized that the goal of Zen Buddhism is not some kind of altered state of consciousness. On the contrary, the aim of Zen Buddhism is to become immune to being conditioned into altered states. In this context, furthermore, "altered states" are defined even more rigorously than in conventional psychological theory, from the perspective of the pure original mind rather from that of the local parameters of conventional consciousness. Guishan (Isan), another great Chinese Zen master of the Tang dynasty, said,

"The mind of people of the Way is straightforward and unartificial, neither ignoring nor inclining, with no deceptive errant mind; at all times their perception is normal. There are no further details. Also, don't shut the eyes and ears; as long as feelings don't stick to things, that is enough."[4]

As suggested by this statement, Zen Buddhism does not teach escapism, chronic withdrawal, or denial of ordinary reality. The late Tang dynasty master Caoshan (Sōzan) said, "There is no need to avoid or escape anything; just know about it, that's enough. If you try to avoid it, it's still affecting you. Just don't be changed or affected by things, and you'll be free."[5]

Nevertheless, the need for practical steps to actually accomplish the liberation of mind from the strictures of temporal conditioning is affirmed in Zen Buddhist teaching, with the provision that such techniques are expedients and not sacred in themselves: as the late Tang master Yangshan (Gyōzan) explained, "From the beginningless past you have turned your back on the light and plunged into darkness; the roots of your illusions are deep and cannot be pulled out all at once. That is why expedient techniques are set up to strip you of coarse consciousness. This is like using yellow leaves to stop a child from crying by pretending they are gold; it is not really so."[6]

Even the "sudden awakening" of which stories abound in Zen lore is not the end of this enterprise to free the mind. Guishan said, "One may become suddenly enlightened to the essence, but as there are still remaining habit energies from beginningless time that cannot be cleared away all at once, one must be taught to get rid of the compulsive habitual flow of consciousness. That does not mean, however, that there is a specific rule to have people practice or aim for."[7]

A typical model of this Zen Buddhist process of mental clarification is the image of death and rebirth. The great Tang dynasty master Dongshan (Tōzan) said, "If you want to know this thing, you should be like a withered tree producing flowers."[8] Caoshan, his Zen successor, explained, "The beginner, knowing there is something fundamental in oneself, turns awareness around to it

6

and then ejects sense data to gain tranquillity. Then, after having accomplished that, one doesn't cling to sense data, is not confused while in their very midst, and lets them be, without hindrance."⁹

The custom of using extracts from ancient Zen lore developed greatly in the tenth and eleventh centuries in China during the colorful Song dynasty. These extracts might be used for illustrative purposes, for testing the mentalities of students through their reactions and interpretations, or as points of meditation concentration. With this activity grew the practice of adding replies, rejoinders, alternatives, substitutions, and comments to the classical materials.

These elaborations might function to describe the pattern of a story or saying to amplify or illustrate the point, to bring out abstruse implications, or to express something left unsaid, particularly a complementary perspective. Zen expressions such as "praising and censuring" and "holding up sideways and using upside down" were coined to refer to this adaptive use of ancient lore in specific teaching situations.

The use of poetry to illustrate Zen stories was particularly popular from the Song dynasty onwards, and Zen literature abounds with such specially crafted works. Several collections of Zen stories with comments in prose and verse were compiled in China between the eleventh and thirteenth centuries, and many more comments on those and other stories are to be found in the recorded talks of the teachers from this and subsequent eras.

The use of old stories and sayings in individual meditation and in the interactions between teacher and student in Chinese Zen is also recorded to some extent, but most of this information is apparently unwritten. It is nevertheless clear from existing evidence that the practice of confronting Zen seekers with anecdotes of ancient Zen masters had become a well-established part of Chinese Zen by the end of the twelfth century.

Specialized institutions for Zen teaching appear to have begun in seventh-century China, during the early Tang dynasty, as the charisma of some of the great Zen masters attracted growing public attention. At the same time, there arose among Zen teachers themselves a tradition of criticizing the very notion of institution-alized teachership, because enlightenment as understood by the Zen masters is not in doctrine and not an external entity to be attained: the classical teacher Baizhang (Hyakujō) said, "If one should say, 'I am capable of explaining, I can understand; I am the teacher, you are the disciple,' this is the same as demonic sugges-tion."[10]

Very early on in their history, Zen masters observed that insti-tutions tend to become, sooner or later, breeding grounds for rivalry and ambition; Baizhang said, "Even to be called a renun-ciant because of the search for unsurpassed enlightenment and ultimate peace is still a false ambition; how much more so is worldly disputation, seeking to prevail, claiming one's own ability and understanding, seeking a following, favoring a particular disciple, becoming attached to a dwelling place, making a pact with a patron for a robe, a meal, a reputation, an advantage."[11]

Large numbers of people were attracted to Zen for a variety of reasons, and many of them entered Zen orders with dubious intentions. The ninth-century Zen treatise *Admonitions* by Gui-shan, who was one of the greatest Zen masters of the late Tang dynasty, is devoted almost entirely to criticizing such discordant elements within the Zen monasteries. The treatise describes a whole syndrome of ills plaguing the Zen communities: lack of individual discipline, lack of communal order, lack of Buddhist learning, primary interest in guaranteed supply of food, clothing, and shelter.[12]

A tenth-century treatise from the Five Dynasties era by Fayan (Hōgen), another leading Chinese Zen master, gives a more de-tailed account of failings in contemporary Zen teachers and stu-dents. Fayan prefaces his treatise with a statement that in thirty years of travels he had found few real adepts among the numerous, well-populated Zen centers he visited; he then proceeds to describe ten forms of corruption he found endemic to institutionalized Zen.

The first problem he analyzes is the age-old sickness of teaching Zen without being enlightened oneself. Since earliest times Zen masters emphasized the need to be actually illuminated oneself before attempting to teach others how to become enlightened.

The second problem is sectarianism, which had already arisen by the tenth century. Here Fayan stresses the point that Zen is not a thing in itself, not a fixed system of doctrine or ritual; as various techniques and schools developed, however, people eventually came to cling to the outgrowths and forget the basic reality. There are many references to the ills of sectarianism throughout Buddhist literature, particularly that of original Zen Buddhism.

The third problem is a corollary of the first: trying to teach Zen without knowing when and how to actually employ the various techniques of Zen method. Here Fayan mentions such common devices as "refuting and upholding," which have to be used at precisely the right time and in the right situation in order to have the desired effect. Fayan complains that many Zennists were just making up imitation teachings based on conceptual models of Zen terminology.

The fourth problem Fayan brings up is a subset of the third; this is the degenerate practice of replying to questions without adequate consideration of the time and situation, failing to see the source of the matter, instead arbitrarily imitating the sayings and actions of ancient teachers. Since ancient times it had been said that every period of true teaching would be followed by a period of imitation.

Fayan then discusses the failure to comprehend both emptiness and phenomena, both absolute and relative realities. Dōgen Zenji was also particularly keen on resolving this problem. Concern with phenomena without realization of emptiness results at best in understanding on an intellectual plane alone, without realizing the liberation of mind. Emphasis on absolute emptiness alone, on the other hand, tends to produce nihilism and decadence.

The next problem analyzed by Fayan is the fashion of making arbitrary personal judgments of Zen koans, sayings, and stories of inner meaning, without refinement and clarification of the mind. This process of clarification, insofar as it concerns Zen stories, involves deep meditation on the stories, both individually and together with an enlightened guide. In Japan, where problems surrounding Zen crypticisms were exaggerated by a language gap, Dōgen Zenji's bilingual Chinese-Japanese presentations of Zen koans address this issue by a process of detailed in-depth analysis.

The seventh form of decadence in Zen schools, according to Fayan's diagnosis, is the practice of memorizing slogans and sticking to a teacher's way without reaching one's own enlightenment and finding the ability to function independently. According to ancient Zen lore, genuine continuation of Zen transmission requires that the disciple ultimately transcend the teacher. This reemphasizes the point made earlier on in the treatise that the aim of Zen is freedom rather than the perpetuation of given doctrines and forms.

The eighth problem Fayan points out is the failure to master the classical Buddhist scriptures and wrongly adducing scriptural proofs for personalistic statements. Here Fayan says that Zen students who do not understand the principles of the scriptures should concentrate on the Zen way rather than glibly misuse the scriptures, while those who just flaunt their scriptural learning should be taught to quiet their minds in the Zen way.

The ninth unwholesome lapse Fayan finds in Zen tradition is the practice of making up songs and verses without proper care for expression and without having arrived at reality. Here Fayan emphasizes the point that literature should be functional in a true Zen sense, and not be allowed to deteriorate into an idle diversion. As a didactic tool, literature should be constructed with knowledge and careful attention to its use and function.

The tenth flaw Fayan saw in the Zen schools was the habit of defensiveness and contentiousness; in their zeal to be considered enlightened Zen masters, people took to putting on airs and trying to outdo others. Self-criticism is a significant part of Buddhist practice, to help improve the moral and mental state; to defend one's own shortcomings is considered worse than the original offense or defect, because it impedes the way to self-correction and self-improvement. It is for this reason that the most telling criticism of Zen schools derives from Zen masters themselves.[13]

In addition to such individual critical works as those of the great classical masters Guishan and Fayan in the ninth and tenth centuries, a great deal of admonitory material appears in the conversations and correspondence of Zen masters of the eleventh, twelfth, and thirteenth centuries. In these we can see mounting concerns over the decadence of Zen communities, with particular emphasis on the role of the abbot. One of the leading Song dynasty masters wrote,

> Recently we see abbots in various places with mind tricks to manipulate and control the members of the community, while members of the community serve the abbot with ulterior motives of influence, power, and profit. Abbots and members trade off, fooling each other. How can the teaching prosper and the communities flourish?[14]

By this time, the main exoteric Zen centers in China were large public monasteries supported by land grants, with the entire public monastic system under the control of the government. There was tremendous interest in Zen on the part of Confucian literati, from among whom came many officials of the Chinese bureaucracy. The close association of secular officials at all levels with Zen establishments provided a breeding ground for ambitions that Zen had long eschewed:

> In nominating abbots for public monasteries, it is imperative to nominate those who preserve the Way, those who are at peace and are modest, those who when nominated will grow stronger in will and integrity, those who won't ruin the communal endowment wherever they go but will fully develop the community, those who are masters of the teaching. They will rescue the present day from decadence. As for wily deceiving tricksters who have no sense of shame, who skillfully flatter and wait on authority, who cleave to powerful upper class families—why should they be nominated?[15]

This kind of teaching also found its way into secular literature, prized for its value in defining ideals of civil leadership as well. As far as the Zen institutions were concerned, the relationship of the abbots to the outside world naturally had its effect on the institution. The relationship of the abbot with the community of Zen seekers and practitioners was also perforce an issue of paramount concern, involving the exercise of special degrees of awareness and effort:

> There is essentially nothing to abbothood but carefully observing people's conditions, to know them all, whatever their station. When people's inner conditions are thoroughly understood, then inside and outside are in harmony. When leaders and followers communicate, all affairs are set in order. This is how Zen leadership is maintained.
>
> If one cannot precisely discern people's psychological conditions, and the feelings of followers is not communicated to the leaders, then leaders and followers oppose each other and affairs are disordered. This is how Zen leadership goes to ruin.
>
> It may happen that the leader will rest on brilliance and often hold biased views, not comprehending people's feelings, rejecting community counsel and giving importance to his own authority alone, neglecting public consideration and practicing private favoritism.
>
> This causes the road of advancement in goodness to become narrower and narrower, and causes the path of responsibility for the community to become fainter and fainter. Such leaders repudiate what they have never seen or heard before, and become set in their ways, to which they become habituated and which thus veil them.
>
> To hope that the leadership of such people would be great and far reaching is like walking backward trying to go forward.[16]

Concern with the quality of leadership also extended to the nomination of monks to perform the tasks of the monastic bureaucracy. Not only did the organizational maintenance and order of the monastic community depend to a great extent on these officers, but these individuals were expected to be models of Zen realization as well. For these reasons, criticism of the spiritual decline in Zen establishments also touched upon the issues and problems involved in choosing people for higher-level duties. Here are important statements on the qualities of officials, made by several of the leading Zen masters of the Song dynasty:

> The position of the leader of the assembly in a Zen monastery is a rank for which the virtuous and wise are to be chosen; but nowadays in various places they don't question whether the monks are good or bad, and all use this post as a steppingstone for their ambitions. This is also the fault of the teaching masters. Now in this age of imitation it is hard to find anyone suitable; if you choose for this rank those whose practice is a bit better and those whose virtue is a bit more complete, who are modest and upright, then that would be better than those who rush ahead precipitously.[17]

> Students with intelligence and perception, truthfulness and integrity, are the best. Those whose intelligence is not so lofty but who are careful and have good judgment are next best. Those who may harbor wrong ambitions and change along with the power structure are really petty people; if you put them in front of others, it will surely destroy the community and pollute the teaching.[18]

> In general, when people are sincere and rightly oriented, even if they are dull they are still employable. If they are flatterers with ulterior motives, even if they are smart they are ultimately harmful. If their attitude is not good, they are in the final analysis unworthy of establishment in positions of service and leadership even if they have talent and ability.[19]

One of the sources of corruption in Zen schools was the misinterpretation of the meaning and place of certain kinds of negation in scriptures and Zen teachings. It is well known that many Buddhist writings contain remarks denying the absolute validity or ultimateness of all doctrines and methods. One purpose of such statements is to call attention to the point that adherence to religious forms is not in itself an indication of real worth. Far from being enlightening, such adherence can even become an obstacle to collective realization of reality, as one Song dynasty Zen master explained in these terms: "When those whose conduct in everyday life is bad, and who have a history of being no good, are known as such in the community, this is not worrisome. What is really worrisome is when people attribute sagehood to those who are inwardly corrupt."[20]

Negation of means, to prevent the habit-forming mind from lapsing into mechanical repetition and lifeless formality, also has the sense of transcending such means *after* they have accomplished their purpose. The classical scriptural simile for this is that of a raft, which is to be left behind once the shore has been reached: "Even the religion is to be abandoned," the famous passage of the *Diamond Cutter Scripture* reads; "how much more that which is contrary to it."

The danger of taking transcendental statements like this as doctrines in themselves, however, is that one may fall into a kind of antinomianism, rejecting the means before the result is effected. Evidently this trend was rife during the Song dynasty, as one of the masters points out: "In the Zen communities wherever you go, there is a false teaching rampant according to which discipline, meditation, and knowledge are unnecessary; and it is unnecessary to cultivate virtue or get rid of craving. Talk like that is not only creating harm to the Zen communities in the present day, it is actually the bane of the teaching for ten thousand ages."[21] There is no doubt that this particular trend of laissez-faire, decadent Zen was transmitted to Japan from Song China; Dōgen was particularly active in rectifying this misconception of Zen.

The idea that Buddhism would eventually become imitative, and finally fall into terminal decay, had itself been a part of Buddhist historical consciousness long before Zen emerged as a distinct movement. This conception does reflect, to a remarkable extent, repeated cycles of rise and decline and renewal of Buddhism in different forms. The notion of this model as referring to one time frame—Buddhism beginning with Gautama Buddha, entering a period of imitation five hundred years later, and going into final decay another five hundred or a thousand years after that—was very strong in some areas, however, and was often used as an excuse for decadence, or as grounds for lament or despair. While

Zen masters definitely criticized the times, nevertheless there are clear denials, in accord with the doctrine of inherent Buddha-nature, that people themselves are inherently or essentially more corrupt in eras of decline:

Virtue, humanity, and righteousness do not belong to the ancients alone. People of today have them too; but because their knowledge is not clear, their study is not broad, their senses are not pure, and their wills are weak, they cannot carry them out powerfully. Eventually they are diverted by what they see and hear, which causes them to be unaware of their own state. It is all due to delusive conceptions and emotional thinking, piling up into a deep accumulation of habit that cannot be eliminated all at once. This is the only reason that people today do not reach the ranks of the ancients.[22]

All people have the spirit—it is just a matter of careful guidance. It is just like jade in the matrix: throw it away, and it is a rock; but cut and polish it, and it is a gem. It is also like water issuing from a spring: block it up and it makes a bog; open a deep channel for it and it becomes a river. So we know that in the ages of imitation teachings and remnant teachings, it is not simply that intelligence is lost or unused; there is also something lacking in the way of education and upbringing.[23]

Discussions of corrective measures in Song dynasty Zen lore often center, as a matter of course, on the qualities and example of the teacher. In the literature of the twelfth and thirteenth centuries there are numerous character sketches of outstanding Zen masters; some of them describe actual people, some represent ideals as defined by Zen teachers. Here again, emphasis is placed on the mental basis of personality and behavior; traditional principles of selflessness and nongrasping remain fundamental in both philosophy and practice:

Anyone called a Zen master should not crave anything at all, for as soon as one craves anything, one is plundered by externals. When you indulge in likes and desires, an avaricious mind arises; when you like getting alms, thoughts of striving and contention arise. If you like obedient followers, then petty flatterers will join you. If you like to score victories, the sense of self and others mounts. If you like to exploit people, there will be voices of resentment. When you get to the bottom of all this, it is not apart from one mind. If the mind is not aroused, everything spontaneously goes away.[24]

Outward cultivation of the person is emphasized in Zen teaching to the extent that it corresponds with inner development, or provides suitable conditions for such development within the individual and society. But in the absence of true mental regeneration, exclusive concern with externals, failing to realize their inner purpose, is considered a sign of decadence in Zen: as one distinguished Song master said, "Among the Zen communities of recent times, there are those who vigorously employ regulations, those who stick to regulations to the death, and those who slight regulations. All of them have turned away from the Path and lost the Principle."[25]

Classical Zen teaching is characterized by freedom from blind clinging to forms, employing forms as instruments rather than perpetuating them as idols, employing forms when, where, and as they are effective, discarding forms when they become obstructions. This approach to method is rooted in the teachings of the great Mahāyāna Buddhist scriptures, and was highlighted in early Zen traditions. It is not, however, invariably practiced in institutionalized settings because it requires supraconventional expertise and defies some of the most deeply seated of human tendencies. A Zen proverb says, "When one person transmits a falsehood, myriad people transmit it as truth."[26] The tendency to dogmatize and hallow the traces of temporary expedients appears again and again in history—not only in religious and cultural history, but also in the history of science. It is for this reason that so much of Zen teaching involves dismantling, superseding, and renewing in the visible dimension, even while its invisible aim remains constant throughout. As one of the greatest Song masters explains:

16

Zen teachers of true vision and great liberation have made changes in method along the way, to prevent people from sticking to names and forms and falling into rationalizations.

Over the course of the centuries, Zen has branched out into different schools with individual methods, but the purpose is still the same—to point directly to the human mind.

Once the ground of mind is clarified, there is no obstruction. You shed views and interpretations based on concepts like victory and defeat, self and others, right and wrong. Thus you pass through all that and reach a realm of great rest and tranquillity.

When an enlightened individual appears in the world and expounds various teachings according to people's mentalities, all of these teachings are expedients, just for the purpose of breaking through obsessions, doubts, intellectual interpretations, and egocentric ideas. If there were no such false consciousness and false views, there would be no need for enlightened people to emerge and expound so many teachings.[27]

THE TEACHINGS OF DŌGEN ZENJI

Buddhism and Methodological Relativism

Both scriptural and Zen Buddhist teachings, such as those cited above, state that the purpose of the enlightening teacher is not to construct a static philosophical or ceremonial system. The aim of Buddhism is in effect, which may be described as twofold: to untie the bonds that constrict the mind, and to help foster its most sophisticated abilities, including the capacity for adaptive evolution. There is an ancient maxim defining the common denominator of all Buddhism in effect as *liberation;* first liberation *from* bondage, then liberation *into* freedom. In pragmatic terms, this means that what Zen teachers *say* needs to be understood in light of what they are trying to *do.*

To approach Buddhism even on the intellectual plane it is helpful, even necessary, to bear in mind two important practical facts. One is that different procedures, which include frameworks of belief or attention as well as specific exercises, may achieve equal results; the other is that identical procedures may turn out to produce different results. There is also the fact that actual results obtained at any given time may or may not be those for which the procedures were originally intended. The sum effect depends on the many variables involved in the constitutions of the particular people concerned and their total milieu.

Mahāyāna Buddhist texts, particularly Zen Buddhist texts, represent these facts as part of their total teaching. Mindfulness of these principles helps those interested in Buddhism or Zen to avoid two extremes that tend to occur in the absence of this background consciousness. On the one hand there is dogmatism or panacea-type thinking on encountering particular descriptions of ways to enlightenment; on the other hand there is cynicism on encountering apparently contradictory statements, or on comparing gross empirical evidences of religious institutions with their professed ideals.

These considerations are especially relevant when considering a body of material as large and varied as the work of Dōgen Zenji, which rivals that of the greatest religious or philosophical authors in any culture. In the two main bodies of Dōgen's work, the *Shōbōgenzō* and the *Eihei Kōroku,* there is much material that is impossible to arrange into an outwardly consistent structure. This is very typical of Zen work, but the sheer mass of Dōgen's writings and speeches, and the nature of the transitional era in which his teaching evolved, make this feature stand out especially prominently in this particular case.

If one adopted the scholastic and cultic practice of assuming that Dōgen had a doctrine or philosophy, completely contradictory statements about it could be "proven" by isolating selected fragments of his writings or sayings. Since he was a Buddhist and a Zen master, however, Dōgen was not dealing in hidebound dogma but in progressive expediency and progressive transcendence, so he was not limited by any standpoint or system. His works thus contain a vast panorama of Buddhist teachings woven into a garland of universal and particular consciousness, not bound to any school or sect. In this they most resemble the structure of the *Flower Ornament Scripture,* which similarly contains the whole range of Buddhist teachings interwoven and was certainly one of Dōgen's major inspirations.

Rinzai Zen and Sōtō Zen

As seen in the treatise of guidelines for Zen schools by the great Chinese master Fayan, sectarianism within Zen had already arisen by the tenth century. When Dōgen went to China in the early thirteenth century, virtually all of the Zen sects but one—the Linji (Rinzai)—had disappeared. Most of the Zen teachers Dōgen consulted in China were of the Linji sect, but the one with whom he studied longest was of the nearly extinct Cao-Dong (Sōtō) sect.

Dōgen first studied Rinzai Zen in Japan, where it was taught along with reformed Tendai Buddhism in a new school founded by Yōsai, a Tendai Buddhist monk and Rinzai Zen master who passed away just as Dōgen was beginning his Zen studies. Yōsai had originally gone to China in the late twelfth century with the intention of traveling the overland route to India, in search of something to revitalize moribund Japanese Buddhism.

Failing to gain safe passage to India, Yōsai turned his attention to China, where he found a form of Buddhism unknown in Japan, which dominated not only China's religious world, but its whole intellectual and artistic world as well. This was the baroque Zen of the Southern Song dynasty, which influenced Confucians and Taoists, poets and painters, as well as Buddhists of all persuasions. Yōsai later returned to China for a longer stay, during which he apprenticed himself to a Rinzai Zen master.

Yōsai was welcomed back to Japan by the central Shogunate, the new military paragovernment, which was seeking a cultural base outside the traditional Tendai and Shingon schools of Buddhism intimately associated with the former social and political elites. A Zen center was built in the old capital of Kyoto; however, because of political pressures from long-established Tendai factions centered in Kyōto, Yōsai actually spent most of his time in a rural temple in one of the provincial islands. His public presentation of Zen, furthermore, was combined with traditional Tendai ritual practices.

Legend says that the teenage Dōgen was privately directed to Yōsai by one of his Tendai tutors, who was also one of his uncles. If Dōgen actually met Yōsai, their acquaintance was brief; most of Dōgen's Japanese Zen study was done with Myōzen, a student and successor of Yōsai. Although Dōgen worked with Myōzen for years and was eventually named his heir in the Yellow Dragon branch of the Rinzai sect, nevertheless Dōgen evidently felt something missing. Thus he ultimately decided to make the pilgrimage to China himself, and he even persuaded Myōzen to go along with him.

As for the rest of the heirs of Yōsai's line, the most prominent of the early Japanese schools of Rinzai Zen, Dōgen was critical of their growing extravagance and lack of discipline. After returning to Japan, Dōgen eventually repudiated this Japanese Zen movement, except for Yōsai himself and Myōzen, who had died in China. He did not repudiate Yellow Dragon Rinzai Zen, however, and quotations from the founder of the branch are prominent in the *Eihei Kōroku,* which generally contains Dōgen's Rinzai Zen teachings.

While Dōgen repudiated sectarianism not only in Zen but in Buddhism as a whole, he also specifically upheld the dignity and honor of his own lineages of transmission. While Dōgen's case against sectarianism is based on the fundamental Buddhist principle that there is only one objective truth in reality, the emphasis he came to place on his own lines of transmission seems to be an accommodation to the mentality of Japanese society.

Intensely concerned with matters of status, prestige, and lineage, Japanese society produced people greatly averse to being seen as doing anything unconventional or unknown. When the political fortunes of the prestigious Willow Branch school of Rinzai Zen rose in Japan under the patronage of the military government, it became necessary for Dōgen, whose background was in the minority sects of Sōtō Zen and Yellow Dragon Rinzai Zen, to reassure his students that their sources were at least as reputable as those of the followers of Willow Branch Rinzai Zen.

Although as an enlightened man Dōgen himself would not be concerned with prestige—and nothing in his life suggests that he ever exploited such prestige as came to him by birth and training— it was undoubtedly necessary for the concentration of his disciples, who by definition were not yet enlightened, to remove this distraction.

Dōgen even went so far as to show how the popularity of Willow Branch Rinzai Zen in Chinese high society had led to its own debasement, warning that this would happen immediately in Japan because the breeding ground had already been long established in the incestuous relationship between religious and political leadership.

The essential issue on which Dōgen thus indirectly focuses is the danger of dilettantism, going from one place to another on the basis of reputation, popularity, or similar superficial attraction. Criticisms of students merely seeking large and prosperous Zen communities appear in Chinese literature long before Dōgen's time. Such criticisms were directed at the attitude of the student, warning that attraction to famous and popular organizations is not a suitable working basis for Zen realization.

Dōgen also directed criticism at Rinzai Zen for a technical shortcoming, one that is also well documented in Chinese critical literature from within the Rinzai school itself. Some criticism is temporary, aiming at dislodging attention from fixation on one level of understanding to perception of another; some criticism is permanent, aiming at dislodging the very habit of fixation itself. In Dōgen's time this was necessary because of the rapid proliferation of Rinzai Zen schools with baffling new features that made it impossible for the Japanese people to discern the real and the complete from the imitation and the fragmentary.

At various points in Dōgen's Japanese *Shōbōgenzō* the same individual figure may be approved or disapproved, according to the quotation or anecdote under discussion. In such cases it is typical for Dōgen to praise or censure the *person,* not simply discuss principles. These are not actually personal or sectarian attacks, but applications of the practice of using the image of a person to represent a principle, one of the so-called Ten Mysterious Gates of Flower Ornament Buddhism. This is a diversionary measure, designed to focus or deflect the attention of the students according to their needs as perceived by the guide.

One characteristic of tactical Buddhist approaches to education is that they are based on the premise that they are, in Dōgen's own words, "facilities of nothingness," in the sense that they exist meaningfully in conditional expediency and are nothing in themselves. It is psychological reality, not philosophical abstractions, that may require something that is counterindicated under current circumstances to be portrayed as in itself useless or wrong. Thus for a teacher to declare something wrong or useless is likely to encounter less emotive resistance than to tell people personally that something is not right for them at this particular time, or that their understanding of it is worthless to them.

In shorter commentaries on Zen koans, hundreds of which are recorded in *Eihei Kōroku.* Dōgen does not use the device of vilifying representative persons. In many cases he brings up one or more sayings of senior Chinese Zen masters about the koan at hand, and then finally presents another perspective. This is traditional Zen commentarial style designed to foster rounded and progressive mental work with a koan; despite its superficial appearance, it is not a claim to having the last word.

There is no end to didactic manipulation of koans in Zen literature, involving techniques with such graphic labels as "praising and censuring," "conceding and denying," "killing and giving life." This activity is not in the realm of doctrine or dispute, but part of the dynamic character of the total work. When Dōgen is read in isolation this aspect of the teaching may seem unusually prominent, but it is actually quite typical of Song dynasty Zen, which was deeply concerned with counteracting mental stagnation at all levels of society, including within its own schools.

It is proverbial in Zen Buddhism that a statement may be "held up sideways or used upside down" by someone who is genuinely enlightened, in order to adapt it to the specific individual and the current situation. Classical commentaries on Zen lore warn against conceiving notions of victory and defeat or conventional right and wrong regarding the symbolic stories of interchanges among Zen illuminates.

In the context of Zen tradition sending down roots in medieval Japan, therefore, Dōgen's infamous vituperations were strategic Buddhist acts of enlightening the habitually ignorant. The personal note so often involved, which may be deceptive to the outside observer thinking in conventional social terms, is a traditional Buddhist symbolic device adapted to a society where the focus of attention and the object of following tend to be represented by persons rather than abstract principles, by historical figures, or mythological entities with personalities.

One of the main vehicles of Dōgen's critique of Rinzai Zen is his attack on the prestigious twelfth-century Chinese Willow Branch Rinzai Zen teacher Dahui (Daie), who was tremendously influential in the world of the Confucian intelligentsia as well as the world of Zen seekers. The influence and prestige of this great master naturally attracted Japanese students newly turning their interest to Zen in large numbers. This enthusiasm blinded them to certain facts. Dahui's fame was partly due to the nature of the specific task of learning he was given by his teacher; his mission in the overall operation of Zen, however important in his time, was limited in technical and temporal scope (and was in any case addressed to a society radically different from medieval Japan); last but not least, the radical methods he employed to promote a new Zen consciousness among Chinese intellectuals in an emergency are traditionally known for being susceptible to a rapid deterioration of effect in the hands of imitators.

What made these facts especially pertinent for Dōgen's own students was that most of them had come from a native Japanese Zen school started by an independent Zen master. This master, Nōnin, had been given approval by a famous Chinese Rinzai Zen master descended from Dahui who had met two of Nōnin's disciples. Most of these people followed their elders into Dōgen's school, for even the leaders of this native Zen school came to study with Dōgen as an authentic Zen master who had personally studied in China and had brought back teachings as yet unknown to them.

When Rinzai schools from China subsequently began to sprout up under military patronage, it would have been natural for Dōgen's students to wish to reestablish a connection with Chinese Rinzai tradition even if they were not necessarily charmed by the current fashion. Since there was widespread degeneration and corruption in Chinese Rinzai Zen, a decadence acknowledged by the masters in China but ignored in Japan, there could be no question but that someone with knowledge of the real situation would have to speak out to inform the people.

Among Japanese sectarians, particular attention has been given to Dōgen's attack on Dahui in the *Shōbōgenzō* essay entitled "Absorption in Self-Realization" *(Jishōzammai)*. Dōgen gives a fragmentary account—including some material of dubious provenance—of Dahui's life as a young Zen student before attaining enlightenment. He then claims that records stating Dahui eventually awakened are not true.

Dōgen also says that Dahui asked for the Zen transmission of the Chinese Cao-Dong (Sōtō) sect, but was rebuffed because of his incompetence. Chinese records, in contrast, attest that Dahui himself repudiated the formalized transmission of Zen then practiced in the Cao-Dong sect, on the basis of the classical principle that enlightenment is not external to one's own inner mind and cannot be passed on and received as if it were a doctrine.

Dōgen's account of Dahui in this essay only deals with some episodes that took place in the Chinese master's early twenties, long before Dahui's great awakening, which is said to have taken place in his late thirties. Dōgen denies that Dahui ever attained Zen awakening, but he offers no explanation of how Dahui's teacher, the great Yuanwu (Engo), a Zen master whom Dōgen regarded highly, could have bestowed his seal of approval and permission to teach upon such an incompetent fool as the Dahui that is portrayed in Dōgen's "Absorption in Self-Realization."

The clumsiness of this essay is such that one Japanese writer, a lay Rinzai Zen master himself, has theorized that it was not actually composed by Dōgen himself but is a later sectarian forgery. While this may very well be true, it may also be true that if Dōgen did actually write this essay he was simply using a few images of Dahui as a bold and impatient youth to paint a negative portrait for didactic purposes, aware that the intensive Zen methods Dahui popularized can also appeal to counterproductive human weaknesses such as impatience and overeagerness.

Other examples of Dōgen's statements about teachers in lineages other than his own will similarly show inconsistencies and contradictions of presentation and logic when compared to one another; often they show no logic at all, being simply declarations. Taken superficially at face value, this aspect of Dōgen's work has provided fodder for sectarian rivalry, and more recently they have become a point around which reconsiderations of Dōgen's character have revolved. All of this, however, loses meaning in the context of Zen teaching, where the point is to strip students of sentimental attachments.

Rivalry between Rinzai and Sōtō Zen factions in Japan is believed by sectarians to have been rooted in China, particularly in the relationship between two outstanding Zen masters of the Song dynasty, the aforementioned Dahui and his contemporary Hongzhi (Wanshi). What certain Western writers on Zen history have called a "controversy" between these two masters appears, however, to be a fiction invented in Japanese sectarian circles to underscore the supposed differences between Rinzai and Sōtō Zen. A similar phenomenon can be seen in the Western Zen sectarian practice of projecting conditions in present-day Japanese and Western establishments back onto ancient schools and traditions, in order to assert the supposed continuity between present-day schools and ancient tradition.

It is true that Dahui criticized something he called "silent illumination Zen," while Hongzhi upheld something he called "silent illumination Zen," but the usage of the term differs in the teachings of the two masters. They may well have done this deliberately as an educational device to show how the same term can be interpreted in different ways; in any case, there is nothing in the Chinese records of these two Zen masters to indicate that they were rivals at all. By *silent illumination* Dahui meant quietism or formalistic pietism, while Hongzhi used it to refer to the harmony of tranquillity-silence and clear awareness-illumination.

In repudiating quietism, furthermore, Dahui did not specifically link it to Sōtō Zen, but spoke of it as a typical error of getting too absorbed in tranquilization exercises: he wrote, "The perfection of quiescence merely stills fragmented false consciousness; if you cling to the quiescence and immediately consider it ultimate, you will be taken in by the false Zen of silent illumination."[28] And far from advocating quietism himself, Hongzhi also repudiates it: "In the present time the understanding of many of the brethren is to keep sitting, producing fault on both sides, being unable to turn around freely and investigate from the side, to go back and forth between the relative and the absolute."[29]

In spite of the fact that Dahui and Hongzhi taught in different ways, which is nothing unusual in the field of Zen, it would be hard to support any claim of rivalry or mutual repudiation. There is no doubt that Dahui criticized degenerate Zen in his time, including degenerate Sōtō Zen, yet he praised Hongzhi for "uplifting the Sōtō school in its decline, treating a serious illness when it had become terminal," and wrote that Hongzhi was a peerless friend who truly understood him. A sign of Hongzhi's high opinion of Dahui is the fact that he even helped out with the material support of Dahui's many Zen students.

In old Japan, ecclesiastical rank corresponded to court rank, and the powerful Buddhist churches were run by and for the aristocracy. Dōgen himself relates how, as a young student of Tendai Buddhism in Japan, he was taught to study in order to become famous and attain a high rank. Dōgen admits to having internalized this attitude, only to repudiate it later in the most emphatic terms along with the whole institutional tradition of Tendai

Buddhism. In view of the reputation of Dahui and his heirs in China, and the prestige of his school in Japan, it is likely that Dōgen feared that the same travesty, of Buddhist institutions becoming fields of status-seeking, would be repeated in Japan with Zen. Sowing doubts about the Zen of Dahui and his school would have been one way to diffuse the momentum of a potentially dangerous fad; and it must be understood that in medieval Japan Dōgen was exercising this option at considerable risk to himself and his reputation, so it could hardly be supposed that he was acting out of personal interests.

Technical matters on which Dōgen criticizes deteriorations of the Zen commonly associated with Rinzai Zen in general, and Dahui's school in particular, are generally three: naturalism, nihilism, and static goal-orientation. In this context, naturalism refers to the idea that since enlightenment is inherent in the mind and reality is all-inclusive in any case, there is no need for cultivation and realization of enlightenment. Nihilism refers to denial of causality because of a subjective sense of aloofness. Static goal-orientation means conscious anticipation of enlightenment in meditation, thus blocking objective realization by the bias inherent in this subjective anticipation.

Nihilism and static goal-orientation are also repeatedly criticized in Dahui's own works, so there can be no doubt that these were common flaws in Zen students of the time. Therefore, Dōgen Zenji's reservations about Rinzai Zen should be understood in the overall context of the political history of Japanese Buddhism and the deterioration of Zen in Song dynasty China, rather than interpreted superficially as a manifestation of sectarian interests.

Dōgen Zenji and Pure Land Buddhism

At the same time that Zen Buddhism was taking root in Japan through the efforts of Dōgen Zenji and other leading teachers of the thirteenth century, Pure Land Buddhism—which, like Zen, was another specialist movement breaking away from the Tendai mother school—was also emerging and establishing an independent presence in medieval Japanese religious life. Like Zen, the Pure Land movement was to become a major stream of Japanese Buddhism, but like Zen it too was at first surrounded by doubt and controversy.

The Pure Land movement explained the decadence of Japanese Buddhism in terms of the old idea that Buddhism would go through three stages of genuine, imitation, and derelict teaching. The belief was that the final derelict age had arrived, and that the majority of the teachings were no longer applicable because the people of the time could not put them into practice.

The method of Pure Land Buddhism in this situation was to give up on attaining enlightenment by the efforts of the ego-ridden self, and instead become absorbed in remembrance of a mystic Buddha representing infinite consciousness and life. This self-forgetting Buddha-remembrance was supposed to result in a spiritual rebirth in the corresponding realm of experience, which is void of barriers to enlightenment.

Dōgen Zenji also recognized the presence of the derelict age, and taught the use of this consciousness as a means of boosting diligence; in a lecture recorded in *Eihei Kōroku,* he says to his students,

You should know that there were already differences in the realization of the teaching among the practitioners of the ages of the genuine teaching and imitation teaching. In later periods of five hundred years there were still differences such as firmness of liberation and firmness of meditation. How much the more so now that we are in the age of the ending of the teaching, the derelict era; even if we are as energetic and vigorous as if we were saving our heads from burning up, we might not equal the people of the times of the genuine teaching and imitation teaching. During the eras of the genuine and imitation teachings in India, there were already those who attained enlightenment and those who did not; this was because of diligence or lack thereof. In the present time of the last remnants of the teaching in this fringe area [Japan], the faculties of the people are vastly different from those of the times of the genuine and semblance teachings.[30]

In an essay in *Shōbōgenzō*, Dōgen also writes, "In these bad times of the derelict teaching, they are not ashamed of not having the right transmission, and are jealous of others who do."[31] Dōgen's perception of medieval Japan as a civilization, furthermore, seems to be that of a morally, intellectually, and spiritually backward country: "Among people of our nation, humaneness and wisdom are not yet widespread, and people are warped besides. Even if they are given straightforward truth, the elixir would probably turn into poison. They are prone to head for fame and profit, and it is hard to dissolve their deluded attachments."[32]

In one of the *Shōbōgenzō* essays translated in this volume, "Sounds of the Valley Streams, Colors of the Mountains," Dōgen pursues the theme of medieval Japanese backwardness in similarly cutting terms: "This country Japan is a remote region out in the ocean. People are extremely stupid. No sage has ever been born here, nor has anyone with inherent knowledge. Even true students of the Way are rare. When one teaches the aspiration for enlightenment to those who do not know it, because truthful words offend the ear they do not reflect on themselves but resent others."[33]

This kind of human failing is not peculiar to medieval Japan, but Dōgen meant it literally as well as metaphorically, referring specifically to the worldliness of established Buddhism. These and similar disparaging remarks about Japan indicate that he was conscious of working in a milieu in which unconventional and extreme statements might be necessary in order to produce specific impressions capable of promoting desirable effects under adverse conditions.

Dōgen has little to say about Pure Land Buddhism, compared with his criticism of fragmentary Zen, yet he did reject the use of the idea of the derelict age to rationalize despair if that led to heedlessness. He also lamented cynical abuse of the notion of free postmortem rebirth in paradise to justify abandonment of the practical aspiration for enlightenment on this earth.

These were characteristic forms of decadence among Pure Land camp followers and dilettantes, but Dōgen seems to have left most of the work of analyzing these problems up to the leaders of the

Pure Land movement, while he himself emphasized, in the traditional manner of Zen Buddhism, the necessity of application in this life as the only chance an individual has for enlightenment.

Regarding the Pure Land practice of Buddha-remembrance by invocation of symbolic names, Dōgen does not go into it very deeply, but he does make mention of it in a general discussion of the relative merits of Zen sitting and other practices more familiar in Japan at that time, in the context of an early *Shōbōgenzō* essay entitled "Talk on Mastering the Way":

> Do you know the virtues gained from such practices as reading scriptures and invoking Buddha names? It is vain to think that simply moving your tongue and raising your voice is meritorious as Buddhist service; to pretend it is the way to enlightenment is even further off.
>
> As far as reading scriptures is concerned, the point is that the Buddha taught models of immediate and gradual practice, and if one understands them and practices according to the teaching, this will surely enable one to attain realization. It is not a matter of vainly expending thought and assuming that is merit for attaining enlightenment.
>
> Trying to reach the Buddha Way by ignorantly making millions of verbal repetitions is like heading north to go south. Reading the literature without knowing how to apply it is like someone who reads prescriptions but forgets about compounding the medicines. What is the benefit? Ceaseless chanting is like frogs in the fields in spring croaking day and night; after all there is no benefit there either.[34]

While this is not a very sophisticated treatment of the subject, in its original context it is given in reply to an unsophisticated challenge. What is noteworthy is that Dōgen does not flatly repudiate other practices, only the presumption that either mechanical performance or mere theory will foster enlightenment.

In another *Shōbōgenzō* essay, entitled "The Mind of the Way," Dōgen himself recommends a practice similar in form and theory to the Pure Land invocational remembrance practice:

When this life ends, the eyes will suddenly go dark; realizing that this time is already the end of life, you should diligently recite, *I respectfully take refuge in Buddha.* Then the Buddhas of the ten directions will extend their sympathy, and even such evils as would cause you to enter bad states will be overridden, and you will be born in heaven, you will be born before Buddhas, and you will honor the Buddhas and hear the teaching expounded by the Buddhas.[35]

Whether one takes statements about death and rebirth in this essay or in Pure Land Buddhism literally or symbolically—and both types of presentation are to be found in both Zen and Pure Land teachings—the correspondence between this particular part of Dōgen's practice and the Pure Land system is an interesting facet of his work transcending conventional sectarian images of Dōgen and his way of Zen. It is, of course, in harmony with the principle of the underlying unity of Buddhism, and illustrates the ultimate futility of drawing sectarian boundaries.

A particularly relevant parallel can be drawn between certain aspects of Dōgen's teaching and that of the popular Japanese saint Ippen (1239–1289), who spread Pure Land practice to millions over a sixteen-year wandering mission. There is evidence of contact between Ippen and both Rinzai and Sōtō schools of Zen, demonstrating a historical relationship as well as a spiritual one. Saint Ippen is even considered by some to have been among those who attained Zen mastery as well as esoteric rebirth in the Pure Land.

One of the most frequently quoted passages of Dōgen's writings comes from the previously mentioned "Talk on Mastering the Way." "Although [enlightenment] is abundantly inherent in everyone, as long as one does not practice it, it is not manifest, and as long as one has not experienced it, there is no attainment."[36] This is commonly cited to illustrate the need for practical cultivation and pragmatic experience of enlightenment, *because* of the inherence of enlightened nature and not in spite of it.

Pure Land Buddhism refers to inherent enlightened nature in terms of "other-power," using the term *other* to mean other than

31

selfish concerns or egocentric efforts. Pure Land Buddhism is often represented, particularly in reference to certain sects, as believing literally in an external savior, but like all Buddhist teachings this is what is called an expedient set-up. While he was a Pure Land saint extolling a way of radical reliance on Other Power, like a Zen master Ippen emphasized the importance of the attitude of the practitioner in making this reliance a pragmatic experience in reality:

> There are no sicknesses or afflictions in the elements of body and mind to plague people, but once you have turned away from awareness of original nature and dwell on desires, eating the poisons of passion and delusion, to suffer the pains of miserable conditions is a natural consequence of your own acts. Therefore, unless you yourself resolve to realize enlightenment, not even the compassion of the Buddhas of past, present, and future can save you.[37]

Both Dōgen and Ippen stressed that salvation, or enlightenment, is in the original nature of humanity, but it remains obscure unless it is discovered and expressed in direct experience. Just as Dōgen thus insisted on the indivisible continuity of practice and realization, Ippen called for absorption in the practice of remembrance to the degree where the very act of invoking Buddha would be identical to the experience of rebirth in the Pure Land.

Dōgen Zenji on Monastic and Lay Zen

In addition to his monumental expositions of Buddhist psychology and philosophy, Dōgen also devoted considerable attention to developing a purified monastic order, and to strengthening the social and spiritual virtues of monastic commitments. Considering the well-known decadence of Buddhist institutions in Japan at that time, and the low opinion Dōgen expressed of Japanese religion, culture, and society, it was undoubtedly natural for him to concentrate particular effort on the cultivation of a select group of earnest seekers. Abused as it was for worldly ends, in medieval Japan monasticism was still virtually the only method available for safeguarding the existence of such a group without armaments.

In later sectarian Sōtō Zen writings, there is a custom of interpreting Dōgen as believing that monastic life itself is the *summum bonum,* or is inextricably connected therewith. If taken as statements of dogmatic truth, rather than as statements intended to produce a calculated effect in a particular group of people under specific circumstances, there are certainly a number of passages that could be extracted from context to support this view of the sectarian Sōtō cult, but it is neither reasonable nor empirically justifiable to do so in an objective study. The issue of the feasibility of lay Zen is one of the points on which Dōgen makes contradictory statements, whose meanings must therefore be sought in historical circumstances and symbolic representation rather than abstract truth in and of itself.

In "Talk on Mastering the Way," Dōgen denies that worldly duties make enlightenment impossible. He states that there are many examples of lay people realizing enlightenment, and goes on to name some of the emperors and ministers of China who were known as Zen students and even recognized as adepts. Dōgen's explanation of this phenomenon is that the matter of enlightenment has nothing to do with whether one is ordained as a mendicant or not, but with whether one has the will or not.

Dōgen also makes the interesting statement that those who believe that worldly duties hinder Buddhism "only know there is no Buddhism in the world, and do not yet know there is nothing worldly in a Buddha." While it is true that infatuation with the world, or clinging to the things of the world, does obstruct enlightenment, the enlightened are in the world without being of the world, and see that the discrimination between worldliness and sanctity is not in phenomena themselves but in the mind of the person concerned. This is a point that is commonly made in Zen writings: a Buddhist proverb says, "If you have sentiments about Buddhist teaching, it becomes a worldly thing; if you have no sentiments about worldly things, they become Buddhist teaching."[38]

Later on, however, after having observed the Japanese scene and the Zen boom among the ruling class for another ten years, Dōgen began to speak in a different vein. In 1231, in his "Talk on Mastering the Way," Dōgen had written:

> In present day China the rulers, ministers, literati, men and women, all set their minds on Zen. Both warriors and people of culture aspire to Zen. Among those who aspire, certainly many illumine the ground of mind. So it is obvious that worldly duties do not hinder the way to enlightenment. . . . When Shakyamuni Buddha was in the world, even bad people with wrong views attained the Way; in the congregations of the Zen founders, even hunters and woodcutters became enlightened."[39]

But in 1243, in his "Thirty-seven Distinct Elements of Enlightenment," an essay on classical Buddhist teachings, Dōgen writes, "During the Buddha's whole lifetime of teaching, not one single lay person ever attained the Way. This is because lay life is not the place to study the Buddha Way, because there are a lot of obstacles."[40] In the same essay he goes so far as to write, in diametric opposition to his earlier statements, "No lay person has ever attained the Way."[41]

Generally speaking, Dōgen extols monastic life, or "leaving home" (*shukke*), specifically in connection with renunciation, poverty, and nonattachment. It would seem that after more than ten years of experience teaching in Japan, during which he had had many contacts with laymen from the Kyoto area, Dōgen felt it was virtually impossible for people there to remain aloof from worldly things as long as they were in the midst of the world. In the "Talk on Mastering the Way" he wrote that "monks in Japan are inferior even to lay folk in China."[42] As a monk himself since youth, Dōgen's interest in monastic reform was natural in view of the deeply materialistic bent of Japanese Buddhism, which included the practices of institutional and magical use of Buddhism to gain material and social benefits.

In the "Thirty-seven Distinct Elements of Enlightenment,"

Dōgen also wrote: "In the last two or three hundred years, people in China claiming to be Zen monks have been saying that lay study of the Way and monastic study of the Way are one. These are just gangs who have become dogs to feed on the urine and feces of lay people."[43] In his *Eihei Kōroku,* however, he is on record as stating, in a letter to a lay grandee and Confucian scholar who studied with him in 1234 and 1235, "As for those who are formally home-leavers but haven't the spirit of home-leavers, how can they be considered home-leavers? Those who are formally men of affairs but have the conduct of home-leavers are superior to home-leavers."[44]

While Dōgen's apparent turnabout on this issue was undoubtedly related to his own experiences and perceptions of the mentality and trend of the times, it is also useful to consider the symbolic value of "home" as "attachment" in the contrast between the adjectives *lay* ("at home") and *monastic* ("home-leaving"). Beyond the specific problems of his time, Dōgen was also addressing the perennial need for the seeker of enlightenment to rise above customary attachments and experience consciousness without the limitations of personal subjective bias.

Another aspect of Dōgen's apparent repudiation of lay Zen was his opposition to the notion that Buddhism and Confucianism are equal. In Song dynasty China, greater opportunities for state employment provided by the civil service examinations contributed to a renewed fervor in Confucian studies. At the same time, there was hardly a Confucian scholar who did not study Zen to some degree. Certainly the revived Confucianism of Song times, known in the West as Neo-Confucianism, owed a great deal to Zen Buddhism; so much so, indeed, that certain leading scholars took great pains to degrade Buddhism and dissociate themselves from it. As a result, Zen teachers, to whom Confucian scholars nevertheless continued to resort in great numbers, took to using quotations from Confucian classics to provide meditation themes for their Confucian students and to undermine conflicts based on blind prejudices.

The ongoing introduction of Song dynasty Zen Buddhism to

Japan in the thirteenth century brought with it the new Chinese Neo-Confucian literature. In dealing with their samurai warrior patrons, Zen teachers in Japan also taught the relatively simple Neo-Confucian ethics, fortified with Zen-like Confucian meditations. This might be construed as an attempt to promote humanism and a peace-oriented sense of society in this new governing class, which had risen to ascendancy through military power.

Dōgen's accounts of the pervasiveness of Buddhist accommodation of Confucianism (and Taoism) appear exaggerated when compared to the literature of the Song Chinese Zen schools, but it may be theorized that his repudiation of this trend was an attempt to forestall another intertwining of government and religion. This was something he saw as an endemic ill of Buddhism in Japan, on the verge of recurring in the process of assimilating Zen into Japanese society.

ON TRANSLATING DŌGEN

Dōgen Zenji is the greatest Japanese thinker in history. His *Shōbōgenzō*, the first and only major Buddhist philosophical text ever composed in the Japanese language, still remains a monument of sophistication, unmatched in its rational elucidation of Zen learning.

While Dōgen played several roles in the history of Japanese Buddhism, his most outstanding contributions were his reconciliation of Zen with the greater tradition of pan-Buddhism and his explicit illustrations of logical procedures in Zen koan meditation. Dōgen exploded the myth, popular then as now, that Zen awakening is an irrational process, thus laying a foundation for a more balanced and complete understanding of Zen Buddhism.

The masterwork of Dōgen is itself a gigantic Zen koan illustrating the politics of knowledge as surely as its contents illustrate the psychology of knowledge. Although it was not publicly burned, as were works of other writers now considered very great thinkers, the transmission of Dōgen's masterwork lapsed altogether for more than four hundred years, "killed by silence," even within the specialist school he himself founded.

It was not until the later seventeenth and early eighteenth centuries that this amazing book began to come to light, partly as a result of political and religious changes in late feudal Japan.

By that time, the Japanese language and culture had changed very considerably, and there was no direct transmission of understanding this text within the specialist school following Dōgen's lineage, so a large body of ad hoc interpretation began to grow up, forming a species of "Dogenism" that was neither like Zen or Buddhism in general nor like the original teaching of Dōgen himself.

Sectarian cultism of this kind was also encouraged by the late feudal Japanese Shogunate, which passed a comprehensive group of laws designed to control the power of institutional Buddhism and make the teachings themselves as irrelevant to the lives of the people as possible, excepting only ceremonial observances and certain public offices such as census-keeping.

Although late feudal Zen institutions also looked after public schooling, the curriculum was decided by the military government, so liberationist or illuminist Buddhism was not included at all. The orthodox curriculum consisted of mechanical repetition of four Confucian classics taught according to the right-wing sociopolitical doctrines of official Neo-Confucian ideology.

In nineteenth-century Japan, with the restoration of an imperial Shintō government, suppression of Buddhism intensified to become active repression. Yet, curiously, the imperial Shintō government suddenly decided to award Dōgen the title of *Daishi,* or "Great Master," over six hundred years after his death.

This would have been doubly strange had it not been for the fact that Dōgen, as the greatest dialectician ever born in Japan, all at once became important to the Japanese Ministry of Education, as a symbol of nationalistic intellectual pride at a time when it had been hurt by the early encounter with Western rationalism and missionary Christianity.

By the early twentieth century, Japanese intellectuals were presenting Dōgen as if he had been a contemporary German academic philosopher, while Japanese religious sectarians were presenting Dōgen as if he had been a contemporary cultist or missionary, whose teaching in either case had little or nothing to do with the rest of Buddhism, or with the world at large, except the supposed desire to get everyone to follow it.

Western works on Dōgen are heir to both trends, the eighteenth- and nineteenth-century reductionist religious cultism and the twentieth-century reductionist academic cultism. Because of the historical process through which Dogenism has become a narrow specialty unto itself, appropriate curricula underlying the basic linguistic and methodological skills needed to translate Dōgen's writing are not yet established in either academic or sectarian Western studies of Buddhism.

The language of Dōgen is full of all sorts of expressions and allusions from other Buddhist schools and a wide variety of texts: it contains classical Japanese, medieval colloquial Japanese, classical Chinese, sutraic Buddhist Chinese, and medieval colloquial Chan Chinese. The background skills necessary for translating this cannot be learned by specializing in Dōgen, and especially not by specializing in Dogenism: they are available only by firsthand experience with the texts and practices of all the major scriptures and schools of Indian and Chinese Buddhism.

The present study of Dōgen is radically different from other works on Dōgen. Its translations are not based on modern Japanese paraphrases and interpolations, and its interpretations are not based on the sectarian and academic cultic presentations of recent times. The translations herein are based exclusively on the original Buddhist hybrid Japanese text that Dōgen himself wrote, and the interpretations are based on the original context of pan-Buddhism and that Dōgen himself studied.

Paragraph-by-paragraph explanations of the inner meanings of Dōgen's intensely concentrated symbolic writing, necessitated by the enormous density of his writing, are also included. Key materials from the classical scriptures and schools of Buddhism are included to illustrate the root patterns of Dōgen's experiential dialectic, and to guide the interested reader in the use of Dōgen's writings as meditation texts.

NOTES

1. *Taishō Tripitaka,* vol. 48, p. 379c.
2. Ibid.
3. Ibid., p. 380c.
4. *Taishō Tripitaka,* vol. 47, p. 577bc.
5. Ibid., p. 530c.
6. Ibid., p. 585c.
7. Ibid., p. 577c.
8. Ibid., p. 509c.
9. Ibid., p. 534a.
10. Thomas Cleary, *The Sayings and Doings of Pai-chang: Ch'an Master of Great Wisdom* (Los Angeles: Center Publications, 1978), p. 36.
11. Ibid., p. 57.
12. *Guishan Jingce, Taishō Tripitaka,* vol. 48, pp. 1042–3.
13. *Zongmen shiguilun. Manji Zokuzōkyō,* vol. 110; see also Thomas Cleary, *Zen Essence: The Science of Freedom* (Boston: Shambhala Publications, 1989), pp. 12–14.
14. Cf. Thomas Cleary, *Zen Lessons* (Boston: Shambhala Publications, 1989), p. 111.
15. Cf. ibid., p. 91.
16. Cf. ibid., pp. 83–84.
17. Cf. ibid., pp. 93–94.
18. *Taishō Tripitaka,* vol. 48, p. 1030a.
19. Cf. *Zen Lessons,* p. 128.
20. Cf. ibid., p. 127.
21. Cf. ibid., p. 102.
22. Cf. ibid., p. 65.
23. Cf. ibid., p. 69.
24. Cf. ibid., p. 57.
25. Cf. ibid., p. 62.
26. There are a number of versions of this proverb, which describes a provisional teaching taken as an absolute truth.
27. *Zen Essence,* pp. 27–28.
28. Ibid., pp. 54–55.

29. *Taishō Tripitaka*, vol. 48, p. 68c.
30. *Eihei Kōroku chūkai zenshō*, vol. II, pp. 261–62.
31. *Shōbōgenzō Kesa Kudoku* (Iwanami edition), vol. I, p. 174.
32. *Shōbōgenzō Bendōwa*, vol. I, p. 75.
33. Cf. p. 122, par. 35.
34. *Shōbōgenzō Bendōwa*, vol. I, p. 61.
35. *Shōbōgenzō Dōshin*, vol. III, pp. 244–45.
36. *Shōbōgenzō Bendōwa*, vol. I, p. 55.
37. *Ippen Hijirie*, in Asayama Endō, ed. *Rokujō Engi* (Tokyo: Sankibō, 1931), p. 65.
38. This is quoted, for example, in National Teacher Musō Soseki's famous *Muchū Mondō*.
39. *Shōbōgenzō Bendōwa*, vol. I, p. 72.
40. *Shōbōgenzō Bodai sanjūshichihin bunpō*, vol. III, p. 30.
41. Ibid., p. 32.
42. *Shōbōgenzō Bendōwa*, vol. I, p. 75.
43. *Shōbōgenzō Bodai sanjūshichihin bunpō*, vol. III, p. 28.
44. *Eihei Kōroku*, vol. III, p. 116.

Universal Book of Eternal Peace

SELECTIONS

FROM

Eihei Kōroku

1

The years of a lifetime are a flash of lightning; who clings to objects? They are empty through and through. Even if you care for the nose hung in front of your face, still be careful and value every moment to work on enlightenment.

This a statement for people in meditation; what about a statement for the seasoned adept on the mountain?

The autumn colors of the thousand peaks
are dyed with seasonal rain;
How could the hard rock on the mountain
follow along with the wind?

2

The saying that having no mind is Buddha originated in India, the saying that mind itself is Buddha began in China.

If you understand accordingly, you are as far off as the sky is from earth.

If you do not understand accordingly, you are just a common sort.

Ultimately, what is what?

In the third month of spring
the fruit is full on the enlightenment tree;
One night the flower blooms
and the whole world is fragrant.

3

A seeker asked a Zen master, "What are you thinking of so intently?"

The Zen master said, "I am thinking of what does not think."
The seeker asked, "How can you think of what does not think?"
The Zen master said, "It is not thought."

Minding already gone,
"mindless" does not quite describe it.
In this life,
purity is foremost.

4

Supreme enlightenment is not for oneself, not for others, not for fame, not for gain. To nevertheless seek unexcelled enlightenment wholeheartedly and singlemindedly, persevering without regressing, is called "awakening the mind for enlightenment."

Once you get this mind to appear, it is not even for the sake of enlightenment that you seek enlightenment; this is the true mind of enlightenment. Without this mind, how can you really practice the way to enlightenment?

Those who are singlemindedly seeking the mind of enlightenment must not weary of this quest; they must not give up. Those who have not yet attained the mind of enlightenment should pray to the Buddhas of former ages, and should also dedicate their good works to the quest for the mind of enlightenment.

Someone once asked a great Zen master, "All things return to One. Where does the One return?"

The Zen master said, "When I was living in such-and-such a place, I made a cloth shirt that weighed seven pounds."

This is how an ancient illuminate spoke. If someone asked me, "All things return to One; where does the One return?" I would say it returns to transcendence.

If asked why I say this, I would say I am within, making offerings to billions of Buddhas.

5

In ancient times a man up in a high tower saw two monks passing by in front of the tower; there were two gods sweeping the road and strewing flowers before them.

Then when the monks came back that way, there were two demons angrily shouting and spitting, wiping away their tracks.

The man came down from the tower and asked the monks the reason for this phenomenon.

The monks said, "As we were going, we were discussing the prnciples taught by the Buddha. On our way back, we were talking about trivia. That must be why it was like this."

The two monks were awakened by this. They repented and went on their way.

Although this is a crude objectification, when you examine it carefully you find it is a most important issue for people studying the Way. Why? Simply because outside objects appear when emotive thoughts arise. If thoughts do not arise, there are no objects that can be apprehended.

In the case of this old story, the gods found a road on which to strew flowers, the demonic spirits found a way to spy: that is why it was like this. What about when the gods find no road on which to strew flowers, and the demons have no way to spy?

Do you want to understand? I will say now what has not been said in former generations.

Buddhas do not appear in the world by virtue of meditation experiences, powers, or occult knowledge. Ordinary people of sharp faculties also practice these meditations, yet they do not realize noncontamination. If the enlightened one explained, they too would realize noncontamination.

6

I didn't go to many monasteries, but I happened to see my teacher and directly found that my eyes are vertical and my nose is horizontal. Then I was not to be fooled by anyone. So I came back with open hands. That is why I haven't got any Buddhism at all; I pass the time leaving it to the flow. Every morning the sun rises in the east, every night the moon sets in the west. When the clouds are gone the ridges of the mountains are bared; when the rain has passed, the surrounding hills hover low. Ultimately, how is it? [*Silence*] One leap year after every three; the rooster crows at dawn.

7

Even acting upon seeing the moment of opportunity is not yet expertise; if you manage by physical manifestation, I still dare not accept it.

That is why it is said, "What thing is it that comes thus?"

What is the principle behind "what thing is it that comes"? [*Silence*]

The true does not cover the false, the crooked does not hide the straight.

8

Cultivating practice for three immeasurable eons,
don't rest when the task is fulfilled.
Realization attained in an instant,
defilement cannot affect it.

An ancient said, "Understanding the meaning according to the scriptures is the enemy of the Buddhas of all times; but a single word's departure from the scriptures is the same as devil talk."

When we do not depend on the scriptures yet do not depart from the scriptures, how do we practice? Do you want to read a scripture?

[*Raising a whisk*]

This is my whisk; what is the scripture?

What follows is lengthy; I leave it for another day.

9

One statement removes obstructing fixations; one statement fills everywhere. Tell me, which statement do the enlightened ones use to help people?

I have a statement that the enlightened ones have never made, and which I will quote to you.

Complete.

10

Even dismantling fixed structures is whirling in the flow of birth and death; even imparting the middle way is still illusion and error.

When you study thus, you are studying along with the Buddhas. When you study it as not thus, you are studying along with your self.

Studying along with the Buddhas and studying along with your self, explaining a furlong and explaining a foot; these are different. Speaking of ten and speaking of nine are different.

What is "not thus"? It is your self. What is "thus"? It is the Buddhas.

When the great Baso was beginning to teach, his teacher Nangaku said to his own group, "Is Baso teaching people?" They said he was. Nangaku said, "I have never seen anyone bring news of this." No one had any reply.

So Nangaku sent a monk to Baso, with these instructions: "When Baso gets up in the hall to lecture, just ask him how he is. Remember what he says and come back."

The monk went and did as he had been told. When he returned, he told Nangaku, "Baso said, 'Ever since the barbarian rebellion, these last thirty years, I have never lacked salt and soup for meals.'"

Making a ball of this story, I offer it to the enlightened ones. There are three people who bear witness: one says it is making offerings of flowers, one says it is making offerings of precious incense, one says it is making offerings of head, eyes, marrow, and brains.

Leaving aside the testimony of these three people, how would the testimony of the whole community have any ordinary people explain?

"In the million years since the barbarian rebellion, I've never lacked salt and vinegar."

11

The lineage of Buddas comes from conditions, the teaching of Buddhas comes from the start. Once you have encountered good conditions, you shouldn't miss them, but should cultivate practical application. In practical application there is refutation and there is accommodation.

Being here, you shouldn't stumble past; you should find out the Way. In finding the Way, there is practice, there is effort; if you break through one day, all things will be complete. If you haven't broken through, all things will be wrong.

Once there was a certain monk in the assembly of one of the great classical masters who was serving as the superintendent of the monastry.

One day the Zen master asked him, "How long have you been here?"

The monk said, "Three years, so far." The Zen master asked, "You are young; why don't you ever ask about the Teaching?" The monk said, "I dare not deceive you. I already attained peace while I was at the place of another Zen teacher."

The Zen master inquired, "By what words did you gain entry?" The monk said, "Once I asked the teacher, 'What is the student's self?' The teacher said, 'The fire god comes looking for fire!'"

Hearing this story, the Zen master remarked, "That is a fine saying, but I'm afraid you didn't understand."

The monk said, "The fire god is in the realm of fire; to seek fire with fire is like seeking self with the self."

The Zen master said, "You really don't understand. If Buddhism were like this, it wouldn't have reached the present."

The monk left in high dudgeon, but on his way out he thought, "This Zen master is the teacher of five hundred people. There must be some point to his warning that I'm wrong."

So he went back to the Zen master and apologized. The master instructed him, "You ask me." The monk said, "What is the student's self?" The Zen master said, "The fire god comes looking for fire!" At this the monk was greatly enlightened.

Before, it was "the fire god looking for fire," and it was "the fire god looking for fire" afterwards too: why wasn't he enlightened the first time, but fell into the road of intellecutal understanding; and why was he greatly enlightened afterwards and shed his nest of cliché?

Do you want to understand?

[*Silence*]

> *The fire god comes looking for fire;*
> *how much light do the pillars and lamps begrudge?*
> *Buried in the ashes, though you search you don't see;*
> *lighting it up and blowing it out,*
> *it goes into action again.*

12

When Sudhana visited Manjushri, Manjushri said to him, "Go outside and get a stalk of medicinal herb."

Sudhana went out and looked all over the earth, finding nothing that was not medicine.

He returned and said to Manjushri, "The whole earth is medicine; what could I bring?"

Manjushri said, "Bring a stalk of medicinal herb."

Sudhana brought a blade of grass.

Manjushri took the blade of grass, then showed it to the assembly and said, "This blade of grass can kill people and can also enliven people."

Before, it was a blade of grass; later, it was a blade of grass: how far apart are before and after?

[*Silence*]

They're a blade of grass apart.

13

Before the day of the full moon, the wind is high, the moon is cool. After the day of the full moon, the sea is calm, the rivers are clear. Right on the day of the full moon the sky and wind go on forever.

> *Having gotten to be thus, it is necessary to be thus.*
> *Advance a step, and the Enlightened Ones arrive;*
> *Step back, and the heart is bare and single.*

Not advancing, not withdrawing, don't say I have no help for people, don't say you people have no realization. Once you have heard of this, do you want to practice in this way?

[*Silence*]

Without turning away from the multitudes of people, body and mind drop off.

14

The king of a country in eastern India invited a Buddhist master to a feast, in the course of which he asked, "Everyone is reciting scriptures; why don't you?"

The master answered, "Breathing out, I do not follow myriad objects; breathing in, I do not dwell on mental or physical elements: I always 'recite' such a 'scripture,' hundreds of thousands of millions of volumes."

Try further to explain the principle.

15

A seeker asked one of the great Zen ancients, "What is the great meaning of the Buddhist teaching?"
The Zen ancient said, "You cannot but know."
The seeker asked, "Is there yet a turning point beyond?"
The Zen ancient said, "The eternal sky does not inhibit the flight of the white clouds."

You can't but know the Buddha's great meaning; it is after all stylish where the style is slight. The eternal sky does not inhibit the flight of the white clouds; this time why bother to ask a Zen master?

16

When the sky becomes one, it is clear; when earth becomes one, it is at rest; when people become one, they are at peace; when time becomes one, it is positive energy. This oneness is eternal; in this eternity Buddhas and Zen masters get their life, and people awaken resolve, cultivate practice, discern the Way, and attain realization of one statement.

Having gained power within eternity, having gained life within eternity, then you make remembrance beads of the bodies of Buddhas and Zen masters, and count off the three hundred and sixty-five days: every time you reach *today,* then you can go on *thus.*

This then is the body-mind of Buddhas and Zen masters, because you can go on *thus.*
[*Silence*]

> *The mind-body of every Buddha now becomes eternal;*
> *the facets of the precious jewels are formed like the skies;*
> *counting, counting, how very long.*
> *The lucky day is when you discover it's all one day.*

17

Once when an ancient Buddhist saint was walking over mud, a novice asked him, "How can you do it yourself, Venerable One?" The saint said, "If I don't do it, who will do it for me?"

Mind like a fan in winter, body like a cloud in a cold valley; if you can see "doing it yourself," then you will see "who will do it." When you don't go by either of these routes, an iron wall stands steep and precipitous.

18

It is rare to hear the truth even in immense eons; that is why the adepts and virtuous ones of the past forgot their bodies, or even lost their bodies, for the sake of truth. There certainly is a meaning to this. Ordinary human beings, animals, ants, mosquitoes, outsiders with erroneous views, all have bodies and life, but as long as they have not yet heard the truth they cannot be honored or esteemed. For innumerable lives, birth after birth, how many times have they been embodied? Yet theirs is not yet a good life. If one gets to hear the truth, that is a good life.

There are three kinds of hearing truth: higher, middling, and lower. The superior beings listen to truth with the spirit, the middling beings listen to truth with the mind, the inferior beings listen to truth with the ears. Since we have spirits, minds, and ears, how will we listen to truth, and what truth shall we listen to?

Haven't you heard how Shakyamuni Buddha said, "By my teaching it is possible to transcend birth, old age, sickness, and death; this teaching is not thought or discrimination"? As for transcending birth, old age, sickness, and death, let them be transcended; and as for denying thought and discrimination, let them be denied. Once you're able to do so, then tell me, when you break open the teaching and take out the marrow of the teaching, then refine the marrow to get the essence of the marrow, then how will you express it?

[*Silence*]

Although aware of the cold wind chilling you, you don't yet know for whose sake the bright moon is white. This is the saying of one who studies from the same source as Shakyamuni; it transcends the teaching and goes beyond the marrow—it is not high, middling, or low.

How do you express the saying of the highest of the high? Do you comprehend?

"When a white heron stands in the snow, they aren't the same color; the bright moon and the white flowers are not like each other."

19

Unless the cold pierces through our bones once, how can we have the apricot blossoms perfuming the whole world?

20

The founder of Zen directed his disciples, "The time is about to arrive; why don't you each say what you have attained?"

His disciple Dōfuku said, "According to what I perceive, not clinging to words and not rejecting words is the function of the Way."

The founder said, "You have attained my skin."

The nun Sōji said, "My understanding is like Ananda seeing the land of Akshobhya, the Immovable Buddha; once seen, it is not seen a second time."

The founder said, "You have attained my flesh."

Dōiku said, "The four gross material elements are empty, the five body-mind clusters are not existent. In my view there is not a single thing that can be grasped."

The founder said, "You have attained my bones."

Finally Eka bowed and stood there.

The founder said, "You have attained my marrow."

Later people assumed there were differences in depth, but this is not what the founder meant.

"You have attained my skin" is like saying "the lamps and pillars."

"You have attained my flesh" is like saying "mind itself is Buddha."

"You have attained my bones" is like saying "mountains, rivers, and earth."

"You have attained my marrow" is like mentioning "twirling a flower and blinking the eyes."

It is not that there are shallow and deep, superior and inferior among these. If you can see the matter in this way, then you will see the founder; then you will see the successor, and then you will get the transmission of the robe and bowl.

If you do not yet believe, listen again to my verse:

> *Great is the power of the wheel of teaching of the enlightened:*
> *It is turned in the whole world, and turned in an atom.*
> *Though the robe and bowl enter hands worthy of transmission,*
> *Hearing the teaching is common to all men and women.*

21

The Seven Sagacious Women were all daughters of kings. On the day of the seasonal festival for appreciating the flowers, hundreds of thousands of people raced to the parks for some enjoyment. Among the Seven Sagacious Women was one who said, "Sisters, we should not go along like everyone else to frolic in the realm of dusts for mundane pleasures. We should go to the forest of corpses."

The other women said, "There are corpses rotting everywhere there; what is good about that?"

The woman said, "Let us just go, sisters; there will be something very good."

When they got to the forest, she pointed to a corpse and said to the other women, "The corpse is here; where has the person gone?"

The women reflected carefully, and at this they realized the Way.

Then they saw celestial flowers raining from the sky, and heard words of praise, saying, "Excellent, excellent!"

The woman said, "Who is showering flowers from the sky and uttering praise?"

From the sky she heard a voice say, "I am Indra, king of gods; as I saw the holy sisters become enlightened, I came with my entourage to shower flowers and give praise."

He also said to the sagacious women, "O sisters, if there is anything you want, I will serve you all my life."

The women said, "Our houses have all the necessities of life, as well as all kinds of riches. We only want three things: a rootless tree, a patch of ground with neither sunlight nor shade, and a valley that does not echo."

Indra said, "I have everything, but I really do not have these three things. Let us go together and tell the Buddha."

So they all went together to see the Buddha and ask about these things. Buddha said, "Indra, none of my disciples who are great saints understand what this means; only the great enlightening beings know these things."

The meaning of the Buddha's great enlightenment is not known by any of the major disciples; there are only the enlightening beings beyond measure, who in gaining the advantage lose the advantage.

Even so, I would say in Indra's stead, "You want a shadowless tree? 'The cypress tree in the yard' is it." If they couldn't use it, I'd hold up my staff and say, "This is it."

"You want a patch of ground with no light or dark? The forest of corpses is it." If they couldn't use it, then "the whole universe in all directions is it."

"You want an echoless valley?" I'd call to them, "O sisters!" And if they responded, I'd say to them, "I've given you the nonechoing valley." If they didn't respond, I'd tell them. "No echo after all."

22

Just see the extreme confusion of the conditioned consciousness; all sentient beings are void of Buddha-nature.

23

A Zen master said, "Birth and death, coming and going, are the real human body."

Another Zen master said, "Birth and death, coming and going, are the real body."

A third Zen master said, "Birth and death, coming and going, are the real human being."

Yet another Zen master said, "Birth and death, coming and going, are the real true body of the Buddhas."

Four masters each express it in their own way. All of them have straight nostrils, and they said it all right; but that's not quite it. If you asked me, I would not agree. Birth and death, coming and going, are just birth and death, coming and going.

24

The autumn clouds and autumn sun are both peaceful and relaxed; they half seem to follow the passage of time, half seem to stay still. I ask my family for a response; I don't know how they'll answer beyond convention.

25
(midautumn)

Having pruned away the tree on the moon, tonight I don't long for any tonight of yore. When a foreigner comes, a foreigner is reflected; when a native comes, a native—the boundless pure light on the fifteenth day of the month.

26

It is clear in everything, existing in everything: everywhere you occupy the ten directions, everywhere you investigate one object. The power of comprehensive investigation is your realization of thusness; the countenance of complete comprehension is your realization of thusness.

When you measure the space in the ten directions, it seems to have no partner; when you realize half emptiness, it seems like freedom and ease. Do you want to understand this principle?

[*Silence*]

Dusky yellow does not stain my clear jewel; when does a clear mirror ever dream of "fine" and "hideous"? Unconsciously the double discs over the oceans of infinite lands turned their light around overnight and are in the corals.

27

Last night a pure breeze descended from the great void; in the morning the cypress tree attained Buddhahood right where it stands.

28

Everybody practices the Way, powerfully effecting a cure. This power in every case itself lies in hope. If every day you just involve

yourself in social affairs, when will the mountains and forests ever
see the time when enlightenment is realized?

29

Exerting strength, twelve faces; being liberal, ten million kinds.
When great doubt is urgent, you cannot get a grasp. How can one
be thus? Do you understand? Explaining in conventional terms is
useless—thoroughly embody the mind of the ancients.

30

Sometimes I speak deeply of entering noumenon, just wanting you
to be in a peaceful state.

Sometimes I set up teaching devices, just wanting you to freely
exercise mental powers.

Sometimes I gallop away beyond the senses, just wanting you to
shed body and mind.

Sometimes I enter into inner absorption, just wanting you to
pick up whatever you may.

If someone suddenly were to come forth and ask me, "What
about transcending all this?" I would just say, "The dawn breeze
polishes the dusky smoke clean; dimly, the green mountains
present a picture."

31

The Zen master Nansen was asked by a grandee, "Please explain
the truth for the people."

Nansen asked back, "How would you have me explain it?"

The grandee said, "Don't you have any methods?"

Nansen said, "What do people lack?"

The grandee said, "What about those living in all sorts of mundane conditions?"

Nansen said, "I do not teach them."

The grandee was speechless.

This mountain savage Nansen did not come down from the mountains for over thirty years, but the ghosts and sprites finally got to him. Though he spoke this way, if it had been up to me, if someone had asked me to explain the truth for the people, I would have said, "I have been explaining it for a long time."

If that person had then asked, "What about those living in all sorts of mundane conditions? I would have said, "Here luckily I can crap once and that is enough—why be concerned about all sorts of mundane conditions?"

32

Life has no whence; it is carrying forth, and carrying forth again.

Death has no whither; it is carrying away, and carrying away again.

Ultimately how is it?

If the mind does not differ, myriad things are one suchness.

33

Everyone holds a luminous jewel, all embrace a precious gem; if you do not turn your attention around and look within, you will wander from home with a hidden treasure.

Have you not heard it said, "In the ear it is like the great and small sounds in an empty valley, none not complete; in the eye it is like myriad images under a thousand suns, none able to avoid casting shadows"?

If you seek it outside of sense experience, you will hinder the living meaning of Zen.

34

The inner ordinary states, the outer ordinary states—bamboo in the mountains, cypresses in the yard. Partial sage, ultimate sage—spring flowers, autumn moon.

When you have attained the realm of Zen, there is no Zen; when you clarify the realm of desire, there is no desire.

There is no one in the whole world who understands Buddhism—everyone is eating leftovers.

To say it is like something would miss it—it is not in the company of myriad things. What stages are there? What do you want with the beyond?

35

Cease and desist, and you are like an ocean taking in a hundred rivers. When you get here, there is no grasping or rejection.

Let go, and you are like a great tide riding on a high wind. When you come to this, there is inside and outside.

Buddhas do not know it exists; housecats do know it exists: do not put the ineffable secret of Zen in your little heart.

36

In sitting meditation, the first thing to do is simply to sit straight with the body upright, and then tune the breathing with presence of mind.

In the small vehicle of Buddhism, there were originally two methods of taming the mind: counting the breaths and contemplating mortality. People in the small vehicle consider counting the breaths to be tuning the breathing.

But the practice of the way of the Buddhas and Zen founders is forever different from the small vehicle. Buddhas and Zen masters have said, "Even if you have the heart of a leprous jackal, do not perform the small vehicle practice of self-control."

The great vehicle of Buddhism also has a method of tuning the breathing: knowing when a breath is long, knowing when a breath is short. The breath goes to the lower abdomen, and then goes out from the lower abdomen.

Impermanence is easy to realize, taming the mind is difficult to accomplish.

My teacher said, "The breath entering comes to the lower abdomen, yet it comes from nowhere; therefore it is neither long nor short. The breath goes out from the lower abdomen, but there is no finding out where it goes; therefore it is neither long nor short."

Since my teacher said this, if someone asked me how I tune my breathing, I would just say, "Though it is not the small vehicle, it is different from the great vehicle." If asked how it is ultimately, I would say, "Exhaling, inhaling, not long, not short."

37

Once Buddha went into meditation concentration while sitting in a forest. A storm arose, with a heavy downpour, thunder, and lightning. Such was the noise that two people who had been plowing their fields died of fright. Then it abruptly cleared.

Buddha rose and began to walk around. Someone followed him and asked, "A while ago when the thunder pealed, two plowmen died of fright at the noise. Didn't you hear it?"

Buddha said, "No."

The man asked, "Were you asleep?"

Buddha said, "No."

The man asked, "Were you in mindless trance where there is no perception?"

Buddha said, "No. I had mindfulness and perception; it's just that I was in meditation."

The man remarked, "This is most wonderful! The meditation

concentration of Buddha is extremely profound, to have mindfulness and perception in meditation, to be aware and yet not to hear
such a loud noise!"

In respectful praise I say that all states of mind on the Path are
summed up in entering meditation concentration with mindfulness and perception.

A different way of presenting the same reality is put to use: in
the meditation hall we reach the end of the mortal coil.

38

The Buddhas of all times and the Zen masters throughout history
carry forth the whole earth and hide it in the earth; they smash
open the world and take out the world.

When you grasp this essential key, you can practice what you
preach. Your body is not a mass of flesh, your mind is a wall. Your
eyebrows are low on the spring mountains, your eyes are blue in
the autumn sea. Hundreds of thousands of meditations appear in
every practice of matter; innumerable teachings emerge from
myriad forms.

39

Harmonious, without edges or seams; clear, without concealment:
though it may have been transmitted to Buddha's successor, how
could it have been given to the heir of the Zen founder?

Manifest everywhere are appropriate words; replete in everyone
is the fragrance of knowing vision.

Space explains, myriad forms listen; ability to bring it out does
not hang on the lips.

People, transients in this world, it fills your eyes and ears twenty-
four hours a day, transcending the passage of time.

Who is self? Who is other?

What is delusion? What is enlightenment?

Do you understand?

Pick up the radishes grown up north; how do they compare to the price of rice down south?

40

There is nowhere that the great Way of the enlightened ones is not present, no thing that does not contain it.

However, only people who have previously planted seeds of wisdom can sustain it.

That is why it is said, "It cannot be seen in form or sought in sound."

> *The wind is still throughout the world;*
> *birds cry, the mountains are quiet.*
> *The crossroads are bright as daybreak,*
> *the doors of the senses cool as autumn.*
> *Half sitting where there is no doubt,*
> *one sees illusion in a floating reflection.*

41

Going into the ocean to count the grains of sand is a vain waste of energy; polishing a tile to make a mirror is useless effort. Do you not see—the clouds on the highest mountain gather and disperse of themselves; what "far" or "near" is there? The flowing water at the bottom of the canyon follows the curves and the straits, without "this" or "that."

The everyday life of people is like clouds and water, but clouds and water are free while people are not. If they would get to be as free as clouds and water, where would people's compulsive mundane routines arise?

42

The body-mind that is "just this" is not the aggregate of material and mental elements; subtly existing, standing out, how could it be an object of emotion?

Without coming or going, it responds to sound and form; returning to the self, it overturns the middle and thence enters the sides.

Beyond relativities, the feet touch the ground. What birth and death are there; the spirit soars to the skies.

43

Freeing yourself here, you release your being on the other side. What is "the other side"? Continuous calm awareness. What is "here"? Continuous open attention.

Leaving aside "the other side" and "here" for the moment, what is such an event?

When the host makes a complete explanation, the guest bears witness; when the guest makes a complete explanation, the host bears witness.

When you make a complete explanation, I bear witness; when I make a complete explanation, you bear witness.

When you and I are speaking, the whisk and staff bear witness; when the whisk and staff are speaking, you and I bear witness.

As for freeing oneself and releasing the being, what expression have these?

A sphere of mutually appropriate explanation, that is complete: when being the guest, you gesture greeting—the host is there all along.

A hundred, a thousand, ten thousand times: so many times has it been said—why do people not understand this time?

44

If one can utter a statement at which the limits of the universe vanish, one is still talking about good and bad luck in a spring dream.

If one can utter another statement that will open up an atom to bring forth a scripture, this is still putting makeup on a beauty.

If one directly illumines the true awakening that is not a dream, then one will see that the universe is not large and an atom is not small.

Since neither is real, on what can a statement be based?

A clam in a well swallows the moon; the jade rabbit at the edge of the sky sleeps by itself in the clouds.

45

When the essential wonder is brought up, the insensitive frown; when there is mystic conversation beyond convention, the liberated go into the mundane world.

If you are ordinary, without a care, and indulge in personal judgments, it is questionable whether you can even save yourself, much less save others.

Apart from this, how do you make an assessment?

Is this not what is meant by the saying, "There's a leap year after every three; autumn comes in September"?

Is this not what is meant by the saying, "A long month is thirty days, a short one twenty-nine"?

In fact, views like this are what is called "being in front of an ass but behind a horse."

And I daresay that even to realize this is still to be in front of an ass but behind a horse.

46

In Zen study, seeking Buddhahood, do not aim for Buddhahood. If you study Zen aiming for Buddhahood, it will become all the more distant.

When obstruction crumbles away and reflection vanishes, what face is it? At this moment, you realize that getting here you need effort.

47

Zen masters in India said that mindlessness is Buddha. A Zen master of China said that mind itself is Buddha. He was not saying that the mind that jumps from one thing to another and the intellect that gallops off in any direction are what Buddha is.

Students in recent times often misunderstand this point. Some say, "Once you return to it, mind itself is Buddha, and there is not another life." If you understand in this way, you are the same as nihilistic heretics.

"Mind is Buddha"—
what religious teaching is this?
If you want to stop a child's crying,
give it a clout.

48

The sitting meditation of the Buddhas and Zen founders is not movement or stillness, not practice or realization.

It does not involve body or mind, it does not depend on delusion or enlightenment.

It does not empty objects, it is not bound to any realm.

How could it value form, sensation, conception, conditioning, or consciousness?

Study of the Way does not use sensation, conception, conditioning, or consciousness; if you practice sensation, conception, conditioning, or consciousness, this is sensation, conception, conditioning, or consciousness—it is not study of the Way.

This being so, how should you concentrate?

"The matter of life and death is important, impermanence is swift."

49

It says in the teachings that all sages and saints realize the unconditioned state, yet there are distinctions.

If someone asked me what the distinct elements are, I would say that once you get involved in distinctions it is not right anymore.

And what is the unconditioned state?

I would say knowledge of distinctions is hard to clarify.

50

A dragon howls in a hidden cave;
heaven and earth are still.
A tiger roars on a precipitous cliff;
the cold valley warms.

NOTES

1. Two perspectives on integration of presence and transcendence: from the point of view of practice, and (in the verse) from the point of view of realization.

    Three practical exercises are presented. One is contemplation of the impermanence of the subject, another is contemplation of the impermanence of objects. The third is alertness in the immediate present.

    "The nose hung in front of your face" is the immediately present awareness, through which consciousness is "breathed." Typically, Dōgen stresses that it is not enough to reach the point of total presence of mind; it is important to be able to use it effectively.

    The verse plays on the contrasts between evanescence and permanence, change and constancy, distinguishing them even as it weaves them together, portraying the Zen mind in the world yet transcending the world at the same time.

2. "Having no mind" is traditionally interpreted in such terms as having no selfish, grasping, deluded mind; not minding pointless superficialities; not minding insult or slight; not dwelling obsessively on any particular function of mind.

    "Mind itself is Buddha" was taught by an early Chinese Zen master to stop people from seeking enlightenment as something to be acquired elsewhere.

    "If you understand accordingly, you are as far off as the sky is from earth." If you understand "no mind" and "this mind" in conventional terms, you wind up identifying mindless blankness or random thought with Buddha.

    "If you do not understand accordingly, you are just a common sort." Having no mind, in the truly liberative, not escapist sense;

realizing the very mind itself, in its essential nature rather than its superficial functions: both are means of transcending the ordinary consciousness.

The symbolism of the first two lines of the verse is self-explanatory. The last two lines mean that when you realize enlightenment in yourself through individual transcendence, your experience of the whole world takes place in a new light.

3. "Thinking" of what does not think refers to the Zen exercise of *ekō henshō,* "turning the light around to shine back," or turning the attention to the innermost mind, to the very seat of consciousness. Elsewhere Dōgen refers to this as the essential art of zazen or sitting meditation.

Just as Dōgen warns people not to take the Zen phrase "this mind is Buddha" to refer to thoughts or the thinking function, he uses this story on "thinking of what does not think" to help ensure that meditators will reach sufficiently deeply into the source.

When the Zen master says "It is not thought," this means that the expression "thinking" here is only a metaphor, and the process of directing the attention in this manner is not "thought" in the sense of conceptualization or mental talk.

This exercise is not unthinking self-absorption, and it is not self-analysis. The verse is a representation of its subtlety and centered balance in practice.

4. See the translation of Dōgen's *Shōbōgenzō* essay "Awakening the Unsurpassed Mind," paragraphs 5, 16, 22, 35.

5. According to ancient Buddhist lore, it is possible to attain occult powers without being enlightened. Of six supernormal powers said to be attained by enlightened Buddhas, only one is believed to be exclusive to them; that is what is called the knowledge of noncontamination. The enlightened Buddhas' unique power of noncontamination refers to their ultimate unaffected freedom in the midst of all phenomena. This cannot be "acquired" by a contrived "practice." On this see the chapter entitled "The Ten Stages" in the *Flower Ornament Scripture,* particularly the sections on stages four, seven, and eight.

6. This passage is a conventional expression of *suchness.*

7. The first passage alludes to the Zen practice called *kōjō,* which means transcendence and also progress, referring to the continuing process of going beyond accomplishment.

The second and third passages allude to the Zen practice called *ekō henshō*, referred to earlier in the notes to the third section of these translations from *Eihei Kōroku*, meaning to turn the attention around to focus on the innermost essence of mind. This practice is not of only one stage; its use is renewed in advanced stages to wean the mind from higher experiences and maintain its essence in complete freedom.

The question "What thing is it that comes thus?" is from an ancient Zen story in which the person thus questioned replies, after eight years of contemplation, "To speak of it as like something would be to miss the mark."

This represents the "unpegged" clear eye that sees objectively: as Dōgen says, in its perspective "the true does not cover the false, the crooked does not hide the straight."

8. Superficial literalism does not yield the real meaning of Buddhist scripture; yet avoiding literalism does not mean ignoring the teachings either. The classical Zen master Baizhang (Hyakujō) interpreted this saying in these terms: "To remain fixedly abiding in the present mirroring awareness is the enemy of the Buddhas of all times; yet anything outside of this is the same as devil talk."

9. Removing obstructing fixations to attain more complete consciousness is an essential part of Zen practice: whether primary attention is given to the "removal" or to the "pervasion" depends upon the stage of progress realized by the individual learner. To pose this as a question of choice, as if it were a matter of preferring one "statement" to the other, is a typical Zen strategic maneuver to make individual hearers think for themselves.

"Complete" is "a statement that the enlightened ones have never made" insofar as the Way never ends. Not only is the Way infinite; there are also infinite ways to see the infinity of the Way. For example, as the object of Buddhas is to enlighten all beings, this process is never complete; as the object of Buddhas is to awaken to all knowledge, this process is never complete. Also, when one attains the "statement that fills everywhere," namely the experience of panoramic awareness, this seems to be complete; but it is only so in a general sense, not in terms of every particular of potential within encompassing consciousness.

10. The first paragraph represents the Buddhist "transcendent wisdom" teaching on the end transcending the means.

The second paragraph introduces the classic Zen terms "thus" and "not thus," which developed through the early Zen handling of the Buddhist teaching of "suchness."

To "study thus" means to receive communication directly from objective reality. To "study it as not thus" means to detach from subjective notions of reality.

Detaching from subjective notions of reality is close to receiving communication directly from objective reality, but not quite the same experience. In Tendai Buddhist terms, this is the difference between a conformative state and a state of realization; one is still affected by deliberate cultivation, the other is spontaneously so of its own nature. This point is illustrated very precisely and in great detail by the differences between the experiences of the seventh and eight stages of enlightenment as described in the core book of the "Ten Stages" in the *Flower Ornament Scripture.*

Baso (Mazu) and Nangaku (Nanyue) were Chinese Zen masters of the middle Tang dynasty. Nangaku is considered a direct disciple of the illustrious Sixth Ancestor of Zen, one of the greatest figures in all of Zen history. Like most of the Sixth Ancestor's disciples, Nangaku is overshadowed in history by his great teacher, and nothing much is really known about him. Baso, on the other hand, ranks almost on a par with his spiritual grandsire in Zen history; he is said to have produced between eighty-four and one hundred and thirty-nine enlightened disciples, a most unusual achievement.

Nangaku and Baso were regarded as ancestors of the Rinzai schools of Zen, and stories about them were popular among followers of Rinzai Zen.

"The barbarian rebellion," an overthrow of the conventional order, symbolizes Zen awakening.

"Salt and soup for meals" refers to living and working in the world after enlightenment. "Thirty years" is a traditional figure representing a period of completion and maturation after awakening.

"Making a ball of this story, I offer it to the enlightened ones." The imagery of this paragraph is from the *Flower Ornament Scripture:* see, for example, the stories of Ratnachuda and the perfumer Samantanetra in the final book of the scripture, the "Entry into the Realm of Reality." The idea of offering both external and internal resources refers to a complete dedication to enlightenment, such as

Dōgen describes in his *Shōbōgenzō* essay "Awakening the Unsur-passed Mind."

"In the million years since the barbarian rebellion. . . ." The essential theme of both the *Lotus* and the *Flower Ornament* scriptures is the eternity of the reality underlying Buddhahood. In Tendai Buddhist terms, here Dōgen shifts perspective from initial enlight-enment, the individual realization that takes place in time ("thirty years"), to fundamental enlightenment, the perennial potential that makes individual realization possible throughout all time ("million years").

11. "Refutation" and "accommodation" are complementary teaching techniques. In abstract terms, a "statement removing obstructing fixations" (see selection 9 above) exemplifies "refutation," while a "statement filling everywhere" exemplifies "accommodation." In concrete terms, it is possible to apply these techniques in general or in particular, so they could take many different forms.

The famous story Dōgen recites gives one example of a concrete practical application of these methods, and recapitulates their ab-stract pattern in his verse. "How much light do the pillars and lamps begrudge?" The reality of suchness is always evident; subjective imaginings are all that screen it. As long as suchness is "buried in the ashes" of mental construction, "though you search you don't see" because of what is in your eyes. "Lighting it up and blowing it out," rousing the self-questioning necessary to penetrate through the very possibility of self-deception, the original mind underlying it all "goes into action again."

12. Sudhana and Manjushri are key figures of the *Flower Ornament Scripture*. Manjushri, personification of wisdom, is one of the main interlocutors of the whole scripture. Sudhana, personification of wholesome learning capacity, is a pilgrim of enlightenment in the extended allegory of the final book of the scripture, the "Entry into the Realm of Reality." In that book Manjushri locates Sudhana and sends him on a journey; ultimately Manjushri appears to Sudhana again on the eve of the consummation of his journey.

In the famous *Discourse on the Flower Ornament,* a Tang dynasty treatise highly regarded in Chinese Zen studies, the symbolism of this final meeting is briefly described in these terms:

> After establishing Sudhana in his own place, Manjushri disappeared, illustrating how after the fruition of Buddhahood

one is not different from when one was among ordinary mortals. After one attains Buddhahood, Buddha is basically nonexistent, so Manjushri "disappeared."

Sudhana saw as many spiritual benefactors as atoms in a billion-world universe, in the sense that knowledge of the body of reality pervades the real universe evenly, so he saw everything everywhere as no different from the body of Manjushri.*

Taking the "blade of grass" in Dōgen's story to stand for suchness, or being-as-is, this first paragraph from the text shows how "this blade of grass can kill people," while the second paragraph shows how "this blade of grass can enliven people."

Death and life are "a blade of grass apart." This means, "How do you see this blade of grass?"

The *Vaipulya*, or "Extended" teachings of Buddhism, in which the whole world is identified with nirvana and Buddha, are said to be poison to those who cannot digest them, clarified ghee to those who can digest them.

13. The "day of the full moon" refers to awakening.

"The wind is high, the moon is cool": the whirl of events in the world may be hectic, but the original mind is unaffected.

"The sea is calm, the rivers are clear": when the whole mind is serene, its functions are lucid.

"Sky and wind go on forever": the eternal unchanging and temporal change are comprehended simultaneously.

"Without turning away . . . body and mind drop off": emotional and intellectual transcendence are attained without rejecting the world and abandoning society.

14. This is a refined breathing-mindfulness exercise, used to attain serenity of mind.

15. "You cannot but know": it is everywhere.

"The eternal sky does not inhibit the flight of the white clouds": realization of the absolute does not extinguish experience of the relative.

"Why bother to ask a Zen master": it is obvious.

16. The *Tao Te Ching* says, "Sky became clear by attaining unity, earth

---

Entry into the Realm of Reality: The Guide, translated by Thomas Cleary (Boston: Shambhala Publications), p. 83.

became steady by attaining unity, spirit was quickened by attaining unity, valley streams were filled by attaining unity, all beings were born by attaining unity."

"Every time you reach *today,* then you can go on *thus":* realization of the awareness of being-as-is goes on from the present to the present; "the lucky day is when you discover it's all one day."

17. "Mind like a fan in winter, body like a cloud in a cold valley": mentally and physically serene and unattached.

"Doing it yourself" represents the practice of diligence; "who will do it" represents the practice of meditation.

"An iron wall stands steep and precipitous" stands for the Zen state that is totally aloof and ungraspable.

18. "Although you are aware of the cold wind chilling you, you don't yet know for whose sake the bright moon is white." The "cold wind chilling you" is "birth, old age, sickness, and death." As long as the idea of something to be transcended remains, this obscures the inherent Buddha-nature.

"When a white heron stands in the snow, they aren't the same color." The heron, snow, moon, and flowers are all "white," yet they are distinct when arrayed together: this is a traditional Zen metaphor representing the experiential integration of the absolute and the relative, in which their unity does not obliterate their distinctness.

19. The "cold piercing the bone" represents the heart of nirvana; the "apricot blossoms perfuming the whole world" represent the knowledge of differentiations. In Tendai Buddhist terms, the cold piercing the bone represents "stopping," the blossoms perfuming the world represent "seeing."

20. Dōgen refers and alludes to this famous story of the founder of Zen and four disciples time and again in *Shōbōgenzō,* similarly emphasizing the importance of seeing it as a whole and not imposing fixed rankings on the statements of realization.

When the "robe and bowl," or Zen successorship, "enters hands worthy of transmission," this is the teaching operating "in an atom." When it is "heard" by virtue of consciousness, wherever it may be, this is the teaching operating "in the whole world."

21. "The corpse is here; where has the person gone?" One of the contemplative exercises that became popular in later Chinese Zen was working on the question, "Who is dragging this corpse around?"

"A rootless tree, a patch of ground with neither sunlight nor shade, and a valley that does not echo": a state without attachment, unaffected by change, not reacting automatically.

22. Ordinarily in universalist Mahāyāna Buddhism it is said that all sentient beings have Buddha-nature. The great mid-Tang dynasty Chinese master Hyakujō seems to have begun saying that "sentient" beings, meaning people deceived by their own senses, effectively lack Buddha-nature, because it is veiled to them.

23. These expressions stand for the integration of the relative and the absolute: but because they speak of union they retain a sense of duality, and therefore stand for the stage of process. In Dōgen's capping phrase, there is no trace of absolute opposed to relative; the inexpressible absolute is in the relative being *just* the relative.

24. The attentive reader will easily understand the symbolism of this passage: the "answer beyond convention" is one's own direct experience.

25. The midautumn full moon is traditionally celebrated as the clearest and brightest of the year.

"The tree on the moon": this is one way the pattern of the craters on the moon was seen. In Zen metaphor, these shadows are flaws in the mirror of awareness, so "pruning away the tree on the moon" stands for clarification of awakened consciousness.

"When a foreigner comes, a foreigner is reflected; when a native comes, a native": pursuing the metaphor of enlightened awareness being like a mirror objectively reflecting whatever it faces.

26. "Space . . . seems to have no partner." This alludes to a meditation exercise in which the whole universe is made into a single point of awareness. It is a way of transcending the realm of particulars, so it leads to realization of "half emptiness," which is formless and immaterial, and so "seems like freedom and ease."

"Dusky yellow" is the color of the "blood" of the "dragons battling in the field" in the symbolism of the ancient Chinese classic known as the *I Ching*, or *Book of Change*. This image occurs at the sixth yin component of the *Earth/Receptive* hexagram, which represents excessive or exaggerated yin. In Zen terms, this refers to nihilism or quietism, an aberration resulting from exaggeration of "half emptiness" and "seeming freedom and ease."

The image of "clarity" for emptiness does not refer to absence of contents, but to freedom from clinging to arbitrary subjectivity: "when does a clear mirror ever dream of 'fine' and 'hideous'?" Here, "fine" stands for nirvana as extinction or quiescence, in contrast to "hideous" samsara as turmoil and confusion. The "clarity" of the mirror of emptiness reflects both the peace of nirvana and the activity of samsara without itself being affected by either.

"Unconsciously the double discs over the oceans of infinite lands turned their light around overnight and are in the corals": in a natural and spontaneous manner the intuitive mind and the rational mind revert to their inherent natures through cessation of conditioned compulsions, and thus arrive at perception of greater objectivity.

27. The voidness aspect of emptiness meditation has a purifying effect, clearing the mind of arbitrary thoughts and ideas, and thus facilitating complete awareness of being-as-is.

28. This is a restatement of the idea that all people, and indeed all living beings, have Buddha-nature, yet it remains dormant unless the thought of enlightenment arouses the determination to realize it mindfully.

29. The supernal enlightening being who represents the embodiment of compassion is often depicted as having twelve faces, while the mythological Buddha of the future is represented as being embodied in ten million different forms. In general terms, these expressions refer to the totality of subjective and objective experience in all their possible forms.

"When great doubt is urgent, you cannot get a grasp." The Zen practice of "great doubt" is not the same as verbally or conceptually formulated intellectual doubt; it is direct confrontation with the ungraspability and inconceivability of ultimate reality in itself. Therefore "explaining in conventional terms is useless."

30. This passage explicitly illustrates the multifaceted character of a Zen master's approach to teaching, demonstrating the folly of attempting to treat Zen teachings as if they were fixed dogmas or rigid systems.

31. Nansen (Nanquan) was a late middle Tang dynasty Chinese Zen master traditionally represented as a symbol of transcending means and living freely beyond things. Virtually all the popular stories featuring Nansen refer to this specific stage and function.

The Transcendent Wisdom Scriptures of Buddhism, which emphasize relinquishment of means when the end is attained, speak of the universalist Buddhist as one who liberates people without having any idea of doing so, or even that there is anyone to be liberated. This is because of not entertaining any notion of self or personality.

"I can crap once and that is enough—why be concerned about all sorts of mundane conditions?" This is an illustration of the transcendent wisdom teaching of universal emptiness, which frees the mind from bondage to material forms and conceptual habits.

32. "Life . . . Death . . ." Typically of Zen teachings, these statements are not intended as philosophical propositions or religious dogma; they are representative of meditation exercises, looking into the "whence" and the "whither" with the inner eye. Traditionally, these two are used both individually and together; they are aimed at opening awareness of the essence of the nature of mind, which is unmodified by fluctuations of thought and therefore perceives suchness directly.

33. Traditional metaphors for Buddha-nature, from the great universalist Mahāyāna *Lotus* and *Nirvana* scriptures fundamental to Tendai Buddhism. To "turn your attention around and look within" is a Zen expression for an exercise to discover this hidden essence. Although this practice is particularly prominent in Zen, it is part of the meditation programs of all complete Mahāyāna Buddhist schools, including complete Tendai, Pure Land, and Flower Ornament Buddhist formats.

In spite of the terminology, "turning your attention around and looking within" does not mean introversion as understood in Western psychology. Here Dōgen says, "If you seek it outside of sense experience, you will hinder the living meaning of Zen," paraphrasing a line from one of the most ancient Zen classics, the *Inscription on Faith in the Mind* by the Third Ancestor: "Do not despise the six senses; the six senses are the same as true awakening."

34. This is a poetic statement of the precise moment of the transcendent present of Zen awakening. "No one in the world understands Buddhism" because as long as there is "someone" to understand "something," this is already secondhand.

35. This section illustrates what Tendai Buddhism calls "stopping and seeing" to attain realization of the integration of the absolute and the relative. "Cease and desist" through focus on the absolute; this is the Tendai exercise of "stopping." "Let go" through focus on the relative; this is the Tendai exercise of "seeing."

"Buddhas do not know it exists": alludes to the aspect of the absolute, subtle beyond all thought. "Housecats do know it exists" alludes to the aspect of the relative, evident in all places and times. "Do not put the ineffable secret of Zen in your little heart": the integration of the absolute and the relative does not mean that the absolute becomes relative or that the relative becomes absolute; it is not a subjective notion objectified.

36. "Even if you have the heart of a leprous jackal, do not perform the small vehicle practice of self-control": if you become absorbed in auto-tranquilization, you deprive yourself of useful stimuli to conscious development. Mahāyāna Buddhists say that this arrests one's individual growth and also stunts the development of compassion and social consciousness.

It may be useful to note that modern Zen sects do actually teach people to use what Dōgen calls the small vehicle method of counting the breaths. Some of them (particularly in the East) do it only for a brief recollective period, to develop concentration before going on to Zen exercises; others (primarily in Western versions) may carry on with this exercise for years.

See also selection number 14 above in connection with this speech.

37. The central point of the story about the Buddha in meditation illustrates a stage beyond the quiescence of all senses and perceptions, which was in Buddha's time regarded as the highest yogic state. The universalist Mahāyāna position is that by remaining poised in the center, neither grasping nor rejecting, it is possible to "not hear"— to be undisturbed—even in the midst of the world, without shutting anything out. The advantage to this method is that it saves the energy of trying to "attain" inner and outer quiescence in order to meditate.

In Tendai Buddhist terms, this is using "seeing" to attain "stopping." The "seeing" that Dōgen says he used—"reaching the end of the mortal coil in the meditation hall"—is referred to in Flower Ornament Buddhism as "stopping by seeing the extinction of the person," which means observing the fact of mortality. In this connection see also the story of the Seven Sagacious Women in selection number 21 above.

38. Rather than a sermon on transcending the dichotomy of subject and object in order to experience reality by direct perception, here Dōgen gives a little description of what it actually feels like to be one with the universe and all things.

39. Here is an example of a meditation method for getting to the union mentioned in the preceding selection by searching the outermost and innermost layers of reality to see where they touch. The *Flower Ornament Scripture* says, "If you want to know the realm of Buddhahood, make your mind as clear as space, unobstructed in all directions." It also says, "Lands teach, beings teach, all things in all times teach."

40. The omnipresence of reality does not obstruct the ubiquitousness of illusion. While reality is all around in objective truth forever, the individual and collective ability to sustain the vision of reality need to be cultivated in actual life experience, in conscious being-time.

   "It cannot be seen in form or sought in sound": it cannot be seen in routines and clichés, it cannot be seen in the terms of the customary world of conditioned mental habit.

   The first two lines of Dōgen's verse represent "stopping," or the heart of nirvana, unaffected by the world. The middle two lines represent "seeing," which while operating in the relative world sees through to the absolute. The last two lines represent practical integration of "stopping" and "seeing."

41. "Going into the ocean to count the grains of sand" symbolizes literalist scholarship; "polishing a tile to make a mirror" symbolizes contrived meditation. Dōgen follows with descriptions of spontaneous detachment and adaptation.

42. The integration of the absolute and the relative in "just this"—not identifying with material or psychological conditions, yet evidently present in the immediacy of reality beyond thought and feeling.

   While the essence of mind is "without coming and going," the functions of mind "respond to sound and form." The absolute neither comes nor goes, the relative depends on conditions.

   "Returning to the self, it overturns the middle and thence enters the sides." A progressive Tendai meditation: contemplation of the conditional nature of phenomena leads into a realization of the emptiness of absolute nature and the relativity of conditional existence. Emptiness and conditional existence, or nirvana and samsara, are the "sides"; they become extreme views when isolated from each other. The "middle" is a state of equipoise attained by shifting back and forth between the absolute and the relative until one can "hover" above their duality.

   Once this is accomplished, one then "returns to the self" by the exercise of looking into the essence of mind to see what it is that realizes the middle. In Tendai meditation this is called "returning," which is practiced after accomplishment of "seeing." This "over-turns" attachment to the middle and enables the free mind to enter into either a nirvanic or a samsaric state without obstruction. The introduction to the "Ten Stages" of the *Flower Ornament Scripture* describes enlightening beings in these terms: "They showed entries into mundane existence and nirvana, while not interrupting the application of means of practices of enlightening beings."

"Beyond relativities, the feet touch the ground. What birth or death are there, the spirit soars to the skies." These lines represent the integration of the absolute and the relative, experienced as integration of the formless awareness of the ineffable, unchanging essence of mind with precise consciousness of everyday reality.

Also compare this selection with number 34 above.

43. The eyes of this selection are the expressions "continuous calm awareness" and "continuous open attention." What follows are descriptions of intimate communion of mind and environment: the "complete explanation" represents suchness, to "bear witness" represents awareness of suchness. Sometimes awakening is described as consisting of "only suchness and knowledge of suchness."

44. "The limits of the universe" represent mental limitations subjectively imposed by temporal conditioning. Even to speak of overcoming these limitations suggests the idea of removing what does not in itself exist; contriving the notion of extinction posits existence. This point is traditionally cited as a central psycho-philosophical basis for the difference between "small vehicle" Hinayāna Buddhism oriented toward self-tranquilization, and "great vehicle" Mahāyāna Buddhism oriented toward universal salvation.

To "open up an atom and bring forth a scripture" is to articulate the lessons of every moment: it is still a description and not the direct experience of the orignial moment itself.

"The universe is not large and an atom is not small" means that magnitude is relative to focal point. Using the Zen technique of spaciousness of mind, sometimes you absorb the world into yourself, sometimes you absorb yourself in the world. Using the vastness of space as you absorb the world into yourself, "the universe is not large." Using the pervasiveness of space to absorb yourself into the world, "an atom is not small."

"Since neither is real, on what can a statement be based?" If everything is relative, how can objectivity be realized? Dōgen goes on to talk about the process of enlightenment.

"A clam in a well swallows the moon; the jade rabbit at the edge of the sky sleeps by itself in the clouds." Clams were a primary source of pearls in China; they were figuratively said to be made by the clams opening up on the night of the full moon and "swallowing" the moonlight. In Chinese Zen this image came to be used for the individual attaining enlightenment by opening up to greater reality. Here in this line of Dōgen's ditty the "well" stands for pinpoint focus of concentration.

"The jade rabbit at the edge of the sky sleeps by itself in the clouds." The jade rabbit is a poetic name for the moon, which stands for enlightenment. The sky is a metaphor for the open, spacious, unobstructed mind. That the moon is at the "edge" of the sky is a treble-entendre summarizing the Tendai practice of triple seeing in one mind: awareness gone to the furthest reaches of both the absolute and the relative, emptiness and conditional existence, and to precisely the point of their meeting. That the moon "sleeps by itself" signifies unobtrusiveness and independence; that it sleeps by itself "in the clouds" signifies its veiled presence in the world.

45. The first two paragraphs should be considered carefully in terms of their evident meanings.

To be "in front of an ass but behind a horse" is a Zen expression for seeing the evident. This basic sobriety is "in front of an ass," because everyone knows that fools do not even see what is obvious; yet it is still "behind a horse," in the sense that the penetratingly enlightened see beyond appearances to what is not obvious on the evident surface of things.

46. The word for "aim" in this passage is not the word for "will" but the word for "calculate," "measure," "scheme." It does not mean aspiration per se, but ambition.

47. The vulgarization of the "mind = buddha" equation with its consequent results in pragmatic expression are a focus of Dōgen's critical eye throughout most of his works, especially *Shōbōgenzō*. The first two paragraphs are one of the simplest summaries of the problem with this point.

As for Dōgen's verse, to "stop a child's crying" is a classical simile for the use of Buddhist teachings and practices to relieve afflictions, intimating therein that these are temporary measures and not dogmatic observances. "Give it a clout" means to provide a transcendent stimulus, something that will jar the mind out of its self-limiting, routine outlook and thinking patterns. "Mind is Buddha" was originally intended to jar people out of their attachment to the externals of the teaching; when it later was debased into a slogan of arbitrary self-approval, it ceased to have its original Buddhistic liberating effect and instead released indulgent tendencies.

48. This is a highly refined, formless "form" of Zen meditation. The inner attention it demands is so subtle that it is not possible to deliberately "concentrate" upon it, only to tacitly merge with it; the outer attention sustaining it requires such empowerment that it needs to focus on what is most urgent. Therefore it is serene but not lax, intensive but not stressssful, lucid but not blank.

49. In the last story of the Zen classic *The Blue Cliff Record*, which Dōgen introduced to Japan, someone asks a Zen master, "What is the sword of wisdom?" The master replied, "Each branch of coral holds up the moon."

50. "Hidden" means there is no trace of conceptual tagging; a "cave" represents concentration or absorption.

A "precipitous cliff" stands for the vantage point of the absolute, inaccessible by relative thought yet directly aware of the suchness of the relative itself.

A "cold valley" represents unbiased perceptivity; "warming" symbolizes becoming lively and active.

This verse also illustrates the integration of the relative and the absolute, including the integration of matter and emptiness, and the integration of practice and realization.

Treasury of Eyes
of True Teaching

SELECTED ESSAYS

FROM

Shōbōgenzō

———

DO NOT DO ANYTHING EVIL

1   An ancient Buddha said; *"Do not do anything evil; do good, and purify the mind yourself—this is the teaching of all the enlightened."*

2   As the general precept of the ancestral school of the Seven Buddhas, this is correctly transmitted from former Buddhas to later Buddhas; later Buddhas have inherited it from former Buddhas. It is not only of the Seven Buddhas—*this is the teaching of all the enlightened.* We should contemplate this principle carefully. What is called the way of the Seven Buddhas must be like the way of the Seven Buddhas. Transmitted and inherited, it is still the *conveying a message* of *herein.* Being *the teaching of all the enlightened,* it is the *teaching, practice, and realization* of *a billion Buddhas.*

3   The evils spoken of here have the evil nature, which is one among the good nature, evil nature, and indeterminate nature. That nature is *unoriginated;* the good nature and indeterminate nature are also *unoriginated, uncontaminated,* and *characteristics of reality,* yet within these three natures there are a number of phenomena.

4   As for evils, there are sameness and difference between the evil of this realm and the evil of other realms, there are sameness and difference between prior times and later times; the evil of the heavens and the evil of the human world are the same and different. How much the more is this so of the way of the enlightened and the world; the evil of the way, the good of the way, and the indeterminate of the way are far different.

5   Good and evil are time, time is not good or evil. Good and evil are phenomena, phenomena are not good or evil. The *equality of phenomena* is the *equality of evil,* the *equality of phenomena* is the *equality of good.* However, in learning *supreme perfect enlightenment,* in listening to teaching, practical application, and experience of results, it is deep, far reaching, subtle.

6   One may hear of this supreme enlightenment from a teacher, or from scriptures. At first, it says *don't do any evil.* If it doesn't say *don't do any evil,* it is not the true teaching of Buddhas; it must be demonic suggestion. You should know that what says *don't do any evil* is the true teaching of Buddhas.

7   "Do not do any evil"—it is not the initiative of ordinary people that makes it this way; in *listening to the teaching* of the explanation of enlightenment, it comes across this way. What comes across this way is an expression which is the word of supreme enlightenment. Since it is the *word of enlightenment,* therefore it *bespeaks enlightenment.*

8   Becoming an expression of supreme enlightenment, put into operation in *being heard,* one aspires to it as *don't do any evil,* and carries it out as *don't do any evil;* in the course of development, where evils are no longer done, the *power of practical application* suddenly becomes manifest.

9   This manifestation is manifest to the amount of the *whole earth,* the *whole world,* the *whole time,* the *whole reality.* The amount of that amount is *not doing. Precisely such a person,* at *precisely such a time,* cannot do evil any more, even though being in places conducive to evil, facing situations conducive to evil, and being in the company of evil-doing companions. Because the *amount of power* of *not doing* becomes manifest, evils naturally do not express themselves as evils; there are no implements fixed as evils.

10 There is a principle of *one picked up, one put down.* At *precisely such a time,* the principle of evil not invading people is known, and the

principle of people not destroying evil is clarified. In applying one's whole mind to practice, applying the whole body to practice, there is *eighty to ninety percent accomplishment* before the event, there is *not doing* after the intent.

11 As you bring your body-mind to practice, as you bring *whose* body-mind to practice, as the power of practical application with the *four elements and five clusters* abruptly becomes evident, it does not defile the *self* of the *four elements and five clusters*. Even the *four elements and five clusters* of *today* go on being cultivated in practice, the power of the *four elements and five clusters* that are the practice of *right now* makes the above *four elements and five clusters* be practice.

12 As it makes even the *mountains, rivers, earth, sun, moon, and stars* practice, the *mountains, rivers, earth, sun, moon, and stars* conversely make us practice.

13 This is not the eye of one time; it is the living eye of all times. Because they are times when the eye is the living eye, they make the enlightened practice, listen to the teaching, realize the result. Because the enlightened have never allowed teaching, practice, and realization to cause defilement, therefore teaching, practice, and realization have never obstructed the enlightened.

14 Therefore, as they make the enlightened practice, there have never been any enlightened ones who have avoided the incipience or aftermath of past, present, or future. When *living beings become enlightened beings,* although they do not obstruct the enlightened beings that have been there all along, they should attentively think about the principle of *becoming enlightened beings* twenty-four hours a day, whatever they may be doing.

15 In *becoming an enlightened being,* this does not destroy the *living being,* or take it away, or lose it; nevertheless, it does mean having shed it.

16   In making good and bad cause and effect cultivate practice, this is not stirring cause and effect, it is not fabrication. When there is cause and effect, it makes us cultivate practice. The *original face* of this cause and effect is already clear: it is *not doing*, it is *no origination*, it is *impermanence*, it is *not obscuring*, it is *not falling*—because it is *shedding*.

17   While studying in this way, evils are manifest as a continuum of being ever *not done*. Inspired by this manifestation, seeing through to the fact that *evils are not done*, one *settles it finally*. At *precisely such* a time, as the *beginning, middle, and end* manifest as *evils not done*, evils are not *born from conditions*—they are only *not done*; evils do not *perish through conditions*—they are only *not done*.

18   If evils are equal, all phenomena are equal too. Those who know that evils are *born from conditions*, but who do not see that these conditions are *not done* of themselves, are to be pitied.

19   Since *the family of Buddhas arises from conditions*, thus *conditions arise from the family of Buddhas*. It is not that evils do not exist, it is just that they are *not done*. It is not that evils exist, just that they are *not done*. Evils are not empty, they are *not done*. Evils are not forms, they are *not done*. Evils are not *not done*, they are just *not done*.

20   For example, spring pines are not nonexistent, not existent; they are *not doing*. Autumn chrysanthemums are not existent, not nonexistent; they are *not doing*. The Buddhas are not existent, not nonexistent; they are *not doing*. The *pillars, lamps, whisk, staff,* and so on are not existent, not nonexistent; they are *not doing*. The self is not existent, not nonexistent; it is *not doing*.

21   Such study is the issue that is at hand, it is the presence of the issue; it works from the host, works from the guest. It being thus, even if one objects to that which is not done as being done, still inevitably this is the power of the work of *not doing*. Therefore, to

hypothesize *not doing* and try to do it is like walking northward to reach the south.

22   The *not doing of evils* is not only *the well looking at the donkey;* it is *the well looking at the well,* it is *the donkey looking at the donkey,* it is the person looking at the person, it is the mountain looking at the mountain. Because there is *expressing the principle of response,* it is *not doing evils.* It is *the reality body of Buddhas being like space, manifesting form in response to beings, like the moon reflected in water.* Because it is *not doing* that is *in response to beings,* it is *not doing* that is *manifesting form. Like space,* it is *clapping on the left, clapping on the right. Like the moon reflected in water,* it is *being unobstructed by the moon in the water.* These *not doings* are manifestations not to be doubted any more.

23   *Do good.* This *good* refers to the nature of goodness among the three natures. Although there is good in the nature of goodness, there has never been good that has become manifest beforehand to await the agent. At *precisely such a time* of *doing good,* there is no good that does not come. Although all that is good is formless, accounting in *doing good* is faster than a magnet attracting iron. That power is stronger than a gale. Even the *earth, mountains, rivers,* the *world,* the *country,* the *dominant power of action,* cannot obstruct the *accounting* of good.

24   However, the principle is the same that the recognition of good is different according to the world. Because of considering recognition as good, *it is like the manner of teaching of the Buddhas of past, present, and future.*

25   "The same" means *teaching in the world* is just time. Because they have also left life span and physical capacity entirely up to time, they *expound no different teaching.*

26   Therefore good in the state of *practicing according to faith* and good in the state of *practicing according to truth* are quite different, while

they seem not to be different teachings. For example, what is keeping precepts for disciples is breaking precepts for enlightening beings.

27 Good does not *arise from conditions* or *perish through conditions.* Though good is all phenomena, all phenomena are not good. Conditions, arising and perishing, and good, are alike *correct in the end* when they are *correct in the beginning.*

28 Although good is performance, it is not self, not known by self, not other, not known by other. As for the cognition and view of self and other: because in cognition there is self and other, and there is self and other pertaining to views, therefore the living eye of each one is in the sun, and in the moon—this is performance.

29 Although at *precisely such a time* of performance, there is the issue at hand, it is not that the issue has just come about, nor that the issue has always been there. Would you still call it past practice?

30 Although *doing good* is *performance,* it cannot be measured. Although the present *performance* is the *living eye,* it is not measurement. It has not come to be to measure anything: the measurement of the *living eye* cannot be the same as the measurement of other things.

31 *Good* is not in the class of existence or nonexistence, form or void; it is just *performance.* Its manifestation in whatsoever place, its manifestation in whatsoever time, must be *performance.* In this *performance* there must be the manifestation of good.

32 Although the *manifestation* of *performance* is the issue, it is not produced and destroyed, it is not *conditional relation.* The entry, abiding, and exit of *performance* are also like this.

33 Where one good among many is already performing, the *whole body of the total teaching* and the *ground of true reality* are together

being performed. The causes and effects of this good are alike *the issue at hand.* Although it is not that causes are before and effects are after, with *causes fulfilled, effects are fulfilled;* the fact is that with *causes equal, phenomena are equal;* with *effects equal, phenomena are equal.* Although effects are experienced awaited by causes, it is not a matter of before and after, because there is a way of such as before and after.

34 In *purifying the mind yourself,* it is the *self* of *not doing,* it is the *purification* of *not doing,* it is the *purification* of *performance,* it is the *the* of *performance,* it is the *self* of *performance.* Therefore it says *this is the teaching of all the enlightened.*

35 *The enlightened* may be like independent celestials. Although there are similarities and dissimilarities in independent celestials, the independent celestials are all not *the enlightened.* This principle should be studied intently. Without studying what *the enlightened* must be like, even though one may vainly seem to struggle, as a living being suffering further this is not *carrying out the way of the enlightened. Not doing* and *performing* are *the business of the horse coming up before the business of the ass is over.*

36 There was a famous statesman and poet of Tang dynasty China who was a lay disciple of a certain Zen master descended from Zen master Baso. When this man was the Inspector of Hangchow, he visited Zen master Dōrin of the Bird's Nest.

37 In the course of that visit, the statesman asked, "What is the great meaning of Buddhism?"

38 Dōrin replied, *"Do not do anything evil, do good."*

39 The statesman said, "If so, even a three-year-old child can say this."

40 Dōrin said, *"A three-year-old child may be able to say it, but an eighty-year-old man cannot practice it."*

41 At this the statesman bowed in thanks.

42 Although this man came from a military background, he was truly
a poet of rare genius. It was said that he had been a literatus for
twenty-four lifetimes. He was sometimes called Manjushri, sometimes called Maitreya.

43 Yet even though he was a famous man of culture, he was a beginner
on the Buddha Way, a newcomer. Indeed, he seems not to have
even dreamed of this teaching of *don't do evil, do good*. He thought
that Dōrin must have been saying, "Don't do evil, do good" only
recognizing intentional contrivance. Thinking this, he spoke as he
did, not knowing or hearing the eternal principle of all enlightened
ones, the *nondoing of evil* and the *doing of good*, thus lacking the
power of the enlightened teaching.

44 Even if fabricated evils are proscribed, and even if fabricated good
is encouraged, it must be the *nondoing* and *performance* of *manifestation*.

45 Generally speaking, enlightened teaching is equal when first heard
from a teacher and in the ultimate result. This is called *correct in
the beginning, correct at the end*, and it is called *sublime cause,
sublime result*, and it is called *enlightened cause, enlightened result*.
As the cause and result of the way of the enlightened is not a
question of such ideas as *differential development* and *equivalent
continuity*, if not for an *enlightened cause* it is impossible to effect
an *enlightened result*.

46 Because Dōrin expresses this principle, he has enlightened teaching.
Even if evils fill the whole world on so many levels, even if evils
have swallowed the whole world on so many levels, this is the
liberation of *not doing*. Since good is *good in the beginning, middle,
and end*, it makes the *nature, characteristic, essence, power, etc.*, of
performance be *thus*.

47   Since the poet-statesman had never tread this pathway, he said it
      could be expressed even by a three-year-old child. He said this
      without the power to correctly express expression. What a pity.
      Sir, *What are you saying?* Since you have not yet heard the Way of
      Buddhas, do you know a three-year-old child? Do you know the
      principle of a child's being born with potential? Anyone who
      knows a three-year-old child would know the enlightened ones of
      past, present, and future. If one does not yet know the enlightened
      ones of past, present, and future, how could one know a three-
      year-old child?

48   Don't think that meeting is knowing, and don't think one does not
      know without meeting. One who knows a single atom knows the
      whole world; one who comprehends one phenomenon compre-
      hends all phenomena. One who does not comprehend all phenom-
      ena does not comprehend one phenomenon. When one who has
      learned comprehension achieves comprehensive penetration, one
      sees all things, and also sees one thing, so one who studies a single
      atom inevitably studies the whole world.

49   To think that a three-year-old child could not speak of the teaching
      of the enlightened, to think that what a three-year-old child would
      say would be easy, is extremely foolish. The reason for this is that
      to understand life and understand death are the conditions of the
      most important matter for Buddhists. An ancient worthy said,
      "When you were first born you had a share of the lion's roar." "A
      share of the lion's roar" is the achievement of *the realized one
      turning the wheel of teaching.* It is truly a most important matter; it
      cannot be easy.

50   Therefore, in trying to understand the practice of conditions of a
      three-year-old child, it is the condition of an even greater matter.
      Because it has both sameness with and difference from the condi-
      tions of practice of the Buddhas of past, present, and future, the
      poet-statesman has foolishly never listened to or heard what a
      three-year-old child can say, and so speaks as he does without even

wondering whether there might be something there. Not hearing the voice of Zen master Dōrin's statement, which is even more pronounced than thunder, in trying to assert inability to articulate it he says, *even a three-year-old child can say this.* This is not hearing the *lion's roar* of a child, and also missing the Zen teacher's *turning the wheel of teaching.*

51 The Zen teacher could not restrain his pity, and went on to say, "Even though a three year-old child may say it, an eighty-year-old man can't practice it." What he meant to say was that there is speech a three-year-old child can say, and one should study this carefully; there is a path that an eighty-year-old man cannot practice, and one should work on it carefully. "I leave the speaking of the child entirely up to you, not to the child; I leave the inability of an old man to practice entirely up to you, not to the old man"—this is what he said.

52 Buddhism makes a principle of discerning, expressing, and getting to the source in this way.

AWAKENING THE
UNSURPASSED MIND

---

1 An eminent teacher in India said, "The Himalaya mountains represent great nirvana." Know that this represents what can be represented. What can be represented is a matter of personal experience, a matter of accuracy. Bringing up the Himalaya is representing the Himalaya, bringing up great nirvana is representing great nirvana.

2 Bodhidharma said, "Each mind is like wood and stone." Mind here spoken of is the *suchness of mind (or mind of objective reality)*, it is the mind of the whole earth; therefore it is the mind of self and other. Each mind, of all the people on earth, as well as the enlightened ones in all worlds, and the celestials and dragons and so on, is *wood and stone*. There is no other mind outside of this.

3 This *wood and stone* is of itself untrammeled by the realms of existence, nonexistence, emptiness, form, and so on. With this *wood and stone* mind one aspires, practices, and realizes. This is because it is *mind wood and mind stone*. By the power of this *mind wood and mind stone*, the present *thinking of what is not thinking* has become manifest. Having seen and heard the *wind and sound* of the *mind wood and mind stone*, for the first time one gets beyond the types of aberrant paths. Before that, it is not the path of enlightenment.

95

4   The National Teacher of Great Realization said, "Walls, tiles, and pebbles are the mind of the ancient Buddhas." One should observe precisely where these *walls, tiles, and pebbles* are; one should inquire *what is it that manifests thus.* The *mind of the ancient Buddhas* is not *on the other side of the king of emptiness,* it is *sufficiency of gruel, sufficiency of rice,* it is *sufficiency of grass, sufficiency of water.* Bringing forth being like this, *sitting Buddha* and *being Buddha,* is called *awakening the mind.*

5   The conditions of awakening the mind for enlightenment are not a matter of bringing forth the mind for enlightenment from elsewhere, but of awakening the mind by bringing forth the mind for enlightenment. Bringing forth the mind for enlightenment is picking up *a blade of grass* and *making a buddha,* picking up a *rootless tree* and *making a scripture.* It is presenting Buddha with sand, it is presenting Buddha with soup. It is giving food to living beings, it is presenting flowers to Buddha. To do some good at the behest of others, to honor Buddha while being disturbed by demons, is also *awakening the mind for enlightenment.*

6   Not only that: it is *knowing home is not home, giving up home and leaving home, entering the mountains to practice the way, acting on faith and acting on principle;* it is *fashioning buddhas and making shrines,* it is reading scriptures and invoking Buddhas, it is explaining the teachings to people, it is seeking out teachers and inquiring into the Way, it is sitting crosslegged, it is honoring the Three Treasures, it is invoking the name of Buddha. Thus the conditions of the eighty thousand sets of Dharma are certainly *awakening the mind.*

7   There have also been those who awakened the mind in dreams and attained enlightenment, those who awakened the mind in the midst of intoxication and attained enlightenment, those who awakened the mind and attained enlightenment from flying flowers and falling leaves, those who awakened the mind and attained enlightenment from peach blossoms and green bamboo, those who

awakened the mind and attained enlightenment in heaven, and those who awakened the mind and attained enlightenment in the ocean.

8   All of these further awaken the mind for enlightenment in the midst of awakening the mind for enlightenment, awaken the mind for enlightenment in body and mind, awaken the mind for enlightenment in the body and mind of the Buddhas, awaken the mind for enlightenment in the *skin, flesh, bones, and marrow* of Buddhas and Masters.

9   Therefore the present building of shrines, fashioning of buddas, and so on, is indeed awakening the mind for enlightenment. It is awakening the mind to *directly arrive at attainment of Buddhahood,* and is not to be destroyed along the way. This is considered unfabricated virtue; this is considered unmade virtue. This is *observation of true suchness,* this is *observation of the nature of things,* this is *absorption in the assembly of Buddhas,* this is *attaining the mental command of the Buddhas.* This is the mind of supreme perfect enlightenment, this is the function of sainthood, this is manifestation of Buddha. Outside of this, there is nothing unfabricated, unmade.

10   Ignorant people on a small vehicle, however, say "Making images and building shrines is fabricated practice, and is not to be done. Stopping thought and freezing the mind is nonfabrication. The unborn and unmade is reality. The practice of contemplating the true characteristics of the nature of things is nonfabrication."

11   It has been a custom to say this in both India and China, past and present. Due to this, even though they commit serious crimes they do not make images or build shrines; even if they are defiled by tangled passions, they do not chant Buddha names or read scriptures. Not only do they ruin the seeds of humanity and divinity, they reject the buddha-nature of the enlightened.

12 It is truly lamentable to live in a time of the Buddha, Dharma, and Sangha, yet have become enemies of the Buddha, Dharma, and Sangha; to climb the mountain of these Three Treasures and return empty-handed, to plunge into the ocean of the Three Treasures and come back with nothing. Even if they live when a thousand Buddhas and myriad masters are in the world, they have no hope of attaining deliverance; they lose the means of awakening the mind.

13 People are like this because of not following the scriptures and not following real teachers. Many are like this because of following false teachers on aberrant paths.

14 You should immediately abandon the view that building shrines is not awakening the mind for enlightenment. You should wash your mind, body, ears, and eyes, and not pay attention to this view. You should follow the Buddhist scriptures, follow true teachers, betake yourselves to the true teaching, and cultivate the way to enlightenment.

15 In the great path of the way to enlightenment, there is a scripture the size of a universe in a single atom, there are infinite Buddhas in a single atom. One plant, one tree—both are body and mind. As myriad phenomena are unborn, one mind too is unborn. As all phenomena are the appearance of reality, one atom is the appearance of reality.

16 So one mind is all things, all things are one mind, are the whole body. If such practices as building shrines were fabrication, then buddhahood, enlightenment, suchness, and buddha-nature would also be fabrications. Since suchness and buddha-nature are not fabrications, then making images and building shrines are not fabrications: they are unfabricated awakening of the mind for enlightenment; they are unfabricated, uncontaminated virtues.

17 You should just firmly believe that such activities as making images and building shrines are awakening the mind for enlightenment.

A billion eons of practical undertakings will grow from this. This is awakening of the mind that cannot be exhausted in billions of trillions of eons. This is called *seeing Buddha and hearing Dharma.*

18 Know that to gather wood and stone, pile up clay, gather gold, silver, and jewels, and fashion buddhas and build shrines, is to gather the one mind and fashion images and build shrines, is to gather every void and make buddhas, is to pick up every mind and fashion buddhas, is to pile up every shrine and build shrines, is to make every Buddha manifest and make buddhas.

19 Therefore scripture says, *when thinking this the Buddhas of the ten directions all appear.* Know that when one thought is *being Buddha,* the thinking Buddhas of the ten directions all appear; when one thing is *being Buddha,* all things are *being Buddha.*

20 Shakyamuni Buddha said, "When the morning star appeared, I and the sentient beings of earth simultaneously attained enlightenment." Therefore, awakening the mind, carrying out practices, enlightenment, and nirvana must be simultaneous awakening, practice, enlightenment, and nirvana. The body and mind of the enlightenment of Buddhas are *plants, trees, tiles, and pebbles,* are *wind, rain, water, and fire.* To turn these around to make them into the enlightenment of Buddhas is itself *awakening the mind.*

21 One should grasp space to build shrines and fashion buddhas; one should scoop up valley stream water to fashion buddhas and build shrines. This is awakening the mind for supreme perfect enlightenment; it is awakening one awakening of the mind for enlightenment hundreds of thousands of myriads of times. Practice and realization are also like this.

22 So to only hear that awakening of the mind is done only once and no more, that practice is infinite, and that realization is one experience, is not hearing the teaching of Buddha, is not knowing the teaching of Buddha, is not meeting the teaching of Buddha. A

billion-fold awakening of mind is certainly the awakening of one awakening of mind; the awakening of mind of a billion people is the awakening of one awakening of mind, one awakening of mind is a billion awakenings of mind. Practice, realization, and teaching are also like this.

23 If not for plants, trees, and so on, how could there be body and mind? If not for body and mind, how could there be plants and trees? Thus it is, for the reason that there are not plants and trees if not for plants and trees.

24 Mastering the Way in sitting meditation is *awakening the mind for enlightenment.* Awakening the mind is not one or different, sitting meditation is not one or different, not two or three, not an arrangement. Everything should be studied this way.

25 If the whole process of gathering plants, trees, or the seven precious substances and making shrines and buddha images is fabrication and cannot effect enlightenment, then the thirty-seven elements of enlightenment must also be fabricated; practicing them with the human and celestial body and mind of the three realms would all be fabrication, and there could be no ultimate state.

26 Plants, trees, tiles, pebbles, and the four elements and five clusters are alike *only mind,* are alike *forms of reality.* All worlds in the ten directions, the nature of enlightenment to reality as is, are alike *phenomena abiding in the normative state.* In the nature of enlightenment to reality as is, how could there be plants and trees? How could plants and trees not be the nature of enlightenment to reality as is?

27 Phenomena are not fabricated, are not unfabricated; they are forms of reality. The forms of reality are forms of reality that are *like this. Like this* is the *body-mind* of *right now.* You should *awaken the mind* with this *body-mind.* Do not be averse to walking on water, walking on stone. Just pick up a blade of grass and make the

sixteen-foot-tall golden body, pick up an atom and build a shrine for an ancient Buddha. This will be *awakening the mind for enlightenment.* This is *seeing Buddha,* is *hearing Buddha,* is *seeing Dharma,* is *hearing Dharma,* is *being Buddha,* is *acting Buddha.*

28 Shakyamuni Buddha said, "Laymen, laywomen, good men, and good women offer the flesh of their spouses and children to the Three Treasures, and offer their own flesh to the Three Treasures: since the monks have received the alms of the faithful, how can they not practice?"

29 So we know that to offer the Three Treasures food and drink, clothing, bedding, medicine, housing, fields, and groves is to offer the Three Treasures one's own body, flesh, skin, bones, and marrow, as well as those of one's spouse and children. When one has entered the ocean of virtues of the Three Treasures, they are one flavor; because they are one flavor they are the Three Treasures. The virtues of the Three Treasures manifesting as the *skin, flesh, bones, and marrow* of oneself, spouse, and children are the diligent work of mastering the Way. Bringing up the essence and character-istics of the Buddha now, one should find out the *skin, flesh, bones, and marrow* of the Buddha's Way.

30 This faithful giving is *awakening the mind.* How could the monks who receive it not practice? It is imperative to start correctly and finish correctly. Due to this, the moment an atom becomes active, the one mind awakens along with it; as soon as one mind awakens, one void awakens.

31 Whenever learners or those beyond learning awaken the mind, for the first time they plant one buddha-nature. Working with the *four elements and five clusters,* if they practice sincerely they attain enlightenment. Working with *plants, trees, fences, and walls,* if they practice sincerely they will attain enlightenment. This is because *the four elements and five clusters* and *plants, trees, fences, and walls* are fellow students; because they are of the same essence, because

they are the same mind and the same life, because they are the same body and the same mechanism.

32 Because of this, in the assemblies of the enlightened ones there have been many cases of mastering the Way *bringing forth the heart of plants and trees;* this is what *awakening the mind for enlightenment* is like. The fifth patriarch of Zen was once a pine-planting wayfarer; Rinzai worked on planting cedars and pines on Mount Ōbaku; and there was an old man Ryū on Mount To who planted pines. They all brought up the sturdiness of pine and cypress to bring out the eyes of the enlightened. This is manifesting the power to *sport living eyes* being *opening clear eyes.*

33 *Making shrines and making buddhas* is *sporting eyes,* is *eating awakening of mind,* is *using awakening of mind.* Without the *eyes* of *making shrines and making buddhas,* it is not the enlightenment of Buddhas and Zen masters. It is after gaining the eye of *making buddhas* that one becomes a Buddha, a master.

34 To say that making shrines eventually turns to dust and earth, and is not real virtue, and that cultivation of nonorigination is stable and undefiled by dust, is not the word of Buddha. If shrines turn to dust and earth, then nonorigination also turns to dust and earth; if nonorigination does not turn to dust and earth, then neither do shrines turn to dust and earth. It is a matter of *where is this to speak of fabricated and unfabricated?*

35 A scripture says, "When bodhisattvas in the midst of birth and death first awaken their minds to the totally dedicated quest for enlightenment, they are firm and immutable; the virtue of that single thought is boundlessly deep and broad, such that a Buddha could not fully explain it in all its particulars, even by the end of time."

36 We should clearly know that to bring forth birth and death to *awaken the mind* is the *totally dedicated quest for enlightenment. That*

single thought must be the same as *one plant, one tree,* because of being *one birth, one death.* Yet the depth of that virtue is boundless, and its breadth too is boundless. Even if the Buddhas were to analyze it using all time for speech, there would be no end. Because even when the ocean dries up the bottom remains, and even though a person dies the mind will remain, it is inexhaustible.

37 Just as that one thought is boundlessly deep and broad, the depth and breadth of *one plant, one tree, one stone, one tile* is also boundless. If *one plant, one stone* is seven feet or eight feet, that one thought is also seven feet or eight feet, and the awakening of mind is seven feet or eight feet, too. Therefore to *go deep into the mountains to contemplate the Way of the enlightened* would be easy; to *build shrines and fashion buddhas* is very hard. Although both are accomplished by diligent effort, there must be a vast difference between bringing forth the mind and being brought forth by the mind. When such awakening of the mind for enlightenment builds up, the enlightened ones manifest.

THE DRAGON HOWL

1   A monk asked Tōsu, "Is there a dragon howl in a dead tree?"

2   Tōsu said, "I say there's a lion roar in a skull."

3   Talk about the *dead tree* and *dead ashes* is originally a deviant teaching. However, the *dead tree* spoken of by deviants and the *dead tree* spoken of by the enlightened ones are very different.

4   Although deviants talk about the *dead tree*, they don't know the *dead tree*, much less hear the *dragon howl*. Deviants think the *dead tree* is dead wood, and practice as if *for it there is no more spring*.

5   The *dead tree* spoken of by the enlightened is the study of the *drying up of the ocean*. The *ocean drying up* is the *death of the tree*, the *death of the tree* is *meeting the spring*. The *nonmoving* of the tree is *dying*.

6   The present *mountain trees, ocean trees,* and *sky trees* are *dead trees*. And *sprouts* are the *dragon howl* of the *dead tree*. Even one with a circumference in the billions is a descendent of the *dead tree*. The *characteristics, essence, substance,* and *power* of the *dead tree* is the *deadwood post* spoken of by the enlightened; it is a *not-dead post*.

7   There are *mountain and valley trees*, there are *field and hamlet trees*. The *mountain and valley trees* are conventionally called *pine and*

cypress, the *field and hamlet trees* are conventionally called *human and celestial. The leaves spread based on the roots*—this is called *the enlightened ones. Roots and branches must return to the source*—this is *participative study.* Being like this is the *long reality body* of the *dead tree*, is the *short reality body* of the *dead tree.*

8　As long as it is not a *dead tree*, it does not make a *dragon howl.* If it is not a *dead tree*, it does not lose the *dragon howl. How many times meeting the spring without changing the mind* is the *dragon howl of total death.* Though it is not among the notes of the musical scale, the notes of the musical scale are *earlier and later two or three children* of the *dragon howl.*

9　However, this monk's statement—*is there a dragon howl in a dead tree*—has become manifest for the first time in a question in measureless eons. It is the *manifestation* of a *saying.*

10　Tōsu's statement—*I say there is a lion roar in a skull*—is a case of *what is hidden*, is a case of *restraining oneself and putting another first*, is a case of *skulls littering the fields.*

11　A monk asked Kyōgen, "What is the Way?"
　　Kyōgen said, "A dragon howl in a dead tree."
　　The monk said, "I don't understand."
　　Kyōgen said, "Eyes in a skull."

12　Later a monk asked Sekisō, "What is a dragon howl in a dead tree?"
　　Sekisō said, "Still joyful."
　　The monk asked, "What are eyes in a skull?"
　　Sekisō said, "Still conscious."

13　A monk also asked Sōzan, "What is a dragon how in a dead tree?"
　　Sōzan said, "The blood line is not ended."
　　The monk asked, "What are eyes in a skull?"
　　Sōzan said, "Not entirely dry."

The monk asked. "Does anyone hear?"

Sōzan said, "There is no one in the world who does not hear."

The monk asked, "What writing does the expression *dragon howl* come from?"

Sōzan said, "I don't know what writing the expression comes from, but those who hear it all die."

14　The *hearer* and *howler* of which an attempt is being made here to speak are not equal to the *howler* of the *dragon howl*. This tune is the *dragon howl*. *In a dead tree* and *in a skull* are not inside or outside, not self or other; they are present and past. *Still joyful* is moreover *the horn on the head growing*. *Still conscious* is *skin and flesh falling away entirely*.

15　Sōzan's saying *the blood line is not ended* is a case of *speaking without avoidance*, is a case of *turning around in the stream of words*. *Not entirely dry* is *the ocean drying up but not reaching the bottom*. Because *not entirely* is *dry*, it is *dryness upon dryness*.

16　To say *does anyone hear* is like saying *does anyone not attain* (or, *does anyone not hear*). As for *there is no one in the world who does not hear*, one should yet ask, leaving aside *there is no one who does not hear*, when there is no world, where is the dragon howl? Speak quickly!

17　As for *what writing does the expression 'dragon howl' come from*, it should be made a question. The *dragon howl* is of itself *making a sound holding forth* that is *in the mind*, it is *breathing out* that is *in the nostrils*.

18　As for *I don't know what writing the expression comes from*, this is *there is a dragon in written expression*. As for *those who hear it all die*, it is *pitiable*.

19　Now the dragon howling of Kyōgen, Sekisō, and Sōzan make clouds and water. I do not say this is speaking, I do not say eyes or skull—this is *a thousand melodies, ten thousand melodies* of *just a dragon howl. Still joyful—a clam howl; still conscious—a worm howl.* Due to this *the blood line is not ended,* and *gourds are heir to gourds.* Because *not entirely dry,* the pillars are pregnant, the lamps face the lamps.

GREAT UNDERSTANDING

---

1   The Great Way of the Buddhas, being communicated, is thorough-going; the effective activity of the Zen masters, manifested, is even. For this reason their *great understanding becomes manifest*, they *arrive on the Way without understanding*, they *have insight into understanding and manipulate understanding*, they *lose understanding and let go*—these are the everyday affairs of the enlightened.

2   There is *using the twenty-four hours* that *brings up*, there is *being used by the twenty-four hours* that *throws away*. There is also *playing with a mud ball* and *playing with the spirit* that even *leaps beyond* this pivot.

3   Although the enlightened always consummate the study that *manifests thus* from *great understanding*, that does not mean that the *undifferentiated understanding* of *great understanding* makes them enlightened, and it does not mean that the *undifferentiated enlightened ones* of the enlightened ones is *undifferentiated great understanding*. Enlightened ones leap beyond the bounds of *great understanding*, and *great understanding* is the aspect of leaping higher than the enlightened ones.

4   However, people's faculties are of many kinds.

5   To be *born knowing* is to pass through free of birth on being born, which means comprehensive investigation in the *beginning, middle, and end* of birth.

6   To *know by learning* is to thoroughly investigate the self by learning, which means to comprehensively investigate the *skin, flesh, bones, and marrow* of learning.

7   There are those with *enlightened knowledge:* this is not knowledge by birth, or knowledge by learning: it is beginningless in *here,* having transcended the bounds of self and other, it is *being unbound* by *knowledge of self and other.*

8   There are those with *teacherless knowledge:* this does not depend on a teacher, or on scripture, or on essence, or on form; although it does not set self in motion, or produce interchange with others, it is clearly evident.

9   Of these various types, one is not recognized as keen and another recognized as dull: together, many types manifest many types of effective activity. So one should inquire into the question of which sentient or insentient beings are not *born knowing.* If there is *knowledge by birth,* there is *understanding by birth,* there is *witness of illumination by birth,* there is *cultivation of practice by birth.*

10   So the enlightened are already masters; this has come to be called *knowing by birth.* It is like this because it is *birth* that has brought up understanding. It must be *understanding by birth* that *greatly understands on fulfillment of study;* it is thus because it is the learning that *brings up understanding.*

11   Therefore one brings up the *three realms* and *greatly understands, brings up the hundred grasses* and *greatly understands,* brings up the *four elements* and *greatly understands,* brings up the *enlightened ones* and *greatly understands,* brings up *public issues* and *greatly understands.* All together bring up *great understanding* and *greatly understand* even more. That *very time* is *right now.*

12   The great teacher Rinzai said, "It's hard to find anyone in the whole vast country of China who doesn't understand."

13 What Rinzai is saying is correctly channeled *skin, flesh, bones, marrow.* There can be nothing incorrect in it. "In China" means *in one's own eyes.* It is not concerned with *the whole world,* it does not stop at *innumerable lands.* Seeking *here* one person *who does not understand,* it turns out such a one is *hard to find.*

14 *Yesterday's self* of the self is not *one who does not understand,* and the *present self* of another is not *one who does not understand* either. In seeking out *not understanding* among *people of the mountains* and *people of the waters,* past and present, it has never been found.

15 If students study Rinzai's statement in this manner, it will not be *a waste of time.* Yet even so, one should study the qualities and works of the school of the living exemplars. That is to say, one should pause to question Rinzai. If one only knows *it is hard to find one who doesn't understand,* and does not know *it is hard to find one who does understand,* then that is not sufficiently correct. It is hard even to call it having thoroughly investigated *the difficulty of finding one who doesn't understand.* Even if it is hard to find one person who *doesn't understand,* there is *half a person* who *doesn't understand,* of a *countenance and dignity outstanding and magnificent*—have you met yet or not?

16 Even if it is hard to find *one who doesn't understand* in all of China, don't consider that ultimate. You should try to find *two or three Chinas* in *one or half a person.* Hard to find? Not hard to find? When you have this eye, you may be considered an enlightened one who has studied fully.

17 Great Teacher Hōshi of Kegon temple was asked by a monk, "How is it when people of great understanding return to confusion?"

18 The teacher said, "A broken mirror does not shine again, fallen leaves cannot climb up a tree."

19 Although this question is a question, it is like a group instruction. It takes the assembly of Kegon to expound it, it takes an heir of

Tōzan to empower it. Truly this must be the seat of an enlightened one who has studied to repletion.

20 *People of great understanding* does not mean those who have always *greatly understood,* nor those who have *greatly understood* externally and stored it. *Great understanding* is not meeting with an aged elder in the public realm. Although it is not forcibly dragged forth from oneself, it is always a matter of *great understanding.*

21 It is not that *not being confused* is considered *great understanding.* And it is not that you should suppose that one only becomes *confused* for the sake of those with the potential for *great understanding. People of great understanding* do *greatly understand* even further; *someone greatly confused* does *further greatly understand.*

22 Just as there are *people of great understanding,* there are *Buddhas of great understanding,* there are *earth, water, fire, air, and space of great understanding,* there are *pillars and lamps of great understanding.*

23 Now the question here is about *people of great understanding.* The question *how is it when people of great understanding return to confusion* is truly asking what should be asked. Kegon unbegrudgingly looks to the ancients in the Zen communities. This must be the developmental work of the enlightened.

24 You should meditate for a while: is the *return to confusion* of *people of great understanding* on a par with that of *people who don't understand?* When *people of great understanding return to confusion,* do they bring forth *great understanding* and create confusion? Do they bring forth confusion from *there,* cover up *great understanding,* and *revert to confusion?*

25 Also, even though *people of great understanding* do not destroy *great understanding* as individuals, do they go on to study *return to confusion?*

26 And does the so-called *return to confusion* of *people of great understanding* refer to bringing forth yet another level of *great understanding* as *return to confusion?*

27 Each of these questions should be studied thoroughly. Also, is it that *great understanding is one hand,* and *return to confusion is one hand too?*

28 You should know that to hear *people of great understanding* have *return to confusion,* in whatever way, is ultimate penetration of study hitherto. You should know there is *great understanding* that makes *return to enlightenment* a personal experience.

29 Thus, *taking a thief to be your child* is not to be considered *return to confusion,* and *taking your child to be a thief* is not to be considered *return to confusion. Great understanding* must be *recognizing a thief as a thief. Return to confusion* is recognizing your child as a child. *Adding a little where there is much* is considered *great understanding. Reducing a little where there is little* is *return to confusion.* Therefore, finding *one who returns to confusion,* one should meet *someone of great understanding* in *holding still.* Is the present self *returned to confusion?* Is it unconfused? You should check—this is considered *going to see the enlightened.*

30 The teacher said, *a broken mirror does not shine again, fallen leaves cannot climb up a tree.* This group instruction expresses the *precise moment of suchness* of the *broken mirror.* So it is not right to study the words *broken mirror* with the mind on the time of the *unbroken mirror.*

31 The essential message of Kegon's saying that *a broken mirror does not shine again, fallen leaves cannot climb up the tree* will probably have been understood to be that *people of great understanding do not shine again,* that *people of great understanding cannot climb up the tree,* that *people of great understanding* do not *return to confusion* anymore. However, it is not such a study. If it were as people

think, it should be asked, *what is the everyday life of people of great understanding?* In reply to this it would be said, *there is a time of return to confusion.*

32 The present story is not this way. Because the question is *how is it when people of great understanding return to confusion,* it is questioning *the very time of return to confusion.* The *spoken manifestation* of *such a time* is *a broken mirror does not shine again,* is *fallen leaves cannot climb up the tree.* When *fallen leaves* are in fact *fallen leaves,* even if one progresses at *the top of a hundred-foot pole,* this is still *fallen leaves.* Because the *broken mirror* is *truly a broken mirror,* even though a certain amount of *livelihood* becomes manifest, just the same it must be the *shining* of *not shining again.*

33 Bringing up the message expressed as *a broken mirror,* expressed as *fallen leaves,* one should study the time when *people of great understanding return to confusion.* That is, *great understanding* is like *being Buddha,* and *return to confusion* is like *sentient beings.* It should not be studied as those who say *returning to be a sentient being* or *sending down traces from the basis.* They speak as if one breaks up great awakening and becomes a sentient being. This story does not say *great understanding* is broken up, it does not say *great understanding* is lost, it does not say *confusion* comes. It is not to be equated with those others.

34 Truly *great understanding* is beginningless, *return to confusion* is beginningless. There is no confusion that blocks *great understanding.* Bringing up *three planes of great understanding,* one makes *half a plane of small confusion.* Hereby there is the Himalaya Mountains *greatly understanding* for the Himalaya Mountains; *wood and stone* greatly understand by means of *wood and stone.* The *great understanding* of Buddhas is *greatly understanding* for the sake of *sentient beings;* the *great understanding* of *sentient beings* is *greatly understanding* the *great understanding of the Buddhas.*

35 One should not be caught up in before and after: the *great understanding* of *right now* is not oneself, is not another self.

Although it has not come, yet it *fills everywhere;* although it does not go, yet *beware of seeking from another.* Why is it so? As it is said, *it goes along with the other.*

36 Master Mai "The Foreigner" had a monk ask Gyōzan, "Do people in the present still need understanding?"

37 Gyōzan said, "It is not that there is no understanding, but what about falling into the secondary?"

38 The monk went back and told master Mai about this. Mai deeply agreed.

39 *The present* is the *right now* of people. *Even if I think of past, future, and present,* no matter how many millions they may be, they are *the present,* they are *right now.* A person's condition is necessarily *the present.* It may be that the *eyes* are considered *the present,* it may be that the *nostrils* are considered *the present.*

40 *Do they still need understanding?* This saying should be calmly investigated, changed into one's heart, changed into one's head. In recent times baldies in China say understanding the Way is the basic aim, and so saying they vainly anticipate understanding. But it seems they are not illumined by the light of the enlightened. They are just lazily stumbling past, neglecting the need to learn from genuine teachers. They would not be liberated even if the ancient Buddhas were active in the world.

41 This saying *do they still need understanding* does not say there is no understanding, does not say there is understanding, does not say it comes; it says do they need it or not. It is like saying, "How has the understanding of present people understood?" For example, if you say they attain understanding, it seems like they have not had it before. If you say understanding comes, it seems like that understanding was somewhere. If you say it has become understanding, it seems like understanding has a beginning.

42 Though not speaking or being this way, when speaking of the manner of understanding, he said, "Do they need understanding?" To this, as he said, "What can be done about understanding falling into the secondary?" This is saying that the secondary too is understanding. *The secondary* is like saying it has become understanding, or one has attained understanding, or understanding has come.

43 So it is like lamenting falling into *the secondary* and eliminating *the secondary*. It also seems like *the secondary* which understanding would have been is really *the secondary*. So even if it is the secondary, or even if it is *the hundred thousandth level,* it still must be understanding. If there is a *secondary* this does not mean it has left a *primary* that is higher than this. For example, it is like though one consider the self of yesterday as the self, yesterday one would call today a second person. The understanding of *right now* I do not say is yesterday, nor has it started now; it is a matter of finding out in this way. This is *great understanding is black,* it is *great understanding is white.*

SOUNDS OF THE VALLEY STREAMS, COLORS OF THE MOUNTAINS

---

1   In the matter of supreme enlightenment, there have been many enlightened forbears who communicated the Way and assigned practices. There are examples of self-sacrifice: study the school of the patriarch who cut off his arm, don't reject the hair laid in the mud. As each of them attained *escape from the shell,* they were unencumbered by previous views and understandings, and what had been long unclear suddenly became manifest. In the *immediate present* of *such a time,* even *I* am *not knowing,* and *who* too is *not cognizing,* and *you* too are *not expecting.* Even the *buddha* eye cannot see it; how can human thought assess it?

2   In Song dynasty China there was a great writer who studied Buddhism, reaching the profound depths and the lofty heights. Once when he went to Mount Lu, he became enlightened upon hearing the sound of a valley stream flowing in the night. He composed a verse on this occasion, which he presented to a Zen master:

> *The sound of the valley stream is the Universal Tongue,*
> *the colors of the mountains are all the Pure Body.*
> *Another day how can I recite*
> *the eighty-four thousand verses of last night?*

116

When he presented this to the Zen master, the Zen master approved it.

3   That Zen master was a spiritual heir of the Yellow Dragon sect of the Rinzai school of Chinese Zen.

4   Once when the writer met another Zen master, that master gave him a religious vestment and Buddhist precepts. The writer often donned religious garb and worked on the Way. He made the Zen master a present of a priceless jade belt. People of the time considered this something beyond the reach of ordinary worldlings.

5   So has the story of enlightenment on hearing the sound of a valley stream no benefit for later followers? They are to be pitied—how many times they seem to have missed out on the teaching activity of *appearing corporeally to expound reality*—why do they still see the colors of mountains, hear the sound of valley streams? Are they one phrase? Are they half a phrase? Are they eighty-four thousand verses? It is regrettable that there are *sound and color* concealed in the *mountains* and *streams*. Yet it is delightful that there are *conditions of time* revealed in the *mountains and streams*. And there is no lapse in the *manifestation of the tongue;* how could there be disappearance of the *form of the body?*

6   However, would you assume the time of revelation near, or would you assume the time of concealment near? Would you consider this one plane? Would you consider it half a plane? There springs and autumns hitherto have not seen or heard the mountains and streams; the *time* of *last night* sees the mountains and streams slightly.

7   Bodhisattvas studying the Way now should open the door of penetrating learning by way of *the mountains flow, the water does not flow.*

8   The day before the night this writer was enlightened, he had asked
     the Zen master about the story of *inanimate things teaching*.
     Although he was not transformed at the words of the Zen master,
     the hearing of the sound of the valley stream was *waves against the
     current* striking the *sky on high*.

9   So would you say the sound of the valley stream startling the writer
     was the sound of the valley stream, or was it the flow from the
     teacher? Perhaps the words of the teacher about *inanimate things
     teaching* were still resonating, and subtly mixed in with the night
     sound of the valley stream. Who would affirm this to be one
     stream, or betake oneself to it as one ocean? Ultimately, was it the
     writer's enlightenment, or was it the enlightenment of the moun-
     tain and water? Whose *clear eyes* would not *quickly focus* on the
     universal tongue and the *pure body*?

10   Also, when Zen master Kyōgen studied the Way in the assembly of
     Zen master Isan, Isan said to him, "You are intelligent and learned.
     Make me a statement about *before the birth of father and mother,*
     one that you have not memorized from writings."

11   Kyōgen tried repeatedly to find something to say, without success.
     Disgusted with himself, he looked through the books he had
     accumulated over the years; but he was still at a loss. Finally he
     burned the writings he had collected over the years, saying, "A
     picture of a cake cannot relieve hunger. I vow not to hope to
     understand Buddhism in this lifetime. I'll just be a monastic
     servant."

12   So saying, he spent several years as a servant. Then he told Isan,
     "My body-mind is dull. I cannot speak. You please tell me."

13   Isan said, "It is not that I refuse to tell you, but I am afraid later
     you would resent me."

14   After spending several years like this, Kyōgen went to Mount
     Wudang looking for the former abode of the National Teacher of

Great Realization. He built a hut where the National Teacher's hermitage had been, and planted bamboo for companionship. One day as he was cleaning the pathway, a spray of rubble hit the bamboo. Hearing the sound, he suddenly was greatly enlightened.

15 Bathing and purifying himself, Kyōgen lit incense, bowed in the direction of the mountain where Isan taught, and addressed him, saying, "Great teacher Isan, had you explained to me back then, how could this have happened today? My debt to you is profounder than that which I owe to my parents."

16 Finally he composed a verse:

> *Forgetting all knowledge at one stroke,*
> *I do not need cultivation anymore.*
> *Activity expressing the ancient road,*
> *I don't fall into passivity.*
> *Everywhere trackless,*
> *conduct beyond sound and form:*
> *The adepts in all places*
> *call this the supreme state.*

He presented this verse to Isan, who said he had penetrated.

17 Also, Zen master Reiun worked on the Way for thirty years. Once when he was traveling in the mountains, as he took a rest at the foot of a mountain he gazed at a village in the distance. It was spring at the time. Seeing the peach blossoms in full bloom, he suddenly was enlightened. He composed a verse which he presented to Isan:

> *For thirty years I've been looking for a swordsman;*
> *How many times have the leaves fallen*
> *and the branches grown anew?*
> *After once having seen the peach blossoms*
> *I have never had doubts any more.*

18 Isan said, "Those who enter by way of conditions never backslide," and gave his approval.

19 Who enters that does not do so by way of conditions? Who enters that backslides? This does not refer only to Reiun.

20 Subsequently Reiun succeeded to Isan. How could this be so if not for the *pure body* of the *colors of the mountains?*

21 A monk asked Zen master Chōsha, "How does one return the mountains, rivers, and earth to oneself?"

22 The master said, "How can one return oneself to the mountains, rivers, and earth?"

23 In this expression, *oneself* is of itself *oneself;* even if you call *oneself* the *mountains, rivers, and earth,* you should not impute any further hindrance to the object of return.

24 Rōya Eshō was a distant descendent of Nangaku. Once a professor of doctrine asked him, "Purity is basically so—how does it suddenly produce mountains, rivers, and earth?"

25 To this question the teacher replied, "Purity is basically so—how does it suddenly produce mountains, rivers, and earth?"

26 Here we realize that the *mountains, rivers, and earth* that are *purity basically so* are not to be mistaken for the *mountains, rivers, and earth.* As teachers of scriptures have never even dreamed of hearing this, they do not know the *mountains, rivers, and earth as mountains, rivers, and earth.*

27 We should know that but for the *colors of the mountains, sounds of the valley streams,* the *raising of a flower* would not expound, and *attaining the marrow* would not *remain in place.* By virtue of the *sounds of the valley streams, colors of the mountains,* the *sentient*

beings of earth attain enlightenment at the same time, and there are Buddhas who *realize enlightenment on seeing the morning star.*

28   Such *skin bags* are sages of the past with very profound determination in seeking reality; people of today should study their examples. Now too, for true study unconcerned with fame or material gain, it is necessary to develop such determination. People who truly seek the reality of Buddhahood are rare; they are not nonexistent, but hard to come across.

29   Many people casually become monastics, and many appear to have left the mundane, yet make Buddhism an avenue to fame and material gain. This is pitiful, lamentable. If they waste this time, and vainly trade in dark deeds, when will they ever become free and enlightened? Even if they encountered a genuine teacher, they would not like a *real dragon.*

30   The Buddhas of the past said such people are to be pitied. This is because of bad causes in former lifetimes. Because by birth they lack the determination to *seek truth for the sake of truth,* when they see *real dragons* they are suspicious of *real dragons,* and when they meet *correct teaching* they are rejected by *correct teaching.* Because of not having been born from truth, this *mind, body, bone, flesh* is incompatible with truth, unreceptive to truth.

31   The teacher-student relation in the ancestral school has continued in this manner for a long time; the aspiration for enlightenment is like talk of a dream long past. What a pity it is to be born on a mountain of jewels yet not to know the treasure, not to see the treasure, much less attain the spiritual treasure.

32   After having aroused the aspiration for enlightenment, even if one migrates through various ways of life, the conditions of that migration all become practical undertakings of enlightenment.

33   Therefore, even if your time has been wasted up until now, as long as this life has not yet ended you should hasten to make this vow:

"May I and all beings hear true teaching in every lifetime from this lifetime onwards, and not doubt it or distrust it when we hear it. When we encounter true teaching, let us relinquish mundane things, accept and hold enlightened teaching, and ultimately attain enlightenment in concert with the sentient beings of the whole earth."

34   When you make a vow in this manner, it will naturally be conducive to correct awakening of aspiration. Do not neglect this psychological technique.

35   Also, Japan is a remote, isolated country; the people are extremely ignorant. Never has a sage been born in Japan, never has one *born knowing* been born here. Even genuine students of enlightenment are rare. When one teaches the aspiration for enlightenment to those who do not know it, because they take offense at sincere words they do not reflect on themselves but resent others.

36   Generally speaking, in the practical undertaking of the aspiration for enlightenment, one should not hope that people of the world will know whether or not one aspires to enlightenment, or whether or not one practices the Way; one should strive not to be known. Thus of course one should not proclaim this of oneself to others.

37   Because people nowadays rarely seek truth, even though they are lacking in the way of conduct and understanding, they seem to look for others who will praise them and say their conduct and understanding accord. This is what is known as *further delusion in the midst of delusion.* This aberrant thinking should be abandoned at once.

38   When studying the Way, what is hard to see or hear is the mental art of correct method. This mental art is something that has been transmitted by the enlightened. It has been transmitted as the *light of the enlightened,* and also as the *enlightened mind.* From the time when the Buddha was in the world up to the present time, there

have been many people who seem to take ambition for fame and gain to be the attitude of study of the Way. Yet even such people will naturally attain enlightenment if they change their attitude on meeting genuine teachers and seek truth.

39 It should be realized that there is a tendency toward this sort of illness in contemporary studies of the Way. For example, whether one is a beginning student or has practiced cultivation exercises for a long time, it may happen that one may get the opportunity for transmission of the Way and prescription of exercises, or one may not get the opportunity. There must be the opportunity to study by looking to the examples of the ancients, and there can also be deranged conditions in which one repudiates them and does not learn. Neither of these should be liked or disliked.

40 How can one not worry or lament? Because those who know the three poisons as three poisons are rare, one does not lament. All the more one should not forget the initial aspiration to seek the way of enlightenment. When first awakening aspiration, one does not seek truth for others, having abandoned reputation and material advantages; not seeking fame or gain, one aims wholly for enlightenment. There is never any anticipation of respect and support from rulers and officials. Nevertheless, now there are such conditions; this is not the basic aim, nor what is sought for. One does not hope to be caught up in the bonds of humans or spirits.

41 However, even if they have aspiration for enlightenment, foolish people quickly forget their original determination and make the mistake of anticipating the support of men and gods, rejoicing in that as evidence of the attainment of the merits of Buddhism. To think that if one gets the allegiance of rulers and officials means one's path is accomplished is one kind of insanity in study of the Way. Though we should not forget to pity this, we should not like it. Haven't you seen how the Buddha has said, *There is much resentment and jealousy even in the Buddha's lifetime.* Thus it is that

the ignorant do not know the wise, and petty beasts despise great sages.

42   Also, the fact that many Buddhist masters in India were destroyed by followers of other paths, followers of the two individualistic vehicles of Buddhism, rulers, and others, does not mean the followers of other paths were better, or that the Buddhist masters lacked foresight.

43   After the founder of Zen came from India to China and took up residence at Shaolin, neither the ruler of southern China nor the ruler of northern China knew about him. At that time there were two dogs, the canonical scholar Bodhiruci and the preceptor Kowtow, who worried that a true man might interfere with their empty reputations and dishonest gains. They were like one who attempts to obscure the sun in the sky; they were even worse than Devadatta in the Buddha's lifetime. How pitiful. The fame and gain with which you are so deeply in love is more despicable than filth to the enlightened.

44   The power of Buddhism does not fail to comprehend this principle. You should realize there are dogs who howl at good people. Don't worry about howling dogs, and don't despise them.

45   You should make a prayer of guidance, in these terms: *You are beasts, yet should awaken the aspiration for enlightenment.*

46   An ancient sage said, "These are animals with human faces."

47   There also should be demons who will render obeisance and support. A past Buddha said, "Don't become familiar with rulers, officials, priests, or laypeople." Indeed these are modes of conduct which those who study the Buddhist Way should not forget. The virtues of the beginning study of enlightenment should accumulate as one progresses.

48   It has also happened, since ancient times, that the king of gods will come to test the will of the practitioner, or the devil will come to interfere with the practitioner's cultivation of the Way. This only happened when people were not free from interest in fame and gain. When one has profound universal kindness and compassion, and the wish to liberate all beings is well developed, these obstacles do not exist.

49   It has happened that the power of developmental practices has spontaneously gained land, and apparently attained worldly success. In such cases, one should further understand it, not become stupefied by it. Fools rejoice over it, like a stupid dog licking a dry bone. Sages avoid it, much as ordinary people avoid filth.

50   Generally speaking, the mental capacity of the beginner cannot measure the way of enlightenment; even though one assess it, this assessment is not accurate. But even though it is not fathomed by the beginner, this does not mean that there is no consummation of the ultimate. The inner sanctum of the stage of penetration is not the shallow consciousness of the beginner. One simply should take practical steps to tread the path of the sages of yore.

51   During this time, in seeking out teachers, inquiring after the Way, there is *climbing mountains and crossing seas*. In seeking guides and spiritual benefactors, they *descend from the heavens* and *emerge from the earth*. In contact with them, as they evoke expression from the sentient and the insentient, one listens in the medium of the body, one listens in the medium of the mind. Although *if you listen with your ears* is an everyday affair, *hearing sound through the eyes* is *why necessarily not necessary*. In *seeing Buddha* too one sees both *self Buddha* and *other Buddha,* one sees *great Buddha and small Buddha.* Don't be startled or frightened by the *great Buddha,* and don't be contemptuous or anxious about the *small Buddha.*

52   It is a matter of temporarily recognizing the so-called *great Buddha and small Buddha* as the *colors of the mountains, sounds of the valley*

streams. In this there is *the universal tongue,* there are *eighty-four thousand verses.* It is *transcendence on mention,* it is *independence on seeing through.* For this reason a worldling said, *it is ever higher, ever harder,* and a past Buddha said, *it encompasses the universe.*

53 There is the elegance of spring pines, there is the excellence of autumn chrysanthemums—this is just being *precisely so.* If one reaches the state of a real teacher, one should be a guide of humans and spirits. If one tries to teach others before reaching this state, one is a great villain. Not knowing the spring pines, not seeing the autumn chrysanthemums, what sustenance can there be, how can one cut through the source?

54 Furthermore, if the mind and body are lazy and insincere, then you should earnestly repent to the Buddhas of yore. When you do so, the power of repenting to the Buddhas of yore will rescue and purify you. This power develops unobstructed pure faith and energy. Once pure faith appears, self and others are alike transformed. The benefits extend to all sentient and insentient beings.

55 The gist of this is as follows: "Even if I have committed many evil deeds in the past, obstructing me on the Way, may the enlightened ones who attained enlightenment by the Way of Buddhas have pity on me, free me from the burden of my deeds, remove the barriers to learning the Way, and fill the whole infinite cosmos with its powerful teaching. Have pity on me: the enlightened ones were in the past such as I, and such as I will in the future be enlightened ones."

56 When you look upon the enlightened, they are one enlightened one; in contemplation of awakening of inspiration too, it must be one awakening of inspiration. When one penetrates pity thoroughly, it is *gaining an advantage,* it is *losing an advantage.*

57 Therefore Rōya said,

126

What you didn't comprehend in past lives
you should comprehend now;
In this life liberate the body, repeatedly born.
Before the ancient Buddhas were enlightened,
they were the same as people now;
Once enlightened, people now
are identical to the ancients.

58 You should quietly look into this saying; this is acceptance of the responsibility of realizing enlightenment.

59 If you repent in this way, there will surely be invisible help from the enlightened ones. By thought and gesture, one should confess to the Buddhas; the power of confession causes the roots of sin to disintegrate. This is uniform correct practice. This is a correct mind of faith, a correct body of faith.

60 When you practice correctly, the *sounds of the valley streams,* the *colors of the valley streams,* the *colors of the mountains,* the sounds of the mountains, freely release eighty-four thousand verses in concert. If you do not cling to the mind and body of fame and gain, the valley streams and mountains too have *such* generosity.

61 Whether or not *the sound of the valley streams and the colors of the mountains* manifest *eighty-four thousand verses,* even be it *last night,* as long as the *total exertion* by which the *streams and mountains* recite the *streams and mountains* is *not yet expedited,* who will *see and hear* you as the *sounds of the valley streams, colors of the mountains?*

NOTES

DO NOT DO ANYTHING EVIL

1. What is evil, what is good? One of the greatest Chinese Zen masters was asked by a disciple, "What should I do?" The master said, "I won't tell you what to do; my concern is that you see straight." This is why Buddhism is not just a matter of doing good and not doing evil; it is necessary to purify the mind.

2. The "Seven Buddhas" refers to specific individuals, but in general it is an expression representing enlightened people of antiquity or prehistory. The seventh of the Seven Buddhas was Shakyamuni Gautama Buddha, who is commonly considered the founder of Buddhism. Other accounts speak of twenty-four ancient Buddhas, or up to an unlimited number of Buddhas; the point of this is the idea that there is only one real truth, and that the enlightened are discoverers of truth, not founders of dogmatic religions.

   According to ancient Buddhist literature, Shakyamuni himself denied that he had founded a religion. He likened himself to one who has discovered an ancient road leading to an ancient city. The road and city were abandoned and overgrown by jungle, but the traces remained; leading others to the same discovery, Shakyamuni Buddha was able to "clear the road and restore the city." This symbolizes the restoration of the original knowledge of humanity, which has in a sense always existed, and is periodically rediscovered and recommunicated.

   According to a most ancient teaching of Buddhism, the general precept of this original knowledge is to refrain from what is bad, to do what is good, and to purify the mind. Dōgen says, "We should contemplate this principle carefully"—this should be given careful

128

consideration in the context of the question of *what human beings are doing on earth.*

It may seem redundant to say that the Way of the Seven Buddhas must be like the Way of the Seven Buddhas, but this actually has a deep meaning: that is to say, just as the Seven Buddhas realized what was good and bad in their times, we too must find out what is good and bad in our times. And just as the Seven Buddhas purified their minds, we too must purify our minds. The Way of the Seven Buddhas does not mean talking about the Way of the Seven Buddhas; it must be *like* the Way of the Seven Buddhas. It must be expressed in the present, it must be a quality of the present being-time, so it must be "herein," which "conveys a message." The message is the living communication of the Way of the Seven Buddhas in the present.

3. "Unoriginated" means that "evil" does not come from itself, but exists only in contrast to "good" and "indeterminate." Since one implies the others, the attribution of evil depends on the attribution of good and indeterminacy; there is no set point of origin in objective reality.

Since there is no definite point of origin, there is no absolute in "evil," so the nature of evil is pure in the sense of being without fixed existence; and this "purity" or "emptiness" is its ultimately real characteristic.

Yet even though there is no absolute good or evil because "evil" is not evil of itself and "good" is not good of itself, nevertheless in the relative world phenomena are good, evil, or indeterminate, in their particular context.

4. What is the same about evils in different places and times is that they are evils, or considered evils, in their place and time. What is different about evils in different places and times is what is specifically evil or considered evil in each specific place and time.

"Evil" might be taken to mean the same thing as "considered to be evil," or it might be taken to mean objectively evil in the sense of militating against the real welfare of the living. These may or may not coincide. The saying of the Zen master quoted earlier, "I am only concerned that you see straight," refers to the actual ability to distinguish between what people want and what people need.

The "evil of the way" is when the way of the way in one time and place is taken to be the fixed way of the way for other, or all, times and places.

The "good of the way" is when the way the way is carried out is really effective in context.

The "indeterminacy of the way" is when there is a possibility of rising from an imitation way to a real way.

In Zen literature these aspects of the way are commonly spoken of in terms of the question of whether the branches are taken for the root, whether the root and branches are understood through each other, or whether one is on the brink of the possibility of connecting the root and branches.

Another meaning of good, evil, and indeterminacy in reference to the way is generally what is good, bad, or indeterminate for spiritual enlightenment. As necessary conditions for this are not coterminous with social requirements, the good, evil, and indeterminacy of the way of the enlightened and the way of the world are different; and this difference is not on the same level, or not in the same dimension, as the differences between good and evil in different worldly realms.

5. Good and evil are manifestations of personal and collective being-time; having no inherently defined nature of its own, being-time is open, manifest in good and evil, manifesting good and evil.

The equality of phenomena is in their emptiness, the absence of fixed inherent nature. Good and evil are time and phenomena, whereas time and phenomena are not good or evil, in that good and evil are themselves (like all times and phenomena) products of relations, not preexisting qualities inhering in the natures of other phenomena.

However, the emptiness of good and evil, meaning their unfixed-ness, relativity, and open-ended quality, does not mean that what is good and bad in terms of learning real enlightenment can be made up or manipulated on a whim. It is a question of actual effect, of learning, application, and experience.

6. At first supreme enlightenment says, "Don't do any evil." On the ordinary level this means that an orderly, safe, and just community is desirable as a basis for higher development. This is because order, safety, and justice free optimum amounts of extra energy that would otherwise be preoccupied with the struggle for material and social survival, or with the struggle for redress. On this level, good and evil refer to the common welfare.

On the level of the Way, this means that the approach to enlightenment has to be correct in order to lead to the right result.

According to the situation, this usually involves doing some things and not doing others. Here good and evil refer to the requirements of higher knowledge.

On the initiatory level, "don't do any evil" means clearing the mind. One of the classical Zen masters said, "The ancients spoke only of the ills of mental impurity and false consciousness."

7. Not doing any evil is not made thus by the initiative of ordinary people for the reason that ordinary people (as the term is understood in Zen Buddhism) are still full of their own subjectivity and do not know beyond that what is good and evil.

   "Listening to the teaching" means real listening, in the sense of setting aside subjective judgments and opening the mind so that the real nature of situations "comes across." True perception of what is what is the word of enlightenment bespeaking enlightenment.

   It is because of the difficulty of bridging the gap between subjectivity and objectivity that the spoken and written teachings of Buddhism have been formulated. Those who cannot at once listen to the teaching from the original source can still find their way to the source by opening their minds to reflections of the source.

8. "Not doing evil" is the stage of aspiration and practice; "evil not being done" is the stage of realization. First there is effort, then spontaneity.

9. The manifestation of not doing is manifest to the amount of not doing. When the whole person is saturated with the ability to not do, then the amount of that nondoing is equal to the amount of everything.

   This means no longer being a slave to compulsion or coercion, whether internal or external. Evils are no longer evil for a nondoing person, in the sense that they have no compelling power and do not express themselves as evils in that person.

   Also, when understood as implements, actions or phenomena have no fixed value in themselves, and are only good or bad according to use. This is one of the secrets of Tantric Buddhism.

10. The one picked up is precisely the one put down: this means being able to use something purposefully without becoming obsessed by it or controlled by it. This should apply to any implements. This is the principle of being in the world but not of it; evil does not invade the person, yet the person does not destroy evil.

131

On another level, "one picked up, one put down" can mean taking to the good and leaving the bad.

Once evil does not invade the person, and the person realizes it is not even possible to destroy evil, thereafter personal character and qualities are refined by ongoing dealing with the relative world in relative terms, while maintaining a state of balance, not tarrying either "here" or "there."

Since situations are continuously changing, even though people may learn how to be inwardly unchanged and evenminded, still they need to learn how to adapt to changes too.

The development of a foundation of impartial objectivity is the "eighty to ninety percent accomplishment before the event," while the ability to avoid being carried away by habit, so as to remain open to the present turning into future, is the "not doing" after the intent.

Another way of looking at this statement is that the development of conscience is not quite sufficient to guarantee probity in the event of circumstances or impulses conducive to wrongdoing; but the ability to "not do" what comes to mind can make up for what foresight and conscience alone cannot accomplish in pragmatic terms.

There is an even deeper and more subtle level of morality in Zen, as noted by the great Chinese Zen master Yuanwu (Engo) when he wrote, "the nondoing of intent is most difficult."

11. "As you bring *whose* body-mind to practice"—*Who* means you! Yes, you! But you won't know who until you work with you as "who," and with "who" as you. In elementary Zen meditation, you are who, through contemplation of who are you.

The power of practical application is not doing; not doing is reached when you become who.

This who, like you, is just a way; it does not apply to the real self of body and mind. What is that real self? Not the you or who you think up.

The body, mind, four elements, and five clusters are still there after you pass through you and who. So what to do? Zen master Dongshan (Tōzan) said, "Every step should tread on this question." Confucius said, "As for those who do not say, 'What should I do? What should I do?'—I cannot do anything for them."

The cultivation of body and mind today must go on; their only power is in ongoing cultivation in the flowing present, and it is only

through this power that mind and body can be practicing enlightenment.

12. And it is not only your own mind and body, because everything is
interrelated. The power of practical application, the not doing of
subjective distortion, makes the whole objective world practice reality; and if we are impartial and objective in seeing the world, the
world will teach us to work in accord with necessity and potential.
So the world real-izes us as we real-ize the world.

13. Seeing objectively is not seeing once and then composing a standard
formula; reality flows. The Japanese Zen master Keizan said, "Don't
sleep, and you won't dream."

When you see the time, in the sense of seeing both the moment
and the flow, then time teaches you.

The living eye is fresh and new. It does not "notch the side of a
moving boat to mark the spot where something fell overboard."

Here, to "cause defilement" means to occasion attachment and
obsession. If people become obsessed with forms of teaching and
practice, or with feelings of realization, they will not get beyond
these to reach real enlightenment. This is especially true when those
forms and feelings belong to a different time.

On the other hand, it is precisely because the enlightened are not
obsessed or blinded by tools that they can assess their appropriate
use and apply them freely without being locked into set patterns.

14. "The enlightened make the enlightened practice" in the sense that it
is your enlightenment that lets you find out what you should do and
what you should be. The degree to which you find your task, what
you can do in pragmatic terms, is the degree to which you can see
clearly.

What you see is a web of times, all interrelated; every time you
focus on one spot or set of time, its relation to other times makes
beginnings, durings, and aftermaths. Someone asked Zen master
Baizhang, "Are greatly cultivated people subject to cause and effect?"
Baizhang said, "They are not blind to cause and effect."

"When living beings become enlightened beings, although they
do not obstruct the enlightened beings that have been there all along,
they should attentively think about the principle of becoming enlightened beings twenty-four hours a day, whatever they may be
doing." Becoming an enlightened being does not mean that this

enlightenment was not there all along; but even though it was there all along, to be a practical reality it has to be carried out all along.

15. Living beings "become" enlightened beings in one sense when they realize their true nature and find that many feelings about living are implanted by conditioning and not part of the real individual. But becoming an enlightened being does not mean becoming a zombie, or having no personality. It does not even mean having no emotion, thoughts, or afflictions. It means being free in the midst of it all, being the master of yourself, able to use or not use at will whatever elements of possibility are available to you as an individual. To nevertheless have "shed" the living being means that one is not enslaved to any of these elements.

16. Therefore becoming enlightened means consciously making cause and effect work. From this point of view, delusion is manifested as a haphazard combination of meddling incompetently in things and allowing oneself to be manipulated by things.

So enlightenment is not "stirring cause and effect," not distorting things, not making things up.

We have to deal with the situation at hand. What we do and do not, that is practice; and today's practice is yesterday's realization, today's realization, and tomorrow's realization.

The "original face" is objective reality—beginningless, ever in flux, naked reality such as it is. When things are subjectively not contrived, but seen impartially, there can be no fixation on anything; and if there is no fixation on any thing, one does not fall under the spell of any thing. This is "shedding."

17. One of the philosophical problems facing the Tendai school of Buddhism from which Dōgen emerged was to explain how evil could exist if the whole of reality was an embodiment of Buddha. To handle this question, Tendai Buddhologists explained that all realms of being were inherent possibilities in the consciousness of all beings, including enlightened beings; the enlightenment of the latter means freedom to choose, to be and to act through free will and not compulsion. Therefore by transcending evil without having to destroy it, "evils are manifest as a continuum of being ever not done."

The science of using "evils" to further human progress is a specialty of one branch of Tantric Buddhism. Some Tantric Buddhism was kept as esoteric lore in the Shingon and Tendai schools in

Japan. Dōgen, however, said that Buddhism in Japan had always been corrupt, so he emphasized nondoing for his time.

Dōgen himself, as is well known, did certain things usually considered "evil" by the standard of exoteric Buddhist precepts: he used harsh language, spoke in a contradictory manner on the conventional level, and attacked people verbally. Some of the attempts by scholars to explain this are truly hilarious, utterly ignoring the didactic purpose of Buddhist "skill in means." One distinguished scholar in Japan has even ventured the opinion that Dōgen was already suffering from *dementia senile* in his early forties!

It is only when evils are evils that it can be said that evils arise or pass away. There is nothing about anything that can definitely make it evil in itself; when evils are not done, they are not born from conditions. "Not done" means that one does not construe anything as something in itself; if nothing is "done"—that is, if nothing is reified, then one cannot treat anything as an entity, concrete or abstract. Only when one realizes by not-doing, by nonreification, that evils are not done, not things, is one really free, really settled. As long as one sets up evils as something to avoid, one still revolves in a circle of one's own making.

18. The equality of evils and the equality of phenomena refer to essence, not to characteristics. It is important to understand this distinction, in order to avoid misapprehension of the Buddhist teaching of equality. Equality and difference are perfectly compatible in the light of Buddhist insight; this is why it can be said that good and evil are equal even though good is good and evil is evil.

    According to the principle of relativity, good and evil do not make themselves, they are products of conditions. The practice of seeing in this way is designed to liberate the mind from fixated notions of good and evil; yet this is not a final liberation, because there is still the view of conditions. Therefore the next step is to see that conditions are not self-determined, "not done of themselves." The idea here is to return awareness to the fluidity of reality, and not let it get fixated anywhere.

19. "The family of Buddhas arises from conditions." This statement from scripture conveys a number of meanings.

    Although we say that Buddhahood, which means full awareness, is the birthright, the original nature, of all living beings, nevertheless the manifestation of this nature is inhibited by taking in and internalizing external influences during the course of mundane life. Therefore the stable manifestation of the original nature of Buddhahood can only come about through effective conditions, the conditions of consciousness-refining practices that will purify the mind of randomly acquired habits, and will also immunize the mind against arbitrary conditioning and will-less behavior. *The Flower Ornament Scripture* says, "The manifestation of Buddha . . . does not come about through just one condition or thing, but by innumerable causes and conditions, innumerable phenomena."

Because individual mind-body equipment and life experiences are different, therefore the conditions that will manifest the original nature are also different for each individual. Sometimes the differences are slight, sometimes they are great. According to these differences, the enlightening conditions and practices differ, so "conditions arise from the family of Buddhas." The family of Buddhas means the potential Buddhas, whose individualities give rise to specific conditions, and also the realized Buddhas, whose knowledge and compassion give rise to the conditions—such as teachings and techniques—to suit the conditions of the potential Buddhas.

The condition of Buddhahood is not annihilation of evil, it is just *not doing* evil. It is important to understand this distinction, otherwise you may wind up like a dog chasing its tail or an imbecile trying to run away from his own shadow.

This "not doing" includes the not doing of thought, so Dōgen shows how to erase the doing of thought about evil: even "not done" is not done. The intent to "not do" is itself a doing, and therefore does not leave its object completely "not done." Thus Buddhas do not try to "not do" evil, but simply let it be "not done."

20. Spring symbolizes growth and life, pine trees symbolize stasis and eternity; therefore "spring pines" represent death within life, being sensitive and effective, yet tranquil and unstirring.

Autumn symbolizes dying, chrysanthemums symbolize living; therefore "autumn chrysanthemums" represent life within death, being tranquil and unstirring yet sensitive and effective.

The not doing of the spring pine is "doing yet not doing," acting without attachment. The not doing of the autumn chrysanthemum is "not doing yet doing," acting spontaneously, without contrivance.

The "pillars, lamps, whisk, and staff" refer to the world of objects; the "self" refers to the mind. The not doing of existence and nonexistence means not grasping the world and oneself, yet not rejecting the world and oneself.

21. This study is really being here, being there. It is presence of mind, mind in the present. Then we see what is really there, not just what we think.

   We step toward reality, reality steps toward us. If we keep on this way, one day "the east wall meets the west wall," and there is union.

   What is there, what is here, being *thus*, one might say that reality is *done*; but reality is not a fabrication of our thoughts, and we can only reach it by the power of the nondoing of falsification. There are all sorts of falsifications, including the falsification of nondoing into doing resulting from the attempt to "do" not doing.

22. In a famous Zen story, a master asked an elder, quoting from scripture, " 'The true reality body of Buddhas is like space; it manifests form in response to beings, like the moon reflected in water.' How do you explain the principle of response?" The elder said, "Like a donkey looking into a well." The Zen master said, "You have said a lot, but that is only eighty percent." The elder asked the master what he would say; the Zen master replied, "Like the well looking up at the donkey."

   The "well looking at the donkey" stands for absorption in objective reality; the same Zen master said, "You are not It, It is you."

   The "well looking at the well" stands for objective being in itself; as an ancient Zen master said in reply to a question about the nature of Buddhism where there are no people, "The large stones are large, the small stones are small."

   The "donkey looking at the donkey" stands for the person realizing self; as a Zen saying has it, "Who is it if not you?"

   The "person looking at the person" and the "mountain looking at the mountain" stand for animate and inanimate beings meeting themselves in spontaneity; a famous Zen master, asked how it is when neither subject nor object is taken away, replied, "The emperor ascends the jeweled throne, the peasants sing hallelujah."

   "Because it is the not doing that is in response to beings, it is not doing that is manifesting form." Not doing evils is the manifestation, or response, of merging with nondoing. This essential nondoing is open, like space; it manifests according to the situation. What is not

137

fabricatd by the acquired personality is the real body of those who are awake.

Manifestation of form in response to beings means the manifestation of knowledge through compassion, resulting in method, means of perceiving reality. Because it is objective and impartial, it is not someone's personal "doing."

This manifestation of openness in form reveals two aspects of reality: nothing that exists can be ultimately grasped, yet nothing that exists can be totally denied. That is "clapping on the left, clapping on the right"—or, as it is said, "Officially, not even a needle can get through; privately, even a horse and buggy can pass."

The moon reflected in water is truth reflected in the world. A manifestation of truth in form is a form proper to the time. If you do not see the truth of a truth in the context of the time, you do not see the whole truth; if you take the form and the time for the truth itself, not only do you not see the truth, you do not even see the form and time.

The sameness and difference of universality and particularity of truth is referred to in Flower Ornament Buddhism as the noninterference of extension and restriction. As a Chinese founder of that school says, truth is there before us all the time, but we make it a field of imagination. This arbitrary imagination is itself the act of "doubting truth."

23. "There has never been good that has become manifest beforehand to await the agent." Like evil, good comes from a combination of conditions, the relation of the mind, word, thought, deed, and situation. The notion of premanifested good awaiting the agent represents fixation on a reification of an idea.

"Precisely such a time" of "doing good" is openness manifesting in form; because it is open, there is no good that cannot come forth in doing, there are no arbitrarily preconceived limitations.

"Accounting" refers to the crystallizations of openness into form, the risings of stillness into movement, which immediately "count" in the world of manifestation of causality.

24. As Dōgen explained before in his discourse on evil, what people call "good" is not the same in different contexts, different communities, and different times. The teaching of Buddhas has been to enable people to recognize what is really good and bad in each situation. Recognition is not the same as supposition; as a classical Zen master

quoted earlier said, "I do not say how you should act; my only concern is that you see accurately."

25. " 'The same' means teaching in the world is just time." Timing in the appropriate use of means depends on knowledge, recognition of what is suitable or unsuitable, useful or otherwise, in a given situation.

   The whole teaching of the enlightened, including their own physical manifestation as teachers, is a matter of the time. The time means the quality of the interactions of minds and objects.

   In the sense that the teachings of the enlightened address themselves to conditions to point to ways out of conditioning, even though the teachings may appear different, in essence there is no different teaching.

26. These are examples of timing. "Disciples" means followers of the individual "small vehicles" of Buddhism, aiming primarily at inner peace and freedom. "Enlightening beings" are followers of the universal "great vehicle" of Buddhism. According to Zen master Baizhang, for "disciples" to devote themselves to meditation concentrations for individual liberation is keeping discipline; while for enlightening beings who are involved in the simultaneous liberation of self and others, devotion to meditation concentrations for individual liberation is breaking discipline.

27. "Good does not arise from conditions or perish through conditions" in the sense that it is none other than the conditions themselves. Good may be anything, but not everything is always and everywhere good. For the result to be right, the conditions must be right; this applies to all acts, words, and thoughts.

28. Good is not what is attributed to oneself, as in the admonition of Jesus of Nazareth: "When you give charity, don't let your right hand know what your left hand is doing." Also, good is not good because it is "good" in the eyes of others: according to the Taoist ancient Lao-tzu, "When 'everyone knows' 'good' is 'good,' this is not good."

   "Self and other" also mean subject and object. "Sun and moon" mean the source and its reflector. The sun/source is "other," pure objectivity, objective truth; the moon/reflector is "self," the subject. The "living eye" is "open" according to the alignment of moon to sun vis-a-vis earth: this means the degree of our ability to reflect truth in the midst of earthy life.

   Note a deep shift in the points of reference of the words "self" and "other" in Dōgen's presentation. In a way this is obvious but in a way it is also subtle.

29. "The issue at hand" is the present interaction of mind and situation. This did not arise out of nowhere; it is a moment in a measureless integral flux of events. Yet that does not mean it has always been there, because the actualization of the moment—be it a measured moment or a measureless moment—is always *now*.

The issue at hand is in part a result of what we have done before, but there is always much more involved. Buddhist teachings speak of five inconceivables, among which is the inconceivability of cause and effect, meaning the totality of cause and effect.

30. Buddhist morality tales illustrate certain kinds of averages in cause and effect relationships, but they are meant to show the principle that actions inevitably cause results; they are not meant to be taken literally to mean that causality is a simple affair of tit-for-tat, of one cause producing one effect.

The same thing goes for the detailed analyses of causality made by early Buddhist philosophers and psychologists who defined phenomena in such terms as primary conditions, enhancing conditions, predominating conditions, and so on: all of these are "measurements" made to perform specific functions, to have certain effects on the perceiving mind. They are not, properly speaking, intended to be comprehensive definitions of objective reality, or to be tenets of belief in theoretical philosophy.

This was clarified by the great Buddhist doctor Nāgārjuna, who unraveled earlier systems to show their definitions to be "empty" of objective reality. "The measurement of the living eye" is the open, nondiscursive awareness freed by this realization of emptiness. Subtended by the realization of emptiness, it is therefore "not the same as the measurement of other things," which are in the nature of conceptual description.

31. According to the classical master Baizhang, not being attached to existence or nonexistence, to form or void, or to any notion at all is considered the elementary level of good. Not dwelling on this goodness is considered the middling level of good. Not making an understanding of nondwelling is called the final good.

32. This passage points out the way to achieve the nondoing of self-reflection in respect to performance of good. "Entry, abiding, and exit" are the "three subtle gates" of all practices. Here Dōgen refers

to the experience of absorption in practice, complete oneness, in which performance is spontaneously manifested without conceptual definition. A Zen proverb speaks of "entering the grasslands without leaving a trace, going into the water without making a ripple."

33. Because all things are interrelated, the performing of one good must directly or indirectly involve all of reality. The causes and effects of this good constitute its nexus of conditions.

From the point of view of universal relativity as illustrated in the Flower Ornament teaching, the relation of cause and effect is not only linear, but radiant, going in all directions in time and space.

The equality of causes, effects, and phenomena means they are all participants in one great matter.

Only part of this can be seen in terms of linear progression of time as we ordinarily think of it and perceive it. "It is not a matter of before and after, because there is a way of such as before and after": there are many ways in which parts of the nexus of conditions can be seen; before and after is one way. There is a totality, which is the vehicle of all possibilities, but it is not itself confined to any given possibility.

34. Each statement here—the interrelation of self, purification, "the," mind, not doing, and performance—is a point to ponder deeply, a koan put here by Dōgen for this purpose.

"The" is the issue at hand; it is the state of the self, of not doing, and of doing. "The" is really too close to be put into words. A classical Zen master said, "As soon as you say it's 'thus,' it has already changed." So one has to ponder and see on one's own.

35. The enlightened may appear in the world in virtually any role, but that does not mean everyone in that particular role is enlightened. And it does not mean the role is enlightened. What it means is that virtually any role can be played in a more enlightened or less enlightened way. Someone who can play a role, or roles, in an enlightened way can teach people through that. This is not the same thing as teaching a role.

"Without studying what the enlightened must be like, even though one may vainly seem to struggle, as a living being suffering further this is not carrying out the way of the enlightened." This passage is a warning against arbitrary adoption of practices. "Spiritual" struggle with practices might be impressive to oneself and others, but this becomes just another slavery.

"The business of the horse coming up before the business of the ass is over" is a stock Zen phrase expressing the ancient formula of "dying and returning to life." The "business of the ass" means learning to "not do" personal follies. The "business of the horse" means learning to act in harmony with necessity rather than sentiment.

That the business of the horse comes up before the business of the ass is done means that objectivity appears in an infinite gradation as subjectivity is lessened or bypassed. It also means that the ultimate annihilation of the subject would mean inability to act constructively in the world.

Therefore the "business of the ass" is never done one hundred percent until death; so we have to keep on doing it, without overdoing it.

36. This statesman was Bo Juyi (Po Chü-i), one of the most revered Chinese poets of all time. Most if not all of China's great poets since the Tang dynasty studied Zen.

The "Bird's Nest" refers to the fact that this particular Zen master lived in a tree. It is said that when Bo Juyi first visited him, the statesman said to the Zen master, "Your position is quite dangerous." The Zen master retorted, "You, sir, are the one in a dangerous position!"

37–41. This story is famous in Zen annals, and is generally used to illustrate the difference between intellectualism and actual Zen practice. According to Bodhidharma, the founder of Zen in China, one of the characteristics of the Zen adept is accord of speech and action. This is often taken as an ethical issue, but it is basically one of ability and work.

42. Manjushri is a supernal enlightening being representing wisdom and knowledge; Maitreya is a supernal enlightening being said to be destined to become the next Buddha on earth.

43. The scholar-poet symbolizes the intellect, which may work marvelously well in its own domain yet misinterpret what is outside that domain by trying to bring everything within its own compass.

Among the things that the intellect likes to think in the present time is that it is in command of itself, that it is in command of oneself, and that what it thinks is in fact true.

In the case of the brilliant scholar-poet, his "only recognizing intentional contrivance" is a typical symptom of self-conscious intellectuals with pride and confidence in their talents, accustomed to thinking of their own abilities as the source of motive and action. Thus he could not even conceive of spontaneous "not doing" and "performing" that transcends subjectively motivated and formulated conduct.

44. Even if fabricated evils are proscribed, the manifestation of this prohibition must be via nondoing. Even if fabricated good is encouraged, the manifestation of this injunction must be by way of performance.

45. "Differential development" and "equivalent continuity" are Buddhist technical terms referring to the conditioning process whereby people evolve in accord with their own actions and those of their environment. This belongs to the domain of mundane habituation, so it is not adequate to describe the process of enlightenment: "but for an enlightened cause"—that is to say, without an enlightened cause, or if it is not an enlightened cause—"it is impossible to effect an enlightened result."

Deluded practice does not make for enlightened realization. The unity of practice and realization of which Dōgen writes in his essay "Talk on Mastering the Way" does not mean, as some cultists believe, that religious exercises are themselves enlightenment; it means that the quality of realization is none other than the quality of practice. In his essay "The Issue at Hand," Dōgen writes that practice and realization based on the ego are delusion, while practice and realization based on objective reality are enlightenment.

46. Once *nondoing* is mastered, it is the nondoing of any and all evils in any and all circumstances; by nondoing, everything evil is transformed into a field of liberation.

"Good in the beginning, middle, and end" is an expression used in earliest Buddhist literature to describe the Dharma, or teaching; for the classical Zen interpretation, see the note to paragraph 31 above.

"Nature, characteristic, essence, power, etc." refer to ten aspects of *thusness,* or *suchness,* as delineated in Tendai Buddhist philosophy.

47. "Do you know the principle of a child's being born with potential?" If you do not know the buddha-nature in a child, you do not know the buddha-nature in yourself, and you do not know the buddha-nature in a Buddha.

"If one does not yet know the enlightened ones of past, present, and future, how could one know a three-year-old child?" According to universalist Buddhist doctrine, the Buddha-nature (which is one and the same in all Buddhas of all times) is none other than the real nature of human beings.

Also, the Buddhas may be taken to symbolize the transmundane, or absolute, while the child symbolizes the mundane, or relative. If one does not know the transmundane absolute, one has no objective perspective on the mundane relative. On the other hand, perfect knowledge of the relativity of the mundane ushers consciousness into knowledge of the transmundane absolute: "Anyone who knows a three-year-old child would know the enlightened ones of past, present, and future."

48. This passage encapsulates the Flower Ornament teaching of universal relativity. The fact that all things are interdependent means that each individual implies the whole in its existence, while the whole implies each individual in its existence. This is explained in great logical detail in the essay "Mirror of the Mysteries" in my *Entry into the Inconceivable: An Introduction to Hua-yen Buddhism.* (Honolulu: University of Hawaii, 1983). One of the most famous images in the *Flower Ornament Scripture* is that of an atom containing a scripture as vast as a universe; the classical Zen master Baizhang used this metaphor very effectively in his teaching, and its pattern is to be found in many passages in Dōgen's *Shōbōgenzō.*

49. A three-year-old child is conscious, alive, and mortal: these are *the conditions of the most important matter.* This aspect of Buddhism—its profound respect for children—is well worth taking into considera- tion today. I don't want to offend anyone here, but in the spirit of Dōgen's criticism of the scholar's slighting remark, I would say that American parents who have tried to wean themselves from babying children or treating them like their possessions, in favor of treating them as essentially equal human beings, have unfortunately, and indeed one would almost have to say inevitably, fallen into the trap of treating children like neurotic, rationalizing, babyish adults. Again I beg of those who read, take heed, not offense: this is precisely why we are studying Buddhism, which really means illuminism, understandingism. Enlightenment is not just for molli- fying our personal spiritual thirst; it is the best of all possible gifts we can give to our children and our children's children.

"When you were first born you had a share of the lion's roar."

According to ancient records, one of the masters of the Chinese Gui-Yang school of Zen actually attained sudden enlightenment on hearing this saying quoted in a teaching hall into which he had just walked. That is how much meaning there is in this consciousness when you take it seriously. "It cannot be easy" also reads, "Don't take it lightly."

50. Here the three-year-old child stands for the beginner, who is the same in essence as the Buddhas but different in practical experience. The scholar is so preoccupied with the lofty ideal that he does not see the immediate practicality. But it is necessary to work with what is at hand. Lao-tzu said, "The journey of ten thousand miles begins at your feet." Because he cannot humble himself to fundamental practicalities, the intellectual does not appreciate the simple teaching of the Zen master quoting a most ancient and honored scriptural passage.

51. Idries Shah the Sufi wrote that it is never too late for some things, and always too late for others. "I leave the speaking of the child entirely up to you, not to the child; I leave the inability of an old man to practice entirely up to you, not to the old man." Zen master Baizhang said of the teaching, "Everything should be referred to yourself."

52. "Buddhism" is defined "like this."

AWAKENING THE UNSURPASSED MIND

The unsurpassed mind is the attitude of enlightenment. Sometimes it may be called the thought of enlightenment, the aspiration for enlightenment, the will for enlightenment, or the spirit of enlightenment. It is not an ordinary thought or desire, and it is not a matter of determining to go from "here" to "there." It is a recognition and an attitude that penetrates time and circumstance.

Because it embraces all yet penetrates all, it is said in the *Flower Ornament Scripture* that with the first arousing of the determination for enlightenment one realizes complete enlightenment; or, as a Zen formulation of this teaching has it, "Pick up a mote of dust, and the whole earth is contained therein."

1. According to Zen legend, Shakyamuni Buddha sat in the Himalaya mountains for six years, shedding attachments to this world and all

worlds. Great nirvana is freedom. The classical Zen teacher Baizhang, (Hyakujō), who lived in China several hundred years before Dōgen's time, used this saying "The Himalaya mountains represent great nirvana" as a signpost for the first stage of Zen meditation, the stage of detachment, freedom from external and internal influences, the mind becoming like space. Baizhang said, "Now if your mind is like space, for the first time your study has some accomplishment."

"This represents what it can represent" in the sense that the expression represents the experience for which it stands, not subjective imaginations or arbitrary emotional or intellectual associations linked to the surface content of the metaphor. "Accuracy" is the accuracy of personal experience, the actuality and not the imagination.

2. Bodhidharma is the symbolic founder of Zen: the image of "each mind like wood and stone" was also used by the seminal teacher Baizhang to point to the experience of the mind being like space. "Suchness of mind," or "mind of objective reality," is not distorted by subjective bias; it is all-embracing, including self and other. This is what is called the original mind, or real mind, which underlies the individual minds of all beings.

3. "Existence, nonexistence, emptiness, form" are points of view. The wood and stone mind is the viewer. The viewer being untrammeled by the view is one of the keys of Zen; only with this art can Zen be practiced in reality.

Yet this practice can be carried out only because the wood and stone mind is not insensitive. Baizhang said that inanimate beings have Buddha nature, whereas sentient beings have not; and he explained that this is a metaphor referring to the matter of whether or not people are slaves of their feelings. In terms of freedom from this slavery, it is called wood and stone mind; in terms of being yet alive, dynamic, and responsive, it is called mind wood and mind stone.

"Thinking of what is not thinking" is what Dōgen refers to as the essential art of Zen meditation. It is a method of direct cutting to the essence of mind, bypassing the feelings and thoughts produced by the function of mind. As the classic *Book of Serenity* points out, however, this technique can be abused: "when the wine is always sweet, it lays out the guests." Only seeing essence, without free manifestation of the unconstrained function, is still an aberration:

therefore one only gets beyond aberrant paths when one has "seen and heard the wind and sound"—experienced the freely functioning dynamic—of the "mind wood and mind stone."

4. Walls, tiles, and pebbles represent the objective world. Observation and inquiry, asking where and what, are what is known in Zen as "the answering is in the questioning." These are questions that are not to be answered as one answers questions of theory, or of consensual fact in the everyday world: the answers are in the experiences provoked by pursuing these questions with the Zen "feeling of doubt" that unsettles fixed assumptions.

"The other side of the king of emptiness" refers to a direction or mode of meditation in a preliminary phase of Zen, used for dissolving occupation with the world of ordinary sense. This is just a doorway into the unlimited universe; in the history of Zen seekers, those who stand by the doorway have been countless. Master Caoshan (Sōzan) said, "The six senses are your teachers: only by following them can you take food."

Dōgen says the mind of the ancient Buddhas is not empty, but full; as a Zen proverb says, "The Reality Body without clothing cannot ward off the cold." It is not only by abstract concentration but also through experience of the world at large that the eternal mind of enlightenment is realized.

"Sitting Buddha" and "being Buddha" comprise the twin practice of stillness and movement, yin and yang, receptivity and creativity.

5. "The conditions of awakening the mind for enlightenment are not a matter of bringing forth the mind for enlightenment from elsewhere, but of awakening the mind by bringing forth the mind for enlightenment." The mind for enlightenment is not acquired, and cannot be faked or forced. Dongshan said, "I am not it, it is me."

"Making a blade of grass a Buddha" means fully recognizing the potential of everything. This is how one's own potential comes out. It is a mutually complementary process—the more one recognizes the potential of each thing, each being, each situation, the more one's own potential is awakened; and the more one's own potential awakens, the more one realizes the potential of everything, everyone, everywhere.

A "rootless tree" is a common metaphor for the body, the mortal being, but it can be used to refer to anything, in the sense of the transience or fluidity of all things. This is the scripture of life.

Observation of impermanence is traditionally considered one of the best ways to arouse the aspiration for enlightenment. At the same time, when one is freed by this observation from the urge to try to fix into a stationary scene what must ever flow, and one thus has no illusions of permanency, then one can read this "scripture" with fearless clarity.

Charity and service are manifestations of the attitude of enlightenment. Generosity is a natural expression of the realization that nothing can be permanently possessed; service is an expression of the realization that change and flux mean ever-renewed opportunities for development and improvement.

All of these awakenings, bringing forth the transmundane while in the midst of the mundane, are beautifully summed up in the expression "to honor Buddha while being disturbed by demons." Honoring Buddha means keeping our Buddha-nature clean, fresh, and alive, even while we are fully involved in the hurly-burly of ordinary life.

6. "Knowing home is not a home" is realizing that this world is only a temporary inn, as Buddhists often say. "Giving up home and leaving home" means not being attached to the world, embodying this realization in life; being fluid and free, not pinned down by mental fixations. Other Zen masters describe this as having no country, abiding in no place.

"Entering the mountains to practice the Way" means being in the world yet somehow removed from the world, a traditional description of Mahāyāna Buddhism; this open space allows the individual to work on the Way to completeness, to realize and experience dimensions of being not included in the social, cultural, and national "homes" that condition the self and train it to ignore the great reality beyond these boundaries.

"Acting on faith and acting on principle" are two stages of practice. At first one does not know or remember, but acts on faith because of an indescribable resonance felt with the teaching. Later one knows, and acts on the basis of principle, what is right and what is so.

The "eighty thousand sets of Dharma" are the myriads of principles and practices that have been and can be used in the process of awakening the mind.

The radical difference between Dōgen's teaching and the doctrines of later sectarian Sōtō Zen Dogenism is abundantly apparent here.

7. Dreams and intoxication are states in which the so-called sixth consciousness, the conceptual faculty, is not so acute, not so powerful, not so dominant; and so there may be unexpected access of impacts that can awaken the mind. Here too, it is a mistake to focus on a fragment of the attendant circumstances rather than the result; the practice, the dream, the intoxication may have played a role in the opening of the mind, but what is important is the effect of the opening. There are many cases of awakenings on sense-impacts, as noted here, but these impacts, like specific practices and mental states, were only a part of a total event, they were not in themselves magic keys.

   This is also true of the meditation states and experiences of expanded consciousness represented by "heaven" and "the ocean." Enlightenment is so pure that it permeates every state in every world—of desire, of form, and without form—yet is not contained in any world. What are in these worlds, from the point of view of the thought of enlightenment, are only experiences that can provoke or trigger awakening beyond the event.

8. Awakening the mind for enlightenment in the midst of awakening the mind for enlightenment means that one does not think or feel "*I* awaken the mind for enlightenment." True awakening takes place at the very source of being, the buddha-nature awakening the buddha-nature, and thus pervades every dimension of being.

9. Shrines and images of Buddhas are representations, bearers of messages, holders of patterns of faith, practice, and understanding. How do you make shrines and fashion buddhas? They are not just material forms, but they are not totally without material forms either: form is empty, emptiness is form. A famous Zen master of Tang dynasty China said in his enlightenment verse, "Before, I looked elsewhere for It; now I see it like ice in fire." Observing suchness, observing the essence of things, being absorbed in the assembly of Buddhas, and attaining the mental command of Buddhas, is all in present being and doing; the Land of Eternally Silent Light (a Tendai Buddhist name for the unfabricated absolute) always pervades all lands.

10. One of the practices of the so-called "small vehicle" of Buddhism involves plunging into formless trances,—absorption in the infinity

of space, infinity of consciousness, infinity of nothingness, neither perception nor nonperception, and cessation of all sensation and perception. Those who are enraptured by these formless trances may easily lapse into the sort of view that Dōgen describes here.

Something similar happens to Zen practitioners who mistake a glimpse of the so-called formless world for *kenshō,* or satori, and reify the experience. This is one of the aberrations in the perennial wisdom tradition of high antiquity that Shakyamuni Buddha corrected, and there are also many later Zen sayings dealing with this historically recurring problem.

The distinguished Song dynasty Chinese Zen master Dahui often stressed the dangers of nihilism and laissez-faire attitudes resulting from counterfeit or misconstrued Zen experience. According to his teaching, people may think and feel that they are free when in fact they are still bound by fixations, and all they have really accomplished by "Zen meditation" is to make the fixation invisible to themselves by arresting certain mental faculties. This is what a Zen proverb calls "covering your ears to steal a bell," or from the point of view of onlookers, "stealing a bell with your ears covered."

11. Nāgārjuna, the Indian Buddhist philosopher who clearly enunciated the principles of emptiness approximately two thousand years ago, wrote that emptiness, according to the Buddhas, is detachment from all views, and that those who hold to "emptiness" as a view are unteachable. In Zen parlance such people are sometimes described as being like small children covering their eyes with their hands and saying nothing is there.

Those who have been accustomed to the sectarian view of Dōgen as proclaiming zazen alone as the way may be interested to note his oblique recommendation of other practices.

12. Buddha, Dharma, and Sangha are the Three Treasures of Buddhism. Buddha is the enlightened one, Dharma is the principle or reality of enlightenment, Sangha is the harmonious community based on the Dharma.

Because the power of self-deception extends from the depths of the realm of desire to the heights of the realm of formless meditations, it is necessary to be acted on by an outside force, like scriptures or teachers. (See the "Ten Stages" scripture in the *Flower Ornament Scripture* for an example of this in the maturation of the Eighth Stage of enlightenment, after the attainment of effortlessness.)

13. Yanshou, who was third patriarch of the Fayan House of Zen in China, ninth patriarch of the Pure Land School, and master of all the other Chinese schools, wrote in his monumental *Source Mirror Record* that nine out of ten people who practice Zen without studying the Buddhist teachings become conceited and go astray.

    Naturally, reception of teachings must also be accurate to be effective, and a teacher that is not genuine can hardly be a guide. Arbitrary understanding and false teachers always continue to exist, even side by side with genuine understanding and real teachers, because the arbitrary and the false are more appealing to people who (whether covertly or openly) want teachings and teachers to flatter them and pander to their wishes.

14. The way to enlightenment requires real effort, both intensive and extensive, purifying both the inner world and the outer world, clarifying the self and expanding the being. If one takes refuge in ignorant nothingness, or in convenient dogmas or sticky relationships with guru/emcee figures, one will never find truth and be real.

15. According to the principles of Flower Ornament Buddhism, every particle and every being is an intrinsic part of the universe, and the whole universe is an intrinsic part of every particle and every being. Enlightenment is reading the patterns of this fabric of totality.

    Because each individual implies all in the whole, and all imply each, there is no beginning, no starting place—this is the meaning of "unborn." When the mind opens up to this, it no longer starts its trips from a constructed mind-set base, so it is also "unborn."

    Then one can appreciate everything in terms of its place in the greater scheme of things, not just in terms of a habitual set of ideas. By opening to the manifestation of reality in the total fabric, one can more completely understand the manifestation of reality in each thread of the fabric.

16. If mind and things were separate, there would be no possibility of awareness of anything. Relative reality and ultimate reality are two only from the point of view of relative reality; from the point of view of ultimate reality they are not two.

    The key to this realization, as indicated in the *Sandhinirmochana-sūtra,* is to detach from descriptions so as to arrive at insight into objective reality. In this context, description refers to imagined reality, reality as subjectively conceived, which conforms to the models inculcated in the process of acculturation and socialization, not to objective reality.

When mind detaches from imagined reality and can penetrate the filter of thought and language, one becomes aware of ultimate reality in relative reality. Then one can act without being contaminated by any notion of reward. Acting without reifying acts, creating without reifying creations, serving life with expectations is the enlightening path of unfabricated, uncontaminated virtue.

17. According to the popular *Vimalakīrti-nirdesha-sūtra,* or Scripture Spoken by Vimalakīrti, just as a castle cannot be built in midair, a pure land cannot be made but on the ground of beings. Making images and shrines means making a pure land.

The emptiness of form means that form is workable and malleable; this is what makes a pure land possible. Myriad enlightening works flow from the actualization of this realization.

The form of emptiness is all forms, but it also has the meaning of forms especially designed to convey the real nature of form. Thus it is said that all the flora and fauna of a pure land are always invoking Buddha and Dharma.

18. A Chinese Zen master said, "In the hubbub of the city there is the Buddha Dharma of the city hubbub; in the quiet of the mountains there is the Buddha Dharma of the mountain quiet."

Once when a famous Zen master of the classical era was herding buffalo, his teacher came by and asked, "Which one is a bodhisattva?" The Zen master replied, "Which one is not a bodhisattva?"

19. The scripture noted is the *Saddharmapundarīka-sūtra,* or *Lotus Scripture,* which says one may see a Buddha once in a lifetime, or never; this means that the thought or moment of mindfulness in which one sees Buddha is total. Seeing the real in the midst of illusion, "seeing the king in the marketplace," with this mindfulness all the Buddhas of the ten directions appear; that is to say, everything is seen at once.

In the *Avatamsaka-sūtra,* or *Flower Ornament Scripture,* when Samantabhadra Bodhisattva, the Universally Good Enlightening Being, enters absorption in the matrix of illumination, he sees all Buddhas; and in the presence of the Buddhas are parallel Samantabhadra Bodhisattvas, all simultaneously aware of one another and of this total nexus, by virtue of concentration on reality.

In Pure Land Buddhist teaching it is said that when you think of

one Buddha, then all Buddhas think of you; when you are mindful
of one Buddha, then all Buddhas are mindful of you.

The Pure Land teaching also says all lands are visible from the
pure land of the Buddha of Infinite Light. The Flower Ornament
teaching says all phenomena are reflected in each other. This is the
awareness of the self-integration and harmony of the universe, such
as becomes accessible to the unbiased mind.

A Chinese Sōtō Zen master was asked, "What is the realm of true
seeing?" He replied, "Nothing interposed." The state of "nothing
interposed" is what Dōgen is writing of as "thinking *this*": it is
"being Buddha," it is being all things, it is being all things being
Buddha.

20. The Chinese proto-Zen Buddhist Sengzhao wrote, "Heaven, earth,
and I have the same root; myriad beings and I are the same body."
Whatever one does simultaneously involves everyone and everything
else at some level or another, whether or not one is aware of it. The
work of enlightenment involves awareness of the implications of
one's acts; awakening the mind involves being enlightened by everything. Dōgen also wrote, "To witness and act on things selfishly is
delusion; to witness and act on the self in the process of things is
enlightenment."

21. Space is open, accommodating, unaffected; valley stream water is
pure, clear, ever flowing: Zen practice and realization may be
described in terms of using these qualities to "build shrines and
fashion buddhas." Every moment, every thought, word, and deed,
should be a rededication, and a reawakening, of this fundamental
awakening.

22. If you think awakening and realization are one-time affairs, you may
think "I have awakened the mind" or "I have experienced realization," and then feel you are now excused. If you think that a practice
is infinite, you may think you never have to do anything else, that
you "have it made."

Note that Dōgen says "only." In a certain sense, awakening the
mind and realization are once and for all experiences, and each
practice that reaches the root is infinite: but if you *only* see in this
way, and do not see the manifold of awakening, practice, and
realization, you do not hear, know, or meet the teaching of Buddha.

The reason for saying this is that the Buddhist awakening of mind
is all-embracing, as the *Flower Ornament Scripture* explains at great

length. Therefore there are no two awakenings, from the "vertical" or transcendental point of view; yet there are countless awakenings, from the point of view of temporal individuality through individual being-times.

All real awakenings go back to the one real awakening, while the one real awakening unfolds in countless awakenings. In the same way, practices, realizations, and teachings are countless *in extension,* while ultimately one *in intention.* It is imperative to see both aspects of this simultaneously, both intention and extension, in order to see the whole body of what is called the Universally Good Enlightening Being.

23. The person and the environment are ultimately inseparable; consciousness and matter-energy are one continuum. "There are no plants and trees but for plants and trees" is Dōgen's version of the bootstrap theory.

This is the same idea, though in reverse formulation, as the bootstrap origination theory of Zen based on the *Shurangama-sūtra,* as posed in this famous dialogue:

Question: "How does fundamental purity suddenly produce the world?"

Answer: "How does fundamental purity suddenly produce the world?"

This calls for close and sustained attention, because meditation on this point leads to realization of what nonorigination really means. This realization is equated with one of the highest forms of tolerance, beyond which there is by nature no regression.

24. It is not unnecessary to say that mastering the Way in zazen, or sitting meditation, requires zazen that masters the Way. In one speech Dōgen even went so far as to say that zazen in the real sense is not practiced until after awakening. Note that the description of zazen that follows is also said to apply to all the other dharmas (principles and practices) as well.

"Not one" means there is no comparison, no antithesis; "not different" means there is no duality in essence. "Not one, not different" is also a classical Tendai Buddhist form of meditation on relativity as equal to emptiness.

"Not two or three" is a famous expression of the *Lotus Scripture* meaning that there is no truth but truth, no completeness but completeness.

154

"Not an arrangement" means that ultimate reality is innocent of the descriptions projected upon it by conceptual and linguistic habits.

25. A classical challenge to the Mahāyāna Buddhist principle of universal emptiness is that if everything were empty there could be no path and no realization. To this Nāgārjuna replies that if everything were not empty there could be no path and no realization, for samsara (birth and death, the domain of confusion and suffering) would be an unalterable world of fixed entities immune to change.

26. Forms of reality are only mind. What is mind? What is only? What reality has forms?

We say we know forms are not ultimately real, they are mental constructs used to impart order and definition to a cosmic chaos of sense experience. Without those forms we could not live efficiently in the world; even though they are not in themselves objective reality, the forms do exist in their way, as *only mind.*

A mistake we habitually make is to deceive ourselves by our own magic. Because of the original usefulness of this power, we are inclined to believe so much in our description of the world that we forget we are just defining something that is in reality far vaster than we could ever imagine. When we forget this, we then allow the world as we have defined it to turn around and define us, thus closing the whole into a confined circle. This is the state of the toolmaker becoming a slave of the tools, the toymaker becoming a puppet of the toys. The disease of materialism, which has also been illustrated in these terms, is just a reflection of this basic self-deception.

According to the *Sandhinirmochana-sūtra,* to get to the ultimate nature of things it is necessary to detach from the imagined nature of things. So we might say, "In true suchness, how can there be specific things?" This calls our attention to the magic of mental construction, and to the fact that its creations are not fixed realities, but can be changed. Detachment from the imagined nature of things does not annihilate it, and does not *annihilate* the faculty of imagination (*māyā,* "magic"). What it does is give us a chance at freedom from illusions about what we are doing, and freedom to make a wider range of choices in the use of this magical faculty.

Everything, after all, is just *such*—reality, relativity, imagination. The specific things we perceive as such are just forms of the reality of only mind. Thus by awakening we break down the illusion of fixed reality, so as to participate in the actualization of fluid reality; we "steal the Buddha's money to buy the Buddha's incense."

27. The *Sandhinirmochana-sūtra* says the constructed is neither constructed nor nonconstructed, and the nonconstructed is neither nonconstructed nor constructed—because "constructed" and "nonconstructed" are themselves just terms representing conceptual glosses.

This scripture goes on to say, however, that this does not mean that nothing is there; the enlightened detach from words, it says, to see naked reality, and then use words as allusions.

One common allusion is "like this," which alludes on the one hand to the indescribability of reality, and on the other to the uniqueness of the *thatness* of everything as it is right now.

"Walking on water" and "walking on stone" mean dealing honestly with both the fluid and the solid aspects of *this right now*. Everything is changing, but temporal forms evolve in their own times; at any given time there is that which can be done and that which cannot.

The combination of initiative and patience this practical realization requires can be balanced only when the ordinary is seen to be sacred—each blade of grass is the beatified Buddha, each grain of soil is a memorial of an ancient Buddha. Then there is neither rush nor lag: everything is as it is, everything can be as it can be, everything is teaching, everything is learning. Seeing this, hearing this, being this, doing this, is awakening the mind.

28. The Three Treasures are the Buddha, Dharma, and Sangha, as noted before: the enlightened, the enlightening teaching, and the harmonious community practicing enlightening teaching under enlightened direction.

Offering flesh means living service. Service of life is making offerings to the Three Treasures. Those who enter religious orders and feel that they are therefore elect representatives of the Three Treasures entitled to consume the alms of the faithful are, in the words of Zen master Bunan, the worst thieves in the world.

One of the perversions of Buddhist teaching is the interpretation of *giving,* the first of the ten perfections, to mean nothing but giving to professional beggars attired in fine robes who do little but sell charms and prayers to temporarily alleviate the superstitious fears that they themselves have carefully fostered for centuries.

29. Whatever enters into the ocean of enlightenment, the ways to enlightenment, and the harmony of the true suchness of enlightenment is itself the Three Treasures. Dōgen says, in effect, don't mistake a model for the real thing, but don't ignore the function of a real model, and don't neglect to need to be able to determine what is a real model of the Three Treasures for your time.

    This manifestation of qualities of enlightenment through the total being of the individual and society is the work of the Way. Essence has no manifestation without characteristics, characteristics have no reality without essence: both are necessary to the whole totality of experience.

    What this means is that enlightened life requires real enlightenment, real knowledge, real wisdom, not just pious hopes and put-on holiness. But knowledge without action is useless, just as action without knowledge is dangerous. Essence and characteristics, wisdom and compassion, truth and expression: with these we find out the skin, flesh, bones, and marrow—the teaching, faith, practice, and attainment—of the way of the enlightened.

30. "This faithful giving is awakening the mind—how could the monks who receive it not practice?" Monk means renunciant, representing renunciation of the ego-centered world view. This "faithful giving," dedication of the total being, or through the total being, is itself renunciation; so by definition of the "monks" who receive it—the people who are liberated from obsession with self by this giving—how could they not practice?

    "It is imperative to start correctly and finish correctly." It is said that if the initial aspiration is faulty, effort will be in vain, leading one even further from enlightenment. Correct starting means starting from "faithful giving." "Faithful" means that you don't worry about getting paid back; "giving" means dedication of being to becoming.

    "The moment an atom becomes active, the one mind awakens along with it." The atom is the *one thought* that is *being Buddha,* the awakening of the thought of enlightenment. This awakening mind awakens the void, the open realm of pure potential, from which countless awakenings and countless works emerge.

31. "Learners" and "those beyond learning" are Buddhist technical terms for those who seek nirvana and those who have attained nirvana. Both still need to *awaken the mind* in the sense of the term as it is used in universalistic Buddhism, which includes the idea of encom-

passing both self and others in a total concern for the liberation and illumination of life. Only then do they transcend their fixation on their own peace of mind, and so "plant buddha-nature." Buddha stands for the comprehensive awareness for which the mind is awakened, which is imbued not only with nirvanic wisdom but also compassionate knowledge. This buddha-nature cannot sprout as long as one is concerned for one's own personal peace of mind alone.

The "four elements and five clusters" are technical terms referring to the human body and mind; "plants, trees, fences, and walls" refer to the environment. Developing the buddha-nature into manifest buddhahood involves working with both person and environment. Body-mind and environment are together in a process of development, as interlocking members of a single organism.

The eye of this paragraph is "if they practice sincerely." The development of buddha-nature, of enlightenment, depends on sincerity, which means being true to that nature, working truly with the essence, mind, life, body, and mechanism of Being.

32. These are famous old stories used to illustrate working in the world as part of enlightenment. When Rinzai's teacher asked him why he was planting trees on a remote mountain (meaning "why work in the world if you are already beyond the world?") Rinzai replied that he had two reasons: to beautify the grounds, and to provide a signpost for future generations. This is indeed a model for *all time*. This is power *sporting living eyes*—acting on knowledge—which is at the same time *opening clear eyes*—enlightening self and others.

33. Making shrines and making buddhas is planting pines and cedars. According to the scripture on the Ten Stages, which is the heart of the *Flower Ornament Scripture,* those in the fifth stage of enlightenment, while they concentrate on perfecting meditation, practice worldly arts and sciences for the common welfare. By the seventh stage they become so skilled that they can carry on their earthly professions spontaneously while progressing in spiritual development. A famous passage of the *Lotus Scripture* says that productive work is consistent with the manifestation of reality.

34. "Nonorigination" is a term for emptiness that means all things are relative and do not exist in isolation or come to be of themselves. The *Scripture on Transcendent Wisdom* says, "Form is not different from emptiness, emptiness is not different from form."

"Where is this to speak of fabricated and unfabricated?" A

paraphrase of the last word in a famous dialogue between the great Chinese Zen master Rinzai and his assistant, this hearkens back to the teaching of the *Sandhinirmochana-sūtra,* which says that the "created" and the "uncreated" are neither created nor uncreated, and that ultimate reality is beyond word and thought.

Form and emptiness are like matter and energy: try to find out the basis of matter, and all that's detected is the formation, movement, and transformation that we call energy; yet try to pin energy down, and all that's detected are the patterns and relations that give the impression of matter.

What is really real, and is such that it manifests in one sense as matter, in one sense as energy, in one sense as form, in one sense as emptiness? Zen proverbs on this point include the famous "Whatever you call it, you miss the mark," and "Even as you are calling it 'thus' it has already changed."

35. Bodhisattvas are enlightening beings, those who live for enlightenment. This passage from the pan-Buddhist *Flower Ornament Scripture* contains an ocean of wisdom: read it, recite it, remember it, ponder it, relate it; for to do so will produce immeasurable merit.

36. Birth and death is called "the great matter" in Zen. "Whence do we come, whither do we go?"—this "great matter" of birth and death has been used as an opening question in Zen schools for centuries. Dōgen adds, "and what are we doing in the meantime?" Using birth and death to awaken the mind is what is called sincerity.

That single thought of enlightenment is one birth, one death: the birth of the great all-embracing mind and the death of the small self-centered mind. So it is each plant, each tree—it is being one with each *being-time.* Although each and every individual *being-time* is finite, *being-time* itself is infinite.

At one with each *being-time,* immersed in the ocean of *being-time,* this is how a Buddha "appears in all worlds in the ten directions without leaving the foot of the tree of enlightenment," as envisioned in the *Flower Ornament Scripture.* Likewise, the Pure Land saint Ippen used to say that the Buddha of Infinite Life, to which Pure Land Buddhists are devoted, is identical to the life of all beings.

37. As that thought, awakening the mind with sincere awareness of birth and death, embraces all *being-time* within it, therefore it is accordingly boundless in depth and breadth. In the same way, because every being and thing is an intrinsic part of the universe, dynamically

related to every other being and thing, then each and every one is infinite.

The degree to which that infinity is apparent is the degree of the thought of enlightenment, the degree of the awakening of mind. A Chinese Zen proverb says, "When Mr. Chang drinks wine, Mr. Lee gets tipsy."

According to another Zen proverb, "Attaining the heart of nirvana is comparatively easy; clarifying the knowledge of differentiation is hard."

Bringing forth the mind is aspiring to transcendence, to join the assembly of the enlightened, which is represented by going deep into the mountains to contemplate the Way. Being brought forth by the mind is acknowledging the commitment of all enlightened ones to return to the world and work for the welfare and liberation of others. The appearance of enlightened people comes about through the equal development of these two aspects of awakening, expressed as self-awakening and other awakening, wisdom and compassion.

THE DRAGON HOWL

1, 2. The dead tree and the skull stand for nirvana, the cessation of compulsive and afflictive mental behavior, which in Zen parlance is also called the great death.

The dragon howl and the lion roar stand for what is known as the great life following great death, the rediscovery and reawakening of the whole potential after liberation from bondage to conditioning.

Zen death means breaking through the perceptual and cognitive boundaries produced by fixation on limited views. This frees the energy that had hitherto been tied up in intellectual and emotional investments in artificially inculcated ideas of oneself and the world. Therefore the dragon howls in the dead tree, the lion roars in the skull.

3. The images of dead tree and dead ashes, commonly used in Zen for nirvana, are deviant teachings insofar as they are presented or interpreted in nihilistic or quietistic terms as escapism or detachment for its own sake.

For the enlightened in the Buddhist sense, detachment (and allied manifestations of this practice, such as iconoclasm and the breaking down of fixed structures) is a means and not an end.

Reification of "emptiness," or of rarefied meditation states originally intended to undermine conditioned convictions, is a "deviation" described in Buddhist technical literature throughout the ages. This is also illustrated in the classic Zen lines, "A dragon does not stay in stagnant water," and "The still pond cannot contain the dragon's coils."

4. Emptiness wrongly practiced does not actually uproot compulsive mental habit energies, but only keeps them in temporary and partial abeyance; therefore this is not really the "dead tree."

Furthermore, working as it does through suppression, deviant emptiness practice also inhibits the lively potential of mind, so it is thus impossible to "hear the dragon howl." This onesided emptiness is death without life, "as if there were no more spring."

5. Drying up the ocean means "stilling" the waves of the "ocean" of birth and death (arbitrarily fluctuating, errant thought) by refraining from fixation on anything in the flux. This stilling stops the inner mind core from being tossed about on the waves of automatic reactions; therefore this stilling is called evaporating the ocean of thirst, or craving.

Thirst, or craving, means the wish to possess a particular condition as an appurtenance of the self; but since conditions come and go, this sticky relation to objects, this craving, is called the cause of birth and death and suffering.

When this stops, there is a great cessation (nirvana) followed by enlivening (represented by springtime): preoccupation with preordained and predefined concerns and wishes falls away, and the vast range of possibility then becomes apparent.

This great cessation, shedding preoccupation, comes about through being unmoved by the waves of consciousness until their power of self-reinforcement and amalgamation into habitual reaction is vitiated.

An ancient master wrote of Zen, "You will get it if your feelings do not stick to things; if feelings do not stick to things, how can things hinder people?"

6. Mountain, ocean, and sky symbolize the Buddhist trinity, the so-called *trikāya* or three bodies of Buddhas.

Mountains stand for what is known as the *nirmānakāya* or emanation body, which means the physical body of a Buddha, and by extension the physical environment.

Ocean stands for consciousness and knowledge, which comprise what is known as the *sambhogakāya* or body of consummate enjoyment.

Sky stands for true emptiness, the so-called *dharmakāya* or body of reality.

All of these are "dead trees" in the same sense that Buddhism teaches all things mundane and transmundane are empty of absoluteness, in that they cannot be objectively grasped as self-existent entities at large.

Zen teaching, resonating with the more ancient Buddhist teaching of *prajñāpāramitā* or transcendent insight, often emphasizes the importance of not reifying anything.

Zen especially stresses the point that reifying "holy" things is harmful because it produces pious possessiveness and pride that is not ordinarily countered by the common ethical convention seeking to identify with what is called "good."

The ninth-century Chinese master Caoshan (Sōzan), spiritual ancestor of Sōtō Zen, is on record as saying that pious attachments that deceptively blinker vision are more pesky problems than coarse grossness that prompts attention.

"Sprouts" represent the regrowth of the primal energy after the stifling effects of conditioning have been stripped away. This is very popular image in Taoist spiritual alchemy, which was closely related to the Zen Dōgen studied in China.

No matter how massive the growth, everything comes from emptiness, in the sense that everything is a temporal formulation grown from the pure potentiality that is emptiness as it is experienced from the perspective known as the relative within the absolute.

Characteristics, essence, substance, and power are a few of the ten kinds of *suchness* or *thusness* (Skt., *tathatā*; J., *shinnyo*) spoken of in the Tendai Buddhism that Dōgen studied. This total suchness is a "deadwood post" in that it is in reality *not* as or what it is made out to be by the fluctuating consciousness playing over superficial appearances and partial definitions.

The negative here is a technical term, as it often is in Zen Buddhism: the symbol of death here is equivalent to a form of negation used as a mnemonic term for objective detachment (*shama-*

tha), one half of the Tendai meditation method of *shi-kan* or "stopping and seeing."

Because "stopping" ("death") introduces "seeing" ("dragon howl," or "meeting the spring"), it is not "dead" in the conventional sense; so it is "a not-dead post."

7. "Mountain and valley" stand for ultimate truth, "field and hamlet" stand for conventional truth. "Pine and cypress" are symbols of unchanging, "human and celestial" beings are representations of temporality. This passage demonstrates two perspectives on emptiness, known as empty and nonempty. Simultaneous awareness of both perspectives, without leaning toward either, is called the center, or middle way.

"The leaves spread based on the roots—this is called the enlightened ones" in the sense that enlightened lives are manifestations of a fundamental enlightenment. The people who are enlightened become channels of knowledge of reality.

"Roots and branches must return to the source—this is participative study." Both enlightenment and its manifestations derive from reality; Zen study involves getting back to this reality.

The "long reality body" and "short reality body" refer to the extensive and intensive aspects of enlightenment: the intensive aspect is *prajñā*, insight or wisdom, while the extensive aspect is comprised of *jñāna*, knowledge, and *karunā*, compassion. Wisdom cuts through directly to the source; knowledge and compassion connect the root and the branches.

8. The true potential does not come forth until arbitrary molds can be set aside. Nevertheless, even in mental bondage no one is ultimately destitute of the true potential.

Yet the awakening of true potential can emerge even before the mundane dross of habit-energy is thoroughly refined away, and this is the reason why apparently "spiritual" experiences can be accompanied by excitement and followed by pride, depression, and other emotions. "Total death," or great nirvana in the midst of life, is when one is no longer affected emotionally by accesses of greater consciousness; "how many times meeting the spring without changing the mind."

The notes of the musical scale represent definition, conventional structure, organization, the relative world of order: total reality does not fit within any convention, but all structures are approximations of ideas projected on reality through a capacity which is itself one part of the potential of that total reality. Thus the notes are limited products from an unlimited source. This passage warns against trying to bring everything within the scope of common or personal convention.

The notes of the musical scale can also be taken to represent the stages of meditation and trance, which are possibilities of consciousness that have been known and described in detail for millennia. One of the main steps Buddha took to restore the perennial wisdom of liberationism from the alienated understanding into which Yoga had fallen in his time was to emphasize that none of these states can be a real goal. This might be paraphrased by saying that all mental states are "two or three children of the awakened consciousness."

9. The answer is always there, but people need the question to bring it out. This question contains all time. The very act of sincerely posing this question—what is beyond what we think—is itself a howl of the dragon.

10. The dragon howl, the lion roar, are never entirely hidden—the question of what is hidden brings up the question of who is hiding it. "What is hidden?" also means "See for yourself." So it is "restraining oneself and putting another first." This is why one teacher said, "Not that I don't want to answer you, but I'm afraid that if I did I'd be bereft of descendants."

To get the answer without truly asking the question can defuse the dynamic power of questioning. "Great doubt, great awakening," says a Zen dictum. One of the great masters who took a very long time to solve a certain problem was told by his teacher, "I want your understanding to come late." The answer that comes too early, that relaxes the doubt before doubt penetrates the whole being, becomes a mere slogan, and the seeker "dies at the words," as a Zen phrase describes it; "skulls litter the fields."

11–14. The hearer and the howler the questioners try to speak of are not equal to the howler of the dragon howl because the former is subjective and the latter objective. "Hearing the name is not as good as seeing the face"—no matter how carefully described, no matter how we imagine it, the real thing is not the same. To realize this is also a note of the dragon howl.

"In a dead tree," "in a skull," mean not in any of the divisions that the mind constructs. "Present and past" mean all time, or rather the total continuity that pervades all time. In this vein Vimalakīrti, the scriptural Golden Grain Buddha, said that all beings are always in nirvana, and do not enter nirvana at a given time.

The "horn on the head growing" commonly means reification in Zen parlance; it can also mean manifestation, activity. Joy is life, but if it is reified as an object of greed, this is "going too far." Joy without clinging represents the enlightening ideal of nonsentimental compassion. Thus joy being called the horn growing is an example of the classic Zen technique of "elevating with one hand while putting down with the other," giving a positive lesson and a negative lesson at one and the same time.

Similarly, "still conscious" is easy to interpret sentimentally, in the sense that one may tend to construe consciousness as one pleases; therefore Dōgen explains that what is meant here is consciousness stripped of accretions, not whatever comes to mind. As a Zen saying has it, "This is It, but as soon as you think *this is It,* then it's not anymore."

15. Sōzan's saying is "not begrudging body and life." The great Zen master Yunmen (Ummon) said, "Even immeasurably great people turn about in the stream of words." Words point to that within which everything flows; the Zen ancient Shitou (Sekitō) wrote, "Hearing words, you should understand the source." Words can kill or enliven—what matters is their function in practice. When to kill and when to enliven are part of the knowledge of an authentic Zen teacher.

The drying up of the ocean is not negation of life and death in the world, it is the realization of the ultimate nirvanic quality of life and death themselves. Therefore the ocean dries up but does not reach the bottom—nothing is left, but nothing is removed. Thus "not entirely" is "dry" in the sense that nonannihilation (compassion) is nevertheless without attachment. Dryness upon dryness is this "wisdom that has gone utterly beyond" the distinction between life in the world and nirvana.

When Zen master Changsha (Chōsha) came back from a ramble in the mountains, he said in reply to a question that he had "gone with the fragrant grasses and come back with the falling flowers." His disciple said, "How springlike," but the master replied, "Cooler than autumn dew dripping from the lotuses." This is a classic story illustrating Dōgen's expressions stating that "not entirely" is "dry" and "dryness upon dryness."

Similarly, a famous Zen saying goes, "as before, mountains are mountains, rivers are rivers," but this is nothing to get excited about. One of the differences between real and false Zen is in the attitude taken toward the awakening to being-as-is.

This applies to both Rinzai and Sōtō schools. Half-baked Rinzais brag about their supposed awakening, while half-baked Sōtōs suppose they are already awake. Half-baked Rinzais tend to mistake altered states for true awakening, while half-baked Sōtōs tend to mistake their own subjectivity for true suchness.

Statements to this effect are to be found widely scattered throughout Dōgen's writings, as throughout authentic Zen lore of all ages.

16. Does anyone hear—does anyone not attain? Nonattainment is most difficult. It is not a consolation prize. It means not being nailed down anywhere.

According to the Buddhist scriptures on transcendental widsom, which are one of the main sources for Zen study, this kind of freedom is terrifying to most people because there is nothing in it they imagine.

Still it is said to be our inmost essence—"who does not hear?" Dōgen tells those interested a way to find this essence—"when there is no world, where is the dragon howl?"

This points to a way of doing one of the basic techniques of Zen meditation. To perform this technique, a classic statement of Zen method says, "the answering is in the questioning."

17. "What writing" should be made a question: this is an iceberg of meaning, of which one tip is "does it matter what writing?" This question also means "what writing matters?"

Then again, as the *Flower Ornament Scripture* says, "There is a scripture in every particle of the universe." In what scripture is the dragon howl found? It is easy to say, "In what scripture is it not found?" It is harder to answer, "What do you call a scripture?"

The *Flower Ornament Scripture* says, "All things in all times teach." What do they teach?

The dragon howl is expressed according to mind; it comes to life according to capacity.

18. "I don't know what writing": Zen proverb says, "All sounds are the voice of Buddha."

"It is pitiable": a Zen proverb says, "Study the living word, not the dead word." Here again Dōgen kills the living and rouses the dead.

19. This is what the technical language of Zen calls the "obvious," or what Dōgen himself calls *genjōkōan,* "the matter at hand."

GREAT UNDERSTANDING

The term "great understanding" used in this essay does not refer to ordinary intellectual understanding, but to satori, a special kind of understanding sometimes translated in Zen literature as "enlightenment."

1. The communication of the Great Way of the enlightened takes place through all phenomena, all aspects of being, and their activity is therefore balanced and equanimous.

   Thus it is that their understanding is manifest, yet the totality of the Way, which is the totality of the universe itself, is ultimately beyond the scope of human understanding.

   However, it is only upon great understanding that this is realized. Therefore the enlightened see into understanding itself and are able to use it deliberately.

   In this process they do not hold on to understanding as a static, reified state, but let go and merge with the events of life.

2. A great Tang dynasty Chinese Zen master said to his disciples, "I use the twenty-four hours of the day; you people are used by the twenty-four hours of the day." This famous saying illustrates the difference between mastery and slavery. It is not the difference between being out of the world and in the world. *Using* brings up potential, *being used* throws it away.

   "Playing with a mud ball" and "playing with the spirit" mean activity of body and mind. Beyond the pivot of using-being used, there is activity that has no "I" that uses or is used; it is a harmonious integration, an interplay, in which it cannot be said that one uses or another is used.

   Perhaps is could be said that all use, all are used; since all are interdependent, using is being used, being used is using.

3. Undifferentiated understanding is only one facet of great under-

standing; according to the *Flower Ornament Scripture,* all of the enlightened have both undifferentiated understanding and differentiated understanding. Therefore undifferentiated understanding is not the sole common characteristic of the enlightened; because they transcend subjectivity and see things as they are, the enlightened also have differentiated understanding.

"Enlightened ones leap beyond the bounds of great understanding, and great understanding is the aspect of leaping higher than the enlightened ones." This refers to the distinction between two kinds of knowledge distinguished in Buddhist psychology, known in Sanskrit as *prajñā* and *jñāna.* The enlightened have both. *Prajñā* is insight into emptiness, seeing through the artificiality of subjectively projected description. *Jñāna* is knowledge of differentiations. *Prajñā* is needed for self-liberation, *jñāna* is needed for teaching others. The enlightened go beyond self-liberating *prajñā* to develop *jñāna* for the edification of others; yet even so *prajñā* is ever aware of the ultimate unreality of forms, and therefore is "leaping higher than the enlightened ones."

In sum, this passage says that enlightenment is more than universal realization of essential emptiness, and it also deals with the characteristics of the relative world. Through realization of emptiness, the ability to be fluid in dealing with the relative becomes manifest; and by realization of relativity, insight into essential emptiness empowers transcendence in the very midst of the relative world.

4. One of the hallmarks of Ekayāna or Unitarian Buddhism, best exemplified by the *Flower Ornament Scripture* and the *Lotus Scripture,* is the adaptation of the teaching to the faculties of the learners.

5. Comprehensive investigation in the beginning, middle, and end of birth refers to the process of meditation whereby one realizes what is called the essencelessness of birth, or birthlessness; the realization that there is no precise beginning to anything. This is explained in the *Sandhinirmochana-sūtra:* since all things are interrelated, there is no starting point in individual phenomena themselves; beginnings are in the boundaries drawn by the mind that makes definitions.

This principle is fairly easy to understand on an intellectual level; it is the Buddhist equivalent of the "bootstrap theory" of modern physics. The meditation, visualization, and inner experience of the principle are more difficult but more rewarding. One traditional exercise is to envision our experience of the world as an interactive combination of sense faculties, sense data, and sense consciousnesses: then, one by one, try to imagine any of these elements without the others. Since none can be grasped but by way of the others, none can be found to be prior. If no element is prior, how can others depending on it come to be? That would mean that all must exist at once, but if they all exist at once, where do they come from? What happens in this classic Tendai Buddhist exercise is a chicken-and-egg situation, a conceptual impasse designed to result in a state of suspension in direct perception of the beginningless *now*.

6. Investigating the self by learning, in the sense of investigating every level of learning, means investigating the process of conditioning that characterizes the self and the world as perceived by the self.

   In terms of the *Prajñāpāramitā* or Transcendent Wisdom teaching, one of the roots of Tendai and Zen, the two kinds of knowledge referred to in this passage are the knowledge of the emptiness of form and the knowledge of the form of emptiness.

7. In terms of the *Yogacāra* or Practice of Union teaching, another root strain of both Tendai and Zen Buddhism, the previous passage speaks of insight into the relative nature of things and the imagined nature of things, whereas this passage speaks of insight into the real or perfect nature of things. This insight is direct and immediate, unobstructed and unbound by dichotomy into subject and object.

8. Teacherless knowledge is what cannot be taught. This is knowledge of the center, or middle way, so it does not lean toward essence (emptiness) or form (characteristics), does not set up self in contradistinction to other. In Tendai Buddhism this is called the Ekayāna, meaning the One (Unitarian) Vehicle, or the Complete Teaching. In oneness there is no other, so in this perspective there is no teacher and no taught.

9. All of these types of knowledge are facets of the great understanding of Buddhism; none should be slighted, none should be emphasized at the expense of others.

   In the Middle Way teaching, and in the Tendai teaching deriving therefrom, these types of knowledge are attained through meditation on relativity. As noted above, Dōgen refers to meditation on relativity as "born knowing" or "knowledge by birth," investigating the premises of origination. This is a fruitful practice, but impatient Zennists have been known to dismiss it just because it looks to them like mere philosophy.

10. Scriptures say that enlightenment is not an acquisition; Zen says it is realization of inherent nature. This realization takes place through examination of that nature.

11. The "three realms" are the domain of desire, of form, and of formless mental states: together they represent the general totality of worldly experience. The "hundred grasses" symbolize manifold phenomena. The "four elements" refer to the physical body. The "enlightened ones" are the manifestations of the true nature of humanity. "Public issues" are Zen stories representing the realizations of the Way. All of these are media of great understanding, and their interweaving totality is an even greater sphere of understanding. That totality is the experience of the being-time of the immediate present.

12. Almost anyone you ask will give you an opinion about things like the supernatural, life after death, extrasensory perception, unidentified flying objects, and so on. As long as opinion is taken for knowledge, it is hard to find anyone who "doesn't understand." This is one way of seeing Rinzai's statement.

    But Rinzai is making another point here. What he is saying is that it is hard to find anyone who does not maintain a subject-object split; and, on another level, the state of mind without the subject-object split is extremely subtle, "hard to find," and naturally cannot be perceived as an object in oneself.

    Also, in the original Chinese, the word *difficult* is commonly understood to mean "impossible" in this sort of construction. Without the subject-object split, the subject cannot be grasped.

13. " 'In China' means in one's own eyes." This refers to the total field of experience. "It is not concerned with the whole world, it does not stop at innumerable lands." It is not delimited by the boundaries of any definitions. It is just here, without separate subject and object; since there is just one whole, the subject "who does not understand" cannot be apprehended. Of this state of transcendence of the sense of a separate self, without the feeling of "I understand," a Zen proverb says, "Demons find no door through which to spy, gods find no road on which to spread flowers."

14. Yesterday's self of the self is a memory, an idea of the self; the present self of another is an objectification. Both involve dualism, splitting into dichotomized subject and object, so neither is "one who does not understand."

    Mountains and waters stand for form and emptiness: here, "people

170

of the mountains" and "people of the waters" are formalists and nihilists. Neither party reaches the nonduality of subject and object, so "not understanding" cannot be found among them.

On another level, "not understanding" cannot be "found" anywhere, because whatever can be "found" is an object, not "not understanding."

15. While it is important in Zen study to learn how to transcend all distinctions, it is also important to learn to deal with the world of distinctions. Therefore, while it is necessary to learn the Zen masters' transcendence of the world, it is also important to study their actions and attributes in the world; it is important to study understanding as well as not understanding.

Then it will be realized that "one who doesn't understand" is only half the person. Furthermore, there are two aspects of "not understanding." One is the aspect of not grasping at the ungraspable, the other is the aspect of fluidity in dealing with the infinite.

In another essay, Dōgen mentions Zen master Rinzai's famous expression "the true human without position," which refers to the free human being; Dōgen then goes on to say that it is not enough to realize this, that one must also know "the true human with position," the free human who nevertheless works in the world and deals with its myriad affairs. It is this to which Dōgen alludes in this passage on not understanding and understanding. He caps his argument in the next passage.

16. Borrowing the terms of an ancient Zen proverb, it is not only necessary to have the heart of nirvana, it is necessary to have clear knowledge of differentiation. "Two or three Chinas" is the relative world; this is included even in realization of voidness ("half a person"), to say nothing of the middle way ("one person").

What this amounts to is that the Buddhist way is to be in the world but not of it. Those who only realize transcendence and cannot work constructively in the world are traditionally said to be stuck in "the deep pit of liberation," or to be "intoxicated by the wine of trance," and lacking in the way of compassion and benefit for the world.

The following passages deal with this issue, but particularly stress that post-awakening return to the world is not the reassertion of the worldly mentality.

17–18. The classical Zen master Baizhang said that a Buddha is someone beyond bondage who comes back into the realm of bondage to help other people out. He also said that the difference between Buddhas and ordinary people is that Buddhas are free to come and go. As Dōgen will explain, this story of the broken mirror and fallen leaves means the same thing: it is not that the liberated do not come back to the ordinary world, but they are no longer bound by worldly things in the same way that people ordinarily are.

19. This is not a matter of theory but of actualization. It can only be explained to those ready to perceive the meaning, and it can only be empowered by those who have succeeded in actualizing the fruit of the teaching.

The Zen master Hōshi (Baozhi) of Kegon (Huayan) temple was an heir of Tōzan Ryōkai (Dongshan Liangjie), one of the most respected of Dōgen's Chinese spiritual ancestors.

20. Great understanding is in accord with our true nature, but it is not really ours, practically speaking, until we "earn" it. Yet even though we may speak of "attaining" great understanding, it is not an acquisition, not something we get from somewhere else.

Great understanding is not, for example, a matter of according with conventional tradition, which Dōgen represents here as "meeting with an aged elder in the public realm." It is also "not forcibly dragged forth from oneself," because the "forcing" is a quality of the false or constructed mentality, which may be contaminated by greed and ambition, or by arbitrary ideas about the "understanding" it is trying to elicit.

21. "It is not that not being confused is considered great understanding." The Zen classic *Merging of Sameness and Difference* says, "Fixation on things is of course delusion; but merging with emptiness is still not enlightenment." When detached from things, although one may not be confused by things, this is still only the level of the "self-tamers" of the "small vehicles" of Buddhism, and thus not sufficient to be considered great understanding.

"And it is not that you should suppose one only becomes confused for the sake of those with potential for great understanding." The bodhisattvas or enlightening beings, practitioners of the universalistic "great vehicle" teaching of Buddhism, return to the world after liberation to help others, but this is not only for the sake of others; it also furthers their own development.

"People of great enlightenment do greatly understand even further." Satori is the beginning of Zen, not the end; after satori one realizes how much there is to learn. In another essay Dōgen writes, "To go on informing the Buddha of today that it is not only today, is the business of going beyond Buddahood."

"Someone greatly confused does further greatly understand." Here "greatly confused" does not mean the same thing as ordinary confusion; it is an expression used by the great Tang dynasty Chinese Zen master Mazu to describe the state of someone who leaves the bounds of conventional knowledge in order to awaken the great understanding that is beyond formal intellect.

22. People of great understanding are on the threshold, starting the way back; Buddhas of great understanding have already come back, and are leading others out.

"Earth, water, fire, air, and space" are five of the six elements of the cosmos in the view of Shingon Mystic Buddhism: these are the body of the microcosm and macrocosm alike, so in Shingon teaching it is said that "self enters Buddha, Buddha enters self."

"Pillars and lamps" is a Zen expression for the perceived world of objects, also used to allude to "suchness."

23. "The question *how is it when people of great understanding return to confusion* is truly asking what should be asked." One of the greatest Tang dynasty Zen masters said in a famous speech, "I don't abide in clarity—do you preserve anything?" Someone asked him, "If you don't abide in clarity, what is there to preserve?" The master said, "I don't know." The questioner continued, "If you don't know, why do you say you don't abide in clarity?" The master said, "Now that you've managed to ask the question, you can go."

A Zen proverb says, "The answering is in the questioning." Zen master Rinzai also emphasized that it is important not to ask questions impulsively or at random; it is important to ask useful questions, for answers come through questioning.

"Kegon unbegrudgingly looks to the ancients in the Zen communities." The Zen master's answer comes from ancient Zen lore. The points Dōgen is making are that his answer is not arbitrary, and that the records of the ancients are there to provide guidance for later people.

24. "Is the return to confusion of people of great understanding on a par with that of people who don't understand?" The Sufi giant Jalāluddīn Rūmī gives the metaphor of two people drinking from the same

173

pond, one through an ordinary reed and one through sugar cane. "Two looked out from prison bars; one saw mud, the other stars."

"Do they bring forth great understanding and create confusion?" Some people think that Zen koans are all illogical, or are meant to stymie the intellect. Dōgen dismisses this idea in his essay "Scripture of Mountains and Waters." If great understanding creates confusion, that is a reflection on the confused; and if it is approached objectively and sincerely, without rationalizing koans as "irrational," this confusion can help to find the way to understanding.

"Do they bring forth confusion from *there,* cover up great understanding, and return to confusion?" Where do the enlightened get the materials which they use to construct "screens" to avoid blinding people with the brilliant light of an understanding that is for the moment beyond them? A Zen proverb says, "Don't ride a golden chariot through a slum." The Taoist expression "diffusing the light to assimilate to the world" is used in Zen to refer to coming back to the world of confusion. It is an advanced stage of practice which protects both the awakened and the unawakened from excitement.

25. The individuality is not obliterated by enlightenment, so individuality does not destroy enlightenment. The question is this: is the return to confusion of the enlightened limited to the individuality as it existed hitherto, or does it involve expansion of the individuality?

26. This follows naturally from the preceding question. Among some Zen practitioners concentrating on detaching from the discriminating mind, there is a tendency to regard the discriminating faculty as of a fixed quantity and quality. In actuality, it is fixed only insofar as it has been trained along certain lines. Buddhist thought shows faculties of discrimination far beyond that of any conventional culture or intellectual tradition.

27. "Each of these questions should be studied thoroughly." There are many such passages throughout Dōgen's work, where he urges students to work through a series of meditations. The Sōtō cult myth that Dōgen's Zen consists of "just sitting" and "nonthinking" cannot be supported by Dōgen's own writings.

28. In *Great Stopping and Seeing,* the classic meditation manual of the Tendai school of Buddhism, the attitude of enlightenment is always described as "seeking enlightenment above, helping others below." The Zen classic *Blue Cliff Record* says, "The more you understand, the more you must study."

Tendai Buddhism speaks of enlightenment as both original and initial. Original enlightenment is the potential that is always there; initial enlightenment is the awakening of the potential. Realization is called "return to the great abode."

29. "Taking a thief to be your child" is a classic Zen metaphor for taking the conditioned consciousness to be the real mind. "Taking your child to be a thief" means to be deceived by the functions of mind, as when one tacitly believes the mental picture of the world is the objective world itself. In his essay "Mind itself is Buddha," Dōgen writes, "When they hear tell of *mind itself,* what the ignorant suppose it means is that ordinary people's thinking awareness without awakened aspiration for enlightenment is itself Buddha. This is a consequence of never having met an enlightened teacher."

Great understanding involves recognizing the falsehood of conditioned consciousness, return to confusion requires recognition that our world is our own doing.

"Adding a little where there is much" means realizing the emptiness of form. "Reducing a little where there is little" means not reifying emptiness either.

"Holding still" means not getting carried away by the activities of body and mind; this is how one meets "someone of great understanding" within oneself while in the very midst of "return to confusion." This involes a practice of self-examination: as Dōgen says, "You should check."

30. The mirror symbolizes being aware without imposing judgments on the contents of awareness; being just like a mirror, which simply reflects whatever comes before it, without grasping or rejecting anything. This is a part of Zen practice, but in it there is still a subtle dichotomy of subject and object, which creates an invisible boundary to awareness. The "broken mirror" signifies the state of realization after breaking through this boundary. The great eighteenth-century Japanese Rinzai Zen master Hakuin referred to this as smashing through the repository consciousness. A Zen saying has it, "Smash the mirror and I'll meet with you."

The "fallen leaves" symbolize the accretions of temporally conditioned consciousness, the illusions we hold to regarding the nature of the world and ourselves. When the leaves have "fallen," we are no longer slaves of habit and automatic thinking.

The "precise moment of suchness of the broken mirror" is the immediate present of being as is, without reflection; it precludes self-consciousness, even of the subtle dimension present in the "mirroring" awareness, and therefore cannot be realized while purposely holding the mind still to achieve the "mirror" effect—"it is not right to study the words *broken mirror* with the mind on the time of the *unbroken mirror.*"

31. Zen master Baizhang said, "Cultivating mundane causes while in the sanctified state, Buddhas enter in among sentient beings, becoming like them in order to guide them. If they only stayed in the sanctified state, how could they go to where others are to talk to them? Buddhas enter various kinds of states of being and make means of liberation for them; like the sentient beings there, Buddhas feel pain, toil, and stress."

32. "The present story is not this way." That is to say, it does not mean, as may be imagined, that the liberated do not reenter the realm of bondage.

The "very time" means entering unreservedly into a situation. A seeker once asked a great Zen master how to escape cold and heat. The master said, "Why not go where there is no cold or heat?" The student said, "Where is there no cold and heat?" The master said, "The cold chills you through and through, the heat heats you through and through."

Cold and heat represent death and life, or the vicissitudes of existence; don't try to avoid or resist them, just let them be "as such," and you will not suffer needlessly.

"Progressing at the top of a hundred-foot pole" is a Zen expression for going beyond nirvana, going beyond detachment into merging; it is parallel to great understanding returning to confusion. Yet it "is still fallen leaves" in that it does not mean reassertion of the former commanding delusions of the ego; even though one returns to life in the world, and "a certain amount of livelihood becomes manifest," it has no more power to delude the person of great understanding.

33. With great understanding, a person is a Buddha; returning to confusion, a Buddha is a person. In Zen this is not understood as an emanation from an transmundane plane into the mundane plane, as suggested by the terms "returning to be a sentient being" and "sending down traces from the basis." In Zen, rather, it means full awakening of both the transcendent *and* earthly side of humanity.

34. "Great understanding" and "return to confusion" are always there;

beginnings are all in the mind. Here, confusion does not block understanding, for understanding understands confusion.

"Three planes of great understanding" are understanding of emptiness, artificiality, and the center. Emptiness means nothing exists in and of itself; definitions of the world are artificial, not referring directly to objective reality. Realization of emptiness comes through using this contemplation to detach from subjective descriptions mentally projected on indescribable reality. The artificial is the ordinary world of common consensus, where things do exist, relative to one another and to the perceiver. The center is the middle way, the ultimate poise of equilibrium, where one neither grasps things as existent nor rejects them as nonexistent; one leans neither toward negation nor affirmation, one is in the world but not of it.

Tendai Buddhism, the parent school of Zen, gives extensive and detailed instructions for meditation on these three planes of great understanding.

These three planes are actually just three perspectives on the same reality. They form one whole, which makes "half a plane of small confusion." "Small" here means empty, not really real; the other half of the half-plane of small confusion is great understanding.

"Hereby there is the Himalaya Mountains greatly understanding for the Himalaya Mountains; wood and stone greatly understand by means of wood and stone." The Himalaya Mountains and wood and stone symbolize the practice of the first plane of great understanding, the realization of emptiness. (Cf. Dōgen's essay "Awakening the Unsurpassed Mind," p. 95, where this symbolic usage is introduced.) In Tendai meditation, according to the capacity of the practitioner one may realize the three planes separately or together; because they are not really separate in themselves but different perspectives on the same reality, the most perfect practice is said to be realization of all three in one mind.

"The great understanding of Buddhas is greatly understanding for the sake of sentient beings; the great understanding of sentient beings is greatly understanding the great understanding of the Buddhas." On one level this illustrates the attitude of enlightenment, "seeking above, helping below." On another level, it illustrates the two-directional communication between the two sides of the mind; as a Zen poet says, "every branch of coral supports the moon," integrating the intuitive and rational modes.

177

35. "Cutting off before and after" is a classic expression illustrating an important transitional experience in Zen. "Right now" is total absorption, so there is no duality in the mind; there is no apartness, no antithesis.

"Right now" does not come or go; it is always "right now." "It goes along with the other" in the sense of oneness with the present being-time; here, "other" means *"That"* without subjectivity. Don't search from another, because there is no nothing apart from *that*.

36–38. This story is used here to refer to the state of absorption in the present, and it can also be taken as an inquiry into the nature of understanding, or the kind of understanding referred to in Zen.

39. Flower Ornament Buddhism teaches the realization of past, present, and future in the present moment. Here Dōgen presents one way of looking at this; past, present, and future are in the thoughts, an all thoughts are qualities of the present being-time.

Someone's condition, the present being-time, may be described in terms of perception ("the eyes"), or in terms of being and doing ("the nostrils," i.e., "breathing").

40. Zen master Dahui, a leading teacher in China somewhat before Dōgen's time who was notoriously critical of deteriorations in Zen study, stressed that Zen meditation must be free from anticipation of enlightenment. This is because the anticipation itself obstructs the practitioner by keeping the mind entangled in subjectivity. It is for this reason that Dōgen said practice and realization are one, not because he thought everyone had to always behave like thirteenth-century Japanese Zen monks to be enlightened. "Don't anticipate enlightenment" and "practice is realization" aim at the same effect, which is total absorption.

41. Zen examination of understanding is investigating whether it is understanding that is separated from being. Is it understanding that is painted on after the fact, or is it understanding that is experience of the fact itself?

This passage also has a more subtle message, which is the question of whether people's understanding is of any use to them, or what use they make of it. If people understand, and then reify that understanding as an acquisition, they will then miss out on the ongoing understanding of the present being-time.

42. "The secondary too is understanding." Dōgen was careful in his teaching to emphasize the point that rational understanding is part

of the total capacity of the enlightened mind. He did this because of the tendency in deteriorated Zen to emphasize nondiscursive awareness alone, resulting in an imbalanced development.

Note that Dōgen says "the secondary" is *like* saying it has become understanding, or one has attained understanding, or understanding has come. Similarly, in the next passage, he says it is *like* lamenting falling into the secondary and eliminating the secondary. Dōgen says that this interpretation is deceptive because the secondary, or even the "hundred thousandth level," is still understanding, and is not apart from the primary. This represents the unity of the absolute and the relative, the consummation of Zen practice.

43. The self of yesterday is part of the experience of the self of today, whereas the self of today is not part of the experience of the self of yesterday. This is why it is said that one has understood and become enlightened when one has understood and become enlightened: even though enlightenment is always there, "it is a matter of finding it out in this way."

So great understanding is "black" and "white" in the sense that it embodies both nondiscursive ("black") and discursive ("white") knowing; it is beyond distinctions ("black"), yet is distinct ("white").

SOUNDS OF THE VALLEY STREAMS, COLORS OF THE MOUNTAINS

1. The Second Ancestor of Zen in China is said to have cut off his arm as a demonstration of sincerity and dedication. Gautama Buddha is said to have laid his hair in the mud to make a clean path for a previous Buddha. These are representations of self-transcendence, which is referred to as "escape from the shell."

When the "shell" of the ego and its appurtenant ideas of reality conditioned by social and personal history is shed, then aspects of reality that had previously been screened from awareness by that shell now become evident.

Because escape from the shell means breaking the force of habit from from the past and the expectations of the future that this force conditions, the experience of the escape is called the "immediate present." Because one's former views of the world no longer obtain, that time is called "such" without further qualification.

Ideas of oneself drop away, so there is no "I" to "know," and the question of "who" has no conceptual referent. At this point, "you"— that is to say, whatever or whoever one faces—is seen without preconception, so one does not act automatically in a way anticipated by habitual patterns.

In this state of freedom, the mind does not rest on anything or reify anything, so it is said that even Buddha's eye cannot see it, much less can human thought assess it; this means that "it is not a thing."

2. This writer was Su Shih (Su Tung-p'o), one of the greatest Chinese poets of all time. He was a scholar, a statesman, and an adept in Buddhism and Taoism. His Zen teacher was an heir of the founder of the Yellow Dragon (Huanglong, Ōryū) branch of Linji (Rinzai) Zen, who was considered one of the greatest masters of the age.

The "universal tongue" is a metaphor for reality expressing itself: though ultimately one, it speaks to all people in accordance with their understanding. So it is said that the universal tongue covers all worlds and speaks all languages.

Similarly, the "pure body" refers to the so-called body of reality, the metaphysical basis of buddhahood. When asked about the body of reality, one Zen master said, "The flowers blooming are like brocade, the brimming stream is blue as indigo."

"Night" represents the time when ordinary linear thinking is shut down; the measureless wealth of the all-at-once totalistic awareness cannot be fully fit into a sequence of linear thought, so the awakened poet says, "Another day how can I recite the eighty-four thousand verses of last night?"

3. The Yellow Dragon and Willow Branch sects of the Rinzai school of Chinese Zen emerged in the eleventh century. Most of the Zen masters in Japan were descendants of the Willow Branch sect. Although Dōgen is mostly known for his mastery of Sōtō Zen, he was also an heir of the Yellow Dragon sect of Rinzai Zen.

4. Giving costly gifts is not something beyond the reach of worldly people; what is beyond the reach of worldly people is giving costly gifts to someone from whom one has no worldly expectations.

5. "Appearing corporeally to expound reality" is represented as a Buddha or a bodhisattva appearing in the world to teach. More generally, as here, it means, in the words of the *Flower Ornament Scripture,* "Beings teach, lands teach, all things in all times teach,

continually, without interruption." If people miss this teaching activity and do not see the reality being taught as it truly is, then "why do they still see the colors of the mountains, hear the sounds of valley streams?"

"Are they one phrase?" Is there anything else? "Are they half a phrase?" Do you see only forms, or do you also see that forms are formless? "Are they eighty-four thousand verses?" How much do you see? Do you only see all in one? Do you also see one in all? All in all? One in one? These are meditations of Flower Ornament Buddhism, designed to help awaken capacities of perception so as to avoid partiality and bias toward one particular view.

"It is regrettable that there are sound and color concealed in the mountains and streams. Yet it is delightful that there are conditions of time revealed in the mountains and streams." It is too bad if you only see what you see and do not see what you do not see; but if you examine what you see, and your seeing of what you see, luckily that will reveal the conditions of your being-time.

A Zen saying goes, "The ass looks into the well, the well looks up at the ass." Often we only know how we see the mountains and streams, and do not realize how the mountains and streams see us. If we knew how the mountains and streams see us, we might really see the mountains and streams, and not just ourselves.

The chance is always there, because the universal tongue and the pure body are always there. By understanding the *conditions of time* revealed, we can uncover the *sound and color* concealed. A Zen poet wrote, "For ever and ever it is revealed to humankind."

6. The "time of revelation" is when nothing is interposed; mind is naked, world is naked. This is nearness without familiarity. The "time of concealment" is when something is interposed; as it is said, "when feelings arise, knowledge is blocked." This is familiarity without nearness.

Are these two visions of one reality? Or are the two visions only half the story, reality itself being the other? "The springs and autumns hitherto" are the life one has led, the conventions that have been instilled by the acculturation process, the habits one has formed. These see only reflections of themselves, not the mountains and streams. "The time of last night" is the experience of opening that takes place when the inner talk of mental habits is stilled. In this there is true seeing, but it is only a little, "slightly," for the inconceivable, incomprehensible whole of objective reality can never be grasped.

7. Here "mountains" represent form, "water" represents emptiness. Form is not absolutely fixed, but relatively fluid; emptiness is constant, never changing: therefore "the mountains flow" while "the water does not flow." Zen requires recognition of the flux of subjective experience and the permanence of objective truth; this is the way to penetrating learning.

8. The story of inanimate things teaching goes back to the Tang dynasty master known as National Teacher of Great Realization, an illustrious heir of the Sixth Ancestor of Zen in China. The gist of the story is that one can "hear" the teaching of the environment when subjective feelings do not interfere with the reception. "Waves against the current" represent an impression outside of convention or expectation; the waves striking the "sky on high" symbolize an unexpected impact opening up access to a higher domain of consciousness, as in the case of the poet attaining Zen awakening on hearing the sound of a valley stream.

9. The issue here is that one does not become enlightened just through the instruction of a teacher, nor only through the impact of personal experience. It is through the appropriate combination of the instruction of a teacher, the attitude and application of the learner, and the impact of experience that awakening takes place.

10–26. The following well-known stories are brought up to illustrate the point that the moment of enlightenment is not just a matter of the immediate circumstances, but also of the effort and preparation of the person involved.

10. Intellectual acumen and learning are manifestations of one part of the function of the mind, externally oriented. This mental activity revolves within its own sphere of experience and does not directly sense the open, unmodified essence of mind. Preoccupation with this aspect of mind accordingly stunts the growth of other modes of mental function; so Zen practice addresses the awakening of unused potential in order to achieve an overall balance.

"Before the birth of father and mother" refers to the essence of mind, represented as a state or mode of consciousness that has not been formulated into a personality and mind-set by the processes of socialization and acculturation. Insight into this essence must naturally be experienced within oneself, and cannot be "learned" in the way that one learns formal intellectual knowledge.

11. In Zen study it may be particularly useful, even necessary, for those who are very much intellect-oriented to be confronted with the limitations of the intellect. This is not presented as a challenge per se, but as a way of being willing to step back and allow other realms of consciousness to emerge from subconsciousness and unconsciousness. This is the function of certain types of Zen koans. In other Buddhist schools, logical conundrums and inconceivable visualizations may be used to accomplish the same purpose.

12. Kyōgen (Xiangyan) was also in the circle of Isan's teacher, where he was already known for his intellectual brilliance. Sharpness and dullness in Zen terms do not mean the same as sharpness and dullness of intellect. Kyōgen's abandonment of his ambitions to be a learned monk was part of a strategy to outwit his own intelligence.

13. If the teacher had given an explanation, the student's intellect would have appropriated that answer, with the result that the student would still be revolving in the self-contained circle of conceptualization. A Zen proverb says, "There is great enlightenment where there has been great doubt." The task of the Zen teacher is not to relieve the tension of doubt prematurely or arbitrarily, but rather to direct it, focus it, and intensify it until the student's inner clinging to holdings, or inner resistance to openness, finally gives way.

14. There are many Zen stories illustrating the awakening of mind at the occurrence of a sense impact while in a state of mental clarity. Sometimes the impact is articulate, such as a saying, a poem, or a line of scripture. Sometimes the impact is inarticulate in the ordinary sense of the word, being a simple sound or physical contact.

    One of the functions of the shouting and striking that have been employed by many Zen teachers for many centuries is to provide this sudden impact at precisely the right time. One of the things that distinguishes the real from the spurious teacher in Zen is that the real teacher sees when to apply an impact, while a spurious teacher does so abitrarily or routinely.

15. Zen students do not realize how much they owe to those who guide them toward enlightenment until they have become enlightened. How many people today would have complained from the start that the teacher wasn't giving them enough attention?

16. "Forgetting all knowledge" became a standard Zen expression for a

183

sudden awakening. Here, "knowledge" does not mean the real knowledge of direct perception, but the "knowledge" of common parlance, a clutter of views, opinions, and random information. Thus to "forget all knowledge" means to experience a sudden penetrating clearing of the mind.

"I do not need cultivation anymore." As long as this mental opening is not subsequently cannibalized by self-consciousness ("*I have awakened*"), real learning can subsequently take place naturally and spontaneously, as one becomes receptive without conscious effort to be receptive.

"Activity expressing the ancient road, I don't fall into passivity." Zen has been called a religion of tranquillity, but this concept is based on mistaking a means for an end. While it is true that there have apparently always been Zennists, even whole Zen schools, that routinely fell into this trap, the classics consistently maintain that it is an aberration and not real Zen.

"Everywhere trackless, conduct beyond sound and form." Being trackless means not sticking to things, events, or acts along the way, not lingering in eddies of self-consciousness or obsession with externals. Because it means not dwelling fixed on anything, it is called conduct beyond sound and form.

17. "Reiun worked on the Way for thirty years." That is to say, he spent thirty years practicing Zen meditation before he experienced his famous awakening upon seeing peach blossoms.

18. The stories of Kyōgen and Reiun (Lingyun) are perhaps the most commonly cited of their kind. Both of them worked for a very long time before they finally awakened, and this is the point Dōgen is emphasizing here.

When people are too attracted to the dramatic, they tend to overlook factors that may be less fascinating but none the less important. A Zen saying goes, "People only like to talk over and over about great achievements of the time, and do not ask about the sweating horses of the past."

19. The "sweating horses of the past" are the preparations, the efforts, the conditions by way of which Reiun and so many other Zen illuminates entered enlightenment. Once the conditions have ripened, they produce corresponding results.

19–20. People may glimpse the "pure body" at times, but unless they have developed corresponding purity of mind, they cannot sustain the perception; if they know the theory of it and have the glimpse without the sustaining refinement, people usually get excited or conceited about their experience, and therefore regress.

This seems to be "entry," but it is not really penetration; it is only a glimpse. Here, "entry" means that one has merged with the "pure body of the colors of the mountains." The following text goes further into this.

21–22. To realize all things as one's own body, it is necessary to realize one's own body as all things. Absorbing the environment into the mind is an elementary form of meditation; it is as if there were a sphere of light and color in an ocean of invisible darkness: one is still within the limits of individual consciousness. Beyond this is the mind being absorbed into the environment; this is forgetting the self and being enlightened by all things. Then there is no more darkness.

23. "Oneself is of itself oneself" means that there is no mental construction, no presumption, no identification, no split in the mind; there is just being as is.

"You should not impute any further hindrance to the object of return" could be read, more simply, "do not hinder what is returned." This means that one should not retain fixed ideas of self or the world. Fixed ideas of self not only cramp the self, they cramp the world as the self experiences it; fixed ideas of the world not only cramp the world, they cramp the self that experiences it. Authentic nonduality can only be realized by "not hindering the object of return" or "not imputing hindrance to the object of return," which means not imputing ineluctable objective reality to mental representations of self and world.

24. The eighth-century Zen master Nangaku was one of the successors of the great Sixth Ancestor of Chinese Zen; Rōya (Langya) was an eminent master of the eleventh century. The professor of doctrine in the story was a noted scholar of the Flower Ornament school who is especially known for his work on the *Shūrangama-sūtra,* or *Heroic March Scripture,* from which the statement in question is taken.

25. The production comes from the questioning itself, or rather from the source of the questioning itself. The Zen master answers by pointing to this source.

According to the Flower Ornament school, purity is like the clarity of a mirror, by virtue of which it can reflect whatever comes before it. In terms of phenomena, it means the indefinite nature of phenomena, which are defined by the working description mentally constructed by the perceiver.

26. Therefore in this sense the mountains, rivers, and earth that are "purity basically so" are not to be mistaken for the mountains, rivers, and earth of common consensus, in that subjective experience and description of what is perceived is not to be mistaken for the reality behind what we imagine we perceive.

   "As teachers of scriptures have never even dreamed of hearing this, they do not know the mountains, rivers, and earth as mountains, rivers, and earth." Mere intellectuals who simply conceptualize this and do not actually detach from imagination do not know the world as just *such* without superficial subjective assessments.

27. According to a famous Zen story, once Buddha raised a flower in the presence of a great assembly; only one person, his disciple Kashyapa the Elder, understood his message.

   In another story, the Zen founder Bodhidharma once asked his disciples to express their understanding. The last to do so said nothing but simply bowed and stood there; Bodhidharma said to him, "You have my marrow."

   The colors and sounds, the raising of the flower and the standing in place, all represent "suchness," being-as-is (*tathatā, yathābhūta, bhūtatathatā*). In terms of the Flower Ornament doctrine of "all in one, one in all," the interpenetration of all realities, the flower represents "one in all," standing in place represents "all in one."

   Similarly, it is said that Shakyamuni Buddha was enlightened on seeing the morning star, and thereupon declared that he and all beings had attained enlightenment together. In other words, when he saw the real nature of the world, he saw the real nature of all beings; all beings have buddha-nature, and when one realizes the buddha-nature in oneself, one realizes the buddha-nature in all beings.

   This effect is like a two-way mirror: ordinary people, on the reflecting side, see reflections of themselves and not the buddha-nature; while Buddhas, on the transparent side, see through the veil of self-reflection and perceive beings just as they are.

28. "Skin bag" is a typically irreverent Zen term for a mortal being. What Dōgen is emphasizing here is that the sages were human beings, in that sense just like anyone else; the difference between

186

sages and ordinary people is that sages had profound determination that took them beyond lesser concerns.

Everyone has the potential, but not everyone truly seeks reality. Depending on fashions, many may pretend to do so, but as an ancient teacher said, "Finding people is not a matter of there being many around."

29. In old Japan, becoming a Buddhist monk was a way of rising socially, politically, and financially. Nowadays it is still for many Buddhist clergy little more than a way of making a living; for most, in fact, it is a hereditary business into which they are born.

But honor and gain does not just refer to the public or professional sphere. There are those who enter the Buddhist orders to fulfill frustrated ambitions of personal importance, those who wish to be part of a mutual reassurance society—a group of people who congratulate themselves daily, so to speak, for having become members of an elite.

Here the order has an economic, social, and psychological function, providing a degree of stability in these realms, but it thereby becomes sterile in terms of transcendent Zen potential, because there is still fixation on worldly selves.

In the absence of true teachers, it is easy for people to mistake relief from material and mental pressures for a sign of spiritual progress. This is one reason such people do not like a real teacher, which Dōgen here calls a "real dragon," because a real teaching situation does not allow any subterfuge on the part of the student. People with ulterior motives do not want them exposed; if they are used to hiding from themselves, they do not even want to be reminded of ulterior motives.

The great master Rinzai said, "Since ancient times our predecessors were disbelieved and thrown out wherever they went. That is how we know their value. As for those with whom everyone agrees, what can they achieve?" A key function of the teacher is to disrupt the nest of attachments that traps the mind of the student.

Those who pander to people's demands may become popular and have a following, but that does not make them Zen teachers. A classical Zen proverb says, "If the medicine doesn't make you dizzy, it isn't potent." It is precisely because truth can only be met with sincerity that Zen teachers have traditionally imposed severe tests and refused to reassure the uncertain or to try to teach all comers.

30. Sincerity means seeking truth for the sake of truth, and nothing for oneself. Those who lack this kind of sincerity are not inclined to take to teachers and teachings that cannot be satisfied with lesser goals. They may think they are rejecting the teaching, but in reality the teaching is rejecting them. Yet this is not indicative of a lack of compassion, or of discrimination on the part of the teacher or teaching; if people are not correctly harmonized or attuned with truth, they cannot in any case perceive or receive it.

So those who seek temporal comforts in the name of spirituality may obtain them, or they may not; they will surely not get anything higher by way of lower aims. Even if one wants enlightenment, this cannot be called really wanting it unless one understands that enlightenment is not available on demand, but requires a transformation of the whole life attitude, an attunement of the mind with truth that has no form.

31. "The ancestral school" refers to Zen. Every form of Buddhist teaching goes through three phases: authentic, imitation, and relic. In Dōgen's time it was widely believed that Buddhism as a whole was generally in the relic phase, and this was the reason for the arising of new forms in that time. Scholars often make the unsubstantiated claim that Dōgen rejected the idea of the relic phase or degenerate age; as can be seen in this passage, and even more explicitly elsewhere in his writings and speeches, Dōgen did consider his time that of a relic or degenerate phase of Buddhism as a whole.

32. This passage is of utmost significance. It is a matter of a fundamental change in attitude, turning all of life into a learning situation. In this vein an ancient Zen master posed the question, "I don't ask about after enlightenment; what about before enlightenment?" and then answered himself, "Every day is a good day."

33. Vowing, or praying, involves consciously directing attention and thought in a certain manner, fostering a particular frame of mind. In this sense Buddhism refers to faith as a faculty that can be developed into a power; it is a means of focusing the mind, whereby a certain type of power is concentrated, just as magnetic power is concentrated by aligning the charges of the molecules in a mass of iron.

Note that the vow or prayer for enlightenment outlined by Dōgen here is made on behalf of all beings. This attitude is a necessary basis of the aspiration for enlightenment as understood in Mahāyāna or Universalistic Buddhism.

34. Here Dōgen makes it clear that he is not talking about a ritual performance, but a "psychological technique" designed to affect consciousness in a specific manner.

35. Dōgen spent five years in China, a vast country on a huge continent with a culture three times as old as that of Japan. For Dōgen, Japan was not the center of the world, and in his view it had not yet been thoroughly transformed by the influence of the great civilizations of China and India to which it was heir.

36. In his talks Dōgen makes much of the historical fact that institutional Buddhism in Japan had always been connected with politics and high society. Reporting that he himself was originally taught to study Buddhism for rank and status, Dōgen apparently considered Japanese Buddhism to have been distorted in its aims. It is important to consider Dōgen's perspective on the state of Japanese civilization in order to understand the intensely critical tone that permeates his works.

37. A proverb says, "Musk is of itself fragrant." It is recorded that Dōgen's Chinese Zen teacher, although abbot of several of the great public monasteries in China, did not publicly reveal his Zen succession until the time of his death.

Advertisement attracts people interested in reputation and outward show, while the reality of the sincere is hidden from the superficial eye. In this way the sincere recognize each other through sincerity, the superficial contact each other through superficialities.

One of the symptoms of hypocrisy in spiritual studies is to seek agreement instead of truth. One function of advertisement is to create ready-made agreements for mass participation. Trading in this kind of agreement is a social and commercial affair, not a spiritual enterprise; Dōgen never seems to tire of making this point, and he was deeply resented in his time for refusing to deal in diplomatic flattery.

39. One may meet genuine teachers and have appropriate exercises prescribed, or one may meet only charlatans and have imitation exercises prescribed. Because of the fact that the opportunity for person-to-person transmission of real teaching may or may not arise, it has been the practice of Buddhists for some two thousand years to make public records of their teachings available.

When the great Chinese Zen master Yunmen was about to die and was asked for final instructions, he is reported to have said, "Buddha has a clear teaching; practice in accord with it." One of the functions of the public record is also to help the would-be student distinguish between genuine and spurious Zen teachers, who do not rely on fixed doctrine.

None of this is any guarantee, of course, because subjective expectations or desires may influence one to become attracted to the spurious and repelled by the genuine. Thus Dōgen says that neither should be liked or disliked—an impartial attitude, free from personal prejudices, is needed to develop the objectivity to discern a real teaching situation.

40. Confucius said, "I wish I could remain silent, but how can I say nothing?" It is those who do not recognize the harm of the poisons of greed, hatred, and ignorance who are not disturbed by their manifestations; yet Dōgen suggests that one should not despair, because those who do recognize the harm are in any case rare, and there is no way for the individual to ameliorate the situation except to personally preserve the aspiration for enlightenment.

This aspiration to seek truth is not "for others," in the sense that it is not for show. Confucius said, "People of the past used to study for themselves; people today study for others." Here studying for oneself means studying to develop oneself, as a service to society; studying for others means studying to gain reputation and position, for profit to oneself.

In *Shōbōgenzō zuimonki,* a record of Dōgen's early talks, Dōgen relates how in his youth he was told to study in order to rise in the ranks of the ecclesiastical hierarchy, which in Japan at that time paralleled the civil hierarcy and meant official court rank with its appurtenant privileges. This was the common custom in Japanese Buddhism in Dōgen's time, widely regarded as a fact of life. Dōgen goes on to relate how he subsequently studied the lives of great Buddhists in China, and thus learned to reject the self-serving attitude that had been instilled in him early on by local custom. So it was that Dōgen, particularly in his early teaching, took special care to stress the necessity of aiming for enlightenment only, truth for the sake of truth.

Nevertheless, Dōgen continues, even when people do not aim to gain honor and support for their religious lives, it may come about naturally. The point here is that this honor and support are by-products, not goals. Bodhisattvas, enlightening beings, are servants of humanity, and service without expectation of reward is one of the keynotes of the bodhisattva path. If they expect honor and support, they are trading in worldly goods, and are therefore still caught up in the bonds of the world.

41. Some organizations that proselytize accord increasing status for successful recruiters: the more members, the more money comes in; the more money comes in, the more privileges the successful recruiters are given. This is then taken as a sign of the efficacy of the doctrine that the organization is selling.

There are also people who have the idea that if someone who is socially or politically prominent is interested in something, then that thing must be worthwhile. This is one reason for the practice of using celebrity endorsements in advertising; people buy image, not the product. This is questionable enough in the case of ordinary commodities; in the case of matters of spiritual worth, Dōgen calls it insanity.

42. As happened among outstanding teachers of other religions, there were great Buddhist adepts who sacrificed their reputations and even their lives in their efforts to demonstrate and teach. It is not a question of winning and losing in an ordinary sense; nor does it mean that Buddhists were not aware of where they were and what they were doing. The *Mahāparinirvāna-sūtra*, or *Scripture of the Great Ultimate Extinction*, teaches that when the true Dharma, or Teaching, is extinguished, in reality the true Dharma is not really extinct: the extinction of the true Dharma is not the extinction of the true Dharma, but the true Dharma itself demonstrating the causes and conditions of the extinction of true Dharma. This is the perspective that makes "every day a good day" in Zen terms, when "everything is teaching."

43. Bodhidharma, the founder of Zen in China, arrived there sometime in the late 400s or early 500s. He taught the inner experiential correspondences of Buddhist formulations, and maintained that forms are only vehicles while truth itself is formless. Thus he incurred the opposition of some who had heavy investments in institutionalized forms. According to legend, Bodhidharma was poisoned six times. On the first five occasions, he healed himself through his medicinal knowledge, which was at that time a common

skill among Buddhist adepts. By the time of the sixth poisoning, the story continues, Bodhidharma's mission had been completed, so he allowed himself to pass on.

Devadatta was a blood relative and ertswhile follower of Shakyamuni Gautama Buddha who later turned on the Buddha and allegedly tried to kill him. Devadatta's name is often invoked as a representation of opposition to Buddhism arising from within its own ranks through the reassertion of egotistical, proprietary, and competitive attitudes.

What is despicable about fame and fortune is not in fame and fortune themselves, but in what people will do and be for the sake of fame and fortune.

44. Like Zen, Taoism lays particular emphasis on not being glad when praised or upset when reviled. In both teachings, ultimate truth is not a question of human feelings, and the seeker of ultimate truth therefore cannot afford to have attention diverted by emotional assessments from another realm of concern.

It is related that once when the prophet and messiah Jesus prayed for people who had reviled him, someone asked him why he had returned kindness for cruelty. Jesus replied, "I could only spend of what I had in my pocket."

Similarly, it is said that when the prophet Muhammad was victimized by aggressors, and someone asked him why he did not curse his oppressors, Muhammad replied that it was not his mission to curse.

45. The Sufi theologian al-Ghazzali wrote in his *Book of Knowledge* that one should "judge people by truth, not truth by people." In the *Mahāparinirvāna-sūtra,* the dying Buddha says that one should "rely on truth, not on personality."

46. The Taoist classic *Tao Te Ching* says, "Only by knowing the sickness of sickness is it possible to not be sick."

47. Some people may oppose you, and some may support you, and either may be right or wrong. Considering truth above human sentiment is the only way to tell for sure. In practical terms, the proverbial saying of the past Buddha, "Don't become familiar with rulers, officials, priests, or laypeople," means that to be enlightened it is essential not to be swayed by public opinion or special interests in matters of real truth.

48. People who practice meditation may have visions or other unusual

sensory experiences, which may be pleasant, exciting, or frightening. The standard rule in Zen is never to allow oneself to become emotionally affected by such experiences. According to Musō Soseki, another distinguished Japanese Zen master, psychological disturbances in mediation occur to those who are covertly seeking to gain something for themselves. This is why the basic attitude of universal compassion is considered the correct basis of meditation.

49. A Chinese Zen master said, "When leaders of Zen communities want to benefit others, first they should conquer themselves, have compassion for others, be humble in mind toward all, and look upon gold and brocade as being like muck and mire."

Another master said, "When fortune produces calamity, it is because when living in ease people indulge in greed and laziness, often becoming arrogant and conceited."

Outward blessings may accrue to people of the Way; but as a proverb says, to indulge in good fortune exhausts good fortune: "Therefore the enlightened person is one who when safe does not forget danger."

50. The problem for the seeker on the Way is not knowing where the Way is going. Thus the need for a guide. Arbitrary preconceptions about what form the teaching and practice will take hinder would-be learners from making a genuine start. Nevertheless, just because the goal is not what may be imagined by the beginner, that does not mean there is no such thing. Zen master Musō also says that the trouble with many people is that they expect to be paid before they have done any work; this is equivalent to expecting the Way to accord with one's own imagination.

51. Study of the Way may involve external travel, but great Zen masters over a thousand years ago emphasized that this is quite different from pseudo-spiritual tourism, which is just another form of sensation seeking.

"In seeking guides and spiritual benefactors, they descend from the heavens and emerge from the earth." This means that guides and spiritual benefactors "descend" from higher consciousness in order to contact people according to their level of understanding, and "emerge" from the most basic ground of experience to contact people who are alienated from it.

Guides teach through fostering particular relationships among

193

people, and between people and the environment. Their guidance is followed through life conduct as well as mental disposition.

"If you listen with your ears . . ." According to a well-known story, when a famous Zen master of old first glimpsed what is known as "the teaching of the inanimate," he said, "If you listen with your ears, you'll never understand; you'll only know when you hear the sound through the eyes."

"In seeing Buddha too one sees both self Buddha and other Buddha, one sees great Buddha and small Buddha." Seeing self Buddha means experiential insight into the essence of mind, seeing other Buddha means seeing all things as the body of Buddha. Seeing self Buddha is when everything is in one's own mind, seeing other Buddha is when one's own mind is in everything. "The donkey looks into the well, the well looks up at the donkey." The small Buddha is the individual, the great Buddha is the totality of Being. Because these are interdependent and in fact part of one another, one should neither be overawed by the great nor slight the small.

52. "Transcendence on mention, independence on seeing through" mean that perceiving the "universal tongue" is a matter of stepping outside the cage of limiting conceptions; as one Zen master says, "leap out of the net and see how vast the ocean is." This is done by seeing through and beyond the barriers maintained by habitual repetition of programmed thoughts and views, to become independent.

There are, however, many who just peep through a chink in the walls, so to speak, or stand by a crack in the door and, dazzled by the infinite light outside, imagine they are free, or illuminated. There are countless warnings about this in Zen lore, reminding interested parties that "it is ever higher, ever harder," and "it encompasses the universe." (The "worlding" was a disciple of Confucius, the "ancient Buddha" was the great classical Zen master.)

According to the Zen view, this is also why the prophet and messiah Jesus said he "had no place to rest his head."

53. Spring is a symbol of life, growth, renewal; the pine is a symbol of perserverance and eternity. Autumn is a symbol of death, destruction, and stripping away; chrysanthemums (which bloom in autumn) are a symbol of life within death. So the spring pines and autumn chrysanthemums stand for nonduality of samsara (birth and death) and nirvana (transcendence), of form/matter and emptiness/reality.

In practical terms, this means being in the world but not of it, like the lotus of traditional metaphor, which grows in the mud yet is unstained by the mud. Dōgen calls this being "precisely so"— nothing is added, nothing is taken away. This represents the Mahā-yāna Buddhist ideal of neither grasping nor rejecting, walking the middle way.

"If one reaches the state of a real teacher, one should be a guide . . ." Having become enlightened oneself, one may be able to enlighten others; if one can enlighten others, one should do so, completing the cycle of the wheel of Dharma.

"If one tries to teach others before reaching this state, one is a great villain." In the case of the kind of life-guidance that Zen Buddhism offers, ancient Zen masters warned people not to attempt to teach without enlightenment. In a ninth-century Chinese booklet of guidelines for Zen schools, written by one of the most eminent masters of that and all times, teaching without enlightenment is listed as the first cause of the degeneration of Zen.

54. Repentance is one of the techniques used by the Tendai school of Buddhism, in which Dōgen received his early training. Repentance ceremonies involve certain postures, gestures, recitations, and thoughts. This practice is used as a means of purifying body and mind.

55–56. The prayer for the pity of the Buddhas is really an attempt to remember the essence of buddhahood in oneself. The fact that delusion is not absolutely real, and can be shed, is itself the mercy of Buddha. Thus this "pity" is gaining an opportunity to realize the true self, losing the opportunity to indulge the false self.

All enlightened people are the same in essence; their differences in individualities are in the realm of expedient means. Similarly, the inspiration for enlightenment may arise through various different circumstances, but its essence is one and the same.

57. Rōya's poem emphasizes the foregoing point further. Buddhas were once ordinary people, ordinary people can be Buddhas: focusing on the common potential is a way to get through the barrier in between.

58. "This is accepting the responsibility of realizing enlightenment." This statement is well worth savoring thoroughly. Accepting this responsibility means acknowledging the reality of our true nature, and also acknowledging the falsehood of falsity.

59. The invisible help of the enlightened ones is what is called "being minded by the Buddhas," which means being mindful of the

buddha-mind in ourselves. The great Buddhist doctor Nāgārjuna wrote that emptiness is compassion: the very fact that delusion has no independent power to bind, that we can turn our attention away from illusion to the nature of mind and be released from false compulsion in emptiness, is the very essence of compassion.

60. The sounds and colors freely release eighty-four thousand verses when we freely accept them. One of Dōgen's own spiritual ancestors asked his Zen teacher, "Why don't I hear the voice of inanimate things teaching?" The teacher replied, "You don't hear it yourself, but you shouldn't hinder that which does hear it." When you do not hinder your own buddha-nature, you realize the generosity of *suchness*.

61. But it is not enough just to *see*. It is also necessary to *be*. It is necessary to live fully as a conscious participant in suchness in order to fulfill the potential we have by virtue of being alive. This is "expediting the total exertion by which the streams and mountains recite the streams and mountains," this is how it is possible to be a mirror of the generosity of suchness, for all who can see to see.

Reference Materials

PROPER NAMES IN
SHŌBŌGENZŌ AND EIHEI KŌROKU
SELECTIONS

Akshobhya: One of the Dhyāni-Buddhas, or Meditation Buddhas, visualized in Tantric practice. The name means "Unshakable."

Ānanda: One of Gautama Buddha's major disciples.

Baso: Mazu, a great Tang dynasty Chinese Zen master, teacher of many outstanding Zen masters, including Baizhang (Hyakujō) and Nanquan (Nansen).

Bodhidharma: An Indian meditation master said to have founded Zen in China around the year 500.

Chōsha: Changsha, a distinguished Tang dynasty Zen master, student of Nansen (Nanquan).

Dōfuku: Daofu, one of the disciples of Bodhidharma.

Dōiku: Daoyu, one of the disciples of Bodhidharma.

Dōrin: Daolin, an outstanding Tang dynasty Zen master; he was popularly called "The Bird's Nest Monk" because he lived up in a tree.

Eka: Huike, the Second Ancestor of Zen, chosen successor to Bodhidharma.

Gyōzan: Yangshan, eminent Tang dynasty Zen master, student of Guishan (Isan); said to be extremely brilliant, Gyōzan was popularly known as "Little Shakyamuni."

Hōshi: Baozhi, a late Tang dynasty Zen master, student of Dongshan (Tōzan).

Isan: Guishan, distinguished Tang dynasty Zen master, student of Baizhang (Hyakujō). Guishan was the author of *Admonitions,* one of the earliest critical works on Zen.

199

Kyōgen: Xiangyan, famous Tang dynasty Zen master, student of Isan (Guishan); noted for his unusual Zen poetry.

Mai "The Foreigner": A well-known Tang dynasty Zen master, student of Isan (Guishan); known as "The Foreigner" because of his bushy beard.

Maitreya: The Buddha of the Future.

Manjushri: A transhistorical personification symbolizing wisdom and knowledge; Manjushri figures in many Buddhist scriptures and Zen stories.

Nangaku: Nanyue, an outstanding Tang dynasty master, heir to the Sixth Ancestor of Zen and teacher of the great Mazu (Baso).

Nansen: Nanquan, an extraordinary Zen master of the Tang dynasty, successor of Mazu (Baso), particularly used as a representation of absolute transcendence.

National Teacher of Great Realization: Huizhong (Echū), one of the most illustrious Zen masters of the Tang dynasty, a direct disciple of the great Sixth Ancestor of Chinese Zen.

Reiun: Lingyun, a Tang dynasty Zen master, successor to Isan (Guishan).

Rinzai: Linji, one of the most famous of the great Zen masters of the late Tang dynasty, after whom the Rinzai sect of Zen is named.

Rōya Eshō: Langya Huizhao, among the very greatest of early Song dynasty Zen masters.

Sekisō: Shishuang, a Tang dynasty Zen master famous for his "dead tree hall" in which mediators sat constantly day and night.

Shakyamuni: "Sage of the Shakya Clan," an epithet of Gautama Buddha; also (in Tendai Buddhism and Dōgen's Zen) a symbol of eternal buddhahood in its manifested aspect.

Sōji: Zongzhi, an enlightened Chinese nun of the sixth century, successor of Bodhidharma.

Sōzan: Caoshan, a brilliant Zen master of the late Tang dynasty, student of Dongshan (Tōzan). The name of the Cao-Dong (Japanese Sōtō) Zen school is said to be derived from the first syllable of the names of Sōzan/Caoshan and Tōzan/Dongshan.

SELECTIONS FROM
CLASSICAL TEXTS

---

from *SCRIPTURE UNLOCKING THE MYSTERIES*

Characteristics of Ultimate Truth

The great enlightening being Dharmodgata said to the Buddha, "In a certain land I once saw a place where there were seventy-seven thousand philosophers and their teachers gathered together in one assembly to consider the characteristics of the ultimate meaning of things. As they thought and assessed and contemplated and searched all over together, they were after all unable to get to the ultimate meaning of all things; just a medley of different interpretations, conflicting interpretations, varying interpretations. They contradicted and argued with one another, then they got out weapons and attacked and wounded each other, finally breaking up and going their separate ways. At that time I thought to myself, 'The appearance of a Buddha in the world is most wonderful; because of the Buddha's appearance in the world it is possible to understand and realize the ultimate truth that is beyond the scope of all thought and deliberation.' "

The Buddha said, "It is so. It is as you say. I have awakened to the ultimate truth which is beyond all thought and reflection; and I explain it to others, revealing and analyzing it, defining and elucidating it. Why?

"The ultimate truth of which I speak is that which is inwardly realized by sages, while the scope of thought and deliberation is that to which unenlightened people testify among themselves. Therefore you should know that ultimate truth transcends all objects of thought and deliberation.

"The ultimate truth of which I speak has no form to which to relate, whereas thought and deliberation operate only in the sphere of forms. Based on this principle you should know that ultimate truth transcends all objects of thought and deliberation.

"The ultimate truth of which I speak cannot be expressed in words, whereas thought and deliberation only operate in the realm of verbalization. Based on this principle you should know that ultimate truth transcends all objects of thought and deliberation.

"The ultimate truth of which I speak has no representation, whereas thought and deliberation only operate in the realm of representation. For this reason you should know that ultimate truth transcends all objects of thought and deliberation.

"The ultimate truth of which I speak puts an end to all controversy, whereas thought and deliberation only operate in the realm of controversy. For this reason you should know that ultimate truth transcends all objects of thought and deliberation.

"Someone who has become accustomed to pungent and bitter flavors as a lifelong habit cannot think of, or assess, or believe in the sweet taste of honey and sugar.

"Someone who in ignorance has an overwhelming interest in desires because of passionate craving, and is therefore inflamed with excitement cannot, as a result, think of, or assess, or believe in the marvelous bliss of detachment and inward effacement of all sense data.

"Someone in ignorance who, because of overwhelming interest in words, clings to rhetoric, therefore cannot think of, or assess, or believe in the pleasure of holy silence with inner tranquillity.

"Someone in ignorance who, because of overwhelming interest in perceptual and cognitive signs, clings to the signs of the world, therefore cannot think of, or assess, or believe in ultimate nirvana that obliterates all signs so that reification ends.

"You should know that just as people in ignorance, because they have various controversies and beliefs involving attachments to self and possessions, cling to mundane contentions and therefore cannot think of, assess, or believe in a utopia where there is no egoism, no possessiveness, no attachment, and no contention, in the same way those who pursue thoughts cannot think of or assess or believe in the character of the ultimate truth that is beyond the sphere of all thought and deliberation."

Characteristics of Phenomena

The Buddha said, "Phenomena have three general natures: first is that to which mere conceptualization adheres; second is dependent origination; third is perfect reality.

"The merely conceptualized nature of phenomena refers to the differences in the intrinsic natures of all things as artificially defined by names to make it possible to talk about them.

"The dependently originated nature of phenomena refers to the fact that the intrinsic nature of all phenomena is conditional production. So when something exists, something else exists; when something is produced, something else is produced. For example, ignorance conditions activities, and so forth, ultimately bringing together a mass of suffering.

"The perfect real nature of phenomena is the true suchness that is equal in all things.

"Enlightening beings can realize this true suchness by diligent effort, right attention, and unperverted thought. Realizing this, gradually cultivating this realization, they will ultimately reach true enlightenment and then witness it fully.

"Furthermore, the conceptualized nature can be known through the association of names and characteristics, the dependent nature can be known through the conceptual clinging superimposed on the dependent nature, and the real nature can be known by not clinging to conceptions superimposed on the dependent nature."

Essencelessness

The Buddha said, "Listen closely and I will explain for you the inner intent of the saying that all things have no essence, have no origin or extinction, are fundamentally quiescent and inherently nirvanic.

"You should know that when I say all things have no essence, I am alluding to their three kinds of essencelessness: essencelessness of characteristics, essencelessness of birth, and ultimate essencelessness.

"What is the essencelessness of characteristics of all things? It is their conceputalized nature. Why? Because the characteristics are defined by artificial names, not by inherent definition. Therefore this is called essencelessness of characteristics.

"What is the essencelessness of birth of things? It is the dependent nature of things. Why? Because they exist dependent on the power of other conditions and do not exist of themselves. Therefore it is called the essencelessness of birth.

"What is the ultimate essencelessness of things? It means that things are said to be essenceless because of the essencelessness of birth. That is, the fact of conditional production is also called ultimate essencelessness. Why? The pure object of attention in things I reveal as ultimate essencelessness. Dependency is not a pure object of attention, so I also call it ultimately essenceless.

"There is also the real nature of things that is called ultimate essencelessness. Why? Because the selflessness of all things is called the ultimate truth and can also be called essencelessness. This is the ultimate truth of all things, and is revealed by essencelessness, so for these reasons it is called ultimate essencelessness.

"You should know that essencelessness of characteristics is like flowers in the sky. Essencelessness of birth is like illusory images, and so is ultimate essencelessness in part. Just as space is revealed only by absence of forms and yet is ever-present, so also is one part of ultimate essencelessness: it is revealed by the selflessness of things, and it is omnipresent.

"It is in reference to these three kinds of essencelessness that I say all things are essenceless.

"Know that it is in allusion to the essencelessness of characteristics that I say all things have no origin or extinction, are fundamentally quiescent and inherently nirvanic.

"Why? If inherent characteristics of things have no existence, they have no origination. If they have no origination, they have no extinction. If they have no origination and no extinction, they are fundamentally quiescent. If they are fundamentally quiescent, they are inherently nirvanic, and there is nothing at all in them that can further cause their ultimate nirvana.

"Therefore I say that all things have no origination or extinction, are fundamentally quiescent and inherently nirvanic, in terms of the essencelessness of characteristics.

"I also allude to ultimate essencelessness revealed by the selflessness of things when I say all things have no origination or extinction and are fundamentally quiescent and inherently nirvanic.

"Why? Because the ultimate essencelessness revealed by the selflessness of things is the eternal and constant real nature of all things, permanent and uncreated, having no relation to any defilements. Because the eternal and constant nature of things is permanent, it is uncreated; because it is uncreated, it has no origination or extinction. Because it is unconnected to any defilements, it is fundamentally quiescent and inherently nirvanic.

"Therefore I say that all things have no origination or extinction, are fundamentally quiescent and inherently nirvanic, in terms of ultimate essencelessness revealed by the selflessness of things.

"Furthermore, I do not define the three kinds of essencelessness because of taking various types of people's particular views of conceptualized nature as essence, or because of taking their particular views of dependent or real natures as essence. I define the three kinds of essencelessness because people add a conceptualized nature on top of the dependent nature and the real nature.

"Based on the characteristics of conceptualized nature, people produce explanations of the dependent and real nature, saying they are such and such, in accord with how people conceptualize them.

"Because the explanations condition their minds, because their awareness conforms to the explanations, because they are lulled by the explanations, they cling to their conceptualizations of the dependent nature and real nature as thus and so.

"Because they cling to their conceptualizations of the dependent and real natures, this condition produces the nature of the dependent state of the future, and due to this condition they may be defiled by afflictions, going through all kinds of psychological states."

Analyzing Application

The enlightening being Maitreya asked the Buddha, "Based on what, abiding in what, do enlightening beings practice *stopping and seeing* in the great vehicle?"

The Buddha replied, "Know that the basis and abode of the practice of *stopping and seeing* in the great vehicle are the provisional setups of the ways of enlightening beings and not giving up the determination for supreme perfect enlightenment."

Maitreya also asked, "The Buddha has said that there are four kinds of domain: one consists of reflections of thought; the second consists of the reflection of nonthought; the third is the totality of all phenomena; the fourth is practical accomplishment. How many of these four domains are focal points of *stopping*, how many are focal points of *seeing*, and how many are focal points of both?"

The Buddha replied, "One is the focal point of *stopping;* that is the reflection of nonthought, without conceptual images. One is a focal point of *seeing:* that is the reflections of thought, with conceptual images. Two are focal points of both *stopping* and *seeing:* the totality of phenomena and accomplishment of tasks."

Maitreya further inquired, "How can enlightening beings seek *stopping and seeing* based on these four domains?"

The Buddha answered, "Enlightening beings listen carefully to the teachings I have devised for them, assimilate them, become familiar with them, reflect on them, and arrive at insight into them. Then in solitude they attentively meditate on these principles for careful reflection. Then they attentively meditate on the inner stream of the meditating consciousness.

"When they practice correctly in this way, they are very calm and stable, giving rise to physical and mental ease. This is called tranquillity, or *stopping.* This is how enlightening beings can attain cessation.

"By attainment of physical and mental ease as a basis, they observe the images on which the concentration within those contemplations focuses intently, and relinquish mental forms; then they are able to correctly discern the knowable meanings of the images of concentration, to discern them to the fullest possible extent, to thoroughly ponder and investigate them, with recognition, appreciation, precise awareness, vision, and contemplation. This is called observation, or *seeing.* This is how enlightening beings can perfect their insight."

from *UNIVERSAL STOPPING AND SEEING*

[meditation on the realm of reality]

As for the stopping and seeing of the mind: sitting straight, correctly mindful, one clears away wrong consciousness and abandons errant thoughts. Don't think at random or grab on to appearances; just focus solely on the realm of reality.

With one thought on the realm of reality, focusing is stopping, and one thought is seeing. When you believe all phenomena are the teaching of Buddha, there is no before or after, no more boundaries. There is no knower, no speaker.

If there is no knowing or speaking, it is not existent or nonexistent. One is neither knower nor nonknower: apart from these extremes, one abides where there is nothing on which to dwell, just as the Buddhas abide, resting in the silent realm of reality. Don't be afraid of this profound teaching.

This realm of reality is also called enlightenment, and it is also called the inconceivable realm. It is also called wisdom and it is also called not being born and not passing away. Thus all phenomena are not other than the realm of reality; hearing of this nonduality and nondifference, do not give rise to doubt.

If one can see in this way, this is seeing the qualities of Buddha. When seeing Buddha, one does not consider Buddha as Buddha; there is no Buddha to be Buddha, and there is no Buddha-knowledge to know Buddha. Buddha and Buddha-knowledge are nondualistic, unmoving, unfabricated, not in any location yet not unlocated, not in time yet not timeless, not dual yet not nondual, not defiled, not pure. This seeing of Buddha is very rarefied; like space, it has no flaws, and it develops right mindfulness.

Seeing the embellishments of Buddha is like looking into a mirror and seeing one's own features. First one sees one Buddha, then the Buddhas of the ten directions. One does not use magical powers to go see Buddhas; one stays right here and sees the Buddhas, hears the Buddhas teaching, and gets the true meaning.

One sees Buddha for all beings, yet does not grasp the form of Buddha. One guides all beings toward nirvana, yet does not grasp the characteristics of nirvana. One produces great adornments for all beings, yet does not grasp the forms of adornment.

No form, no sign, no seeing, no hearing, no cognition; Buddha does not witness. This is considered wonderful, because Buddha is identical to the realm of reality—for the realm of reality to witness the realm of reality would be a contradiction. There is no witness, no attainment.

One sees the appearances of beings as like the appearances of Buddhas, the extent of the realm of beings as like the extent of the realm of Buddhas. The extent of the realm of Buddhas is inconceivable, and the extent of the realm of sentient beings is also inconceivable. The abode of the realm of sentient beings is the abode of space.

By the principle of nondwelling, by the principle of signlessness, abiding in transcedent wisdom, one does not see anything profane, so what is there to abandon? One does not see anything holy, so what is there to grasp? Thus it is also of samsara and nirvana, defilement and purity—not rejecting, not grasping, one just abides in reality.

In this way one sees living beings as the true reality realm of Buddha. One sees desire, anger, folly, and other afflictions as forever being the practice of tranquillity. This is immutable practice, neither samsaric nor nirvanic, practicing the Way of Buddha without abandoning views, and without abandoning the uncreated.

It is not practicing the Way, yet not not practicing the Way. This is called correct abiding in the reality realm of afflictions.

[contemplating evil]

We know that evil does not obstruct the Way. And the Way does not prevent evil either: one disciple of Buddha had ever mounting lust, another was still arrogant, yet another became angry; yet what loss or gain was there in their noncontamination? Just as in space light and darkness do not remove each other, the enlightenment of Buddhas is revealed. That is the sense of this.

If people are by nature very greedy and very impure, and though they try to quell and subdue this, it becomes more acute, they should just let their inclinations be. Why? If veils do not arise, they cannot practice contemplative seeing.

It is like when you go fishing with hook and line. If the fish is strong but the line is weak, you cannot fight with the fish to pull it in; you just let it take the bait and let it run with it as far as it will, diving or surfacing. Before long you can take it in.

The same goes for practicing contemplative observation of mental veils. The veils are the bad fish, the observation is the hook and bait. If there is no fish, there is no use for the hook and bait. So as long as there are fish, be they many or large, that is all right—just follow them with hook and bait, never giving up, and before long the veils can be overcome.

[a model procedure for arriving at the emptiness of mental veils]

What is seeing? When desire is about to arise, observe desire carefully, in terms of four aspects: before desiring, incipient desire, desiring, and after desiring.

Is it that incipient desire arises when the state before desire passes away?

Is it that incipient desire arises without the state before desire passing away?

Is it that incipient desire arises when the state before desire has both passed away and not passed away?

Or is it that incipient desire arises when the state before desire has neither passed away nor not passed away?

If the incipient state arises when the prior state has passed away, are that passing away and arising identical or separate? If it is supposed they are identical, yet arising and passing away are opposites. But if the arising is separate, that arising has no cause.

If the incipient state arises without the state prior to desire passing away, are they identical or separate? If identical, the arisings of the two states happen together, and there would thus be no end. If separate, again the arising has no cause.

If the incipient state arises with the prior state having both passed away and not passed away, if it arises from the passing away there is no need for the not passing away; if it arises from the not passing away, there is no need for the passing away—how can an indefinite cause produce a definite result? If their actuality is one, yet their natures are mutually contradictory; but if their actualities are different, they do not interrelate.

If incipient desire arises when the state before desire has neither passed away nor not passed away, are the objects of double denial existent or nonexistent? If existent, how can it be called denial? If not, how can nothing produce anything?

In this way, with the tetralemma, you do not see incipient desire arising; turning the tetralemma around, you do not see the state before desire passing away. The arising of the incipient state, the nonarising, both arising and not arising, neither arising nor not arising, are also as explained above.

Seeing the veil of desire as ultimately empty, while simultaneously being aware of both its emptiness and conditional existence, is as explained above. This is called the hook and bait. As long as veils continue to rise, this seeing continues to illuminate; you neither see arising nor see illumination, yet illumine whenever there is arising.

Also contemplate what sense field this veil arises from: is it from form, or from other fields? What action does it arise from—is it from walking, or from other actions? If it is based on form, is it before seeing, about to see, seeing, or after seeing? If it is based on walking, is it before doing it, about to do it, doing it, or after doing it? For what does it arise—for breaking precepts, for getting followers, for deception, for jealousy, for humanity and deference, for good meditation, for nirvana, for the qualities of the spiritual body, for the perfection of transcedent ways, for liberative concentrations, for the innumerable aspects of Buddhahood?

When you see in this way, there is no receiver of data, and no objectifier—yet the reception of sense data and the focusing of sense faculties on objects are both illumined clearly. Phantasms, emptiness, and the nature of reality do not obstruct each other.

Why? If the veils obstructed the nature of reality, the nature of reality would break down; if the nature of reality obstructed veils, the veils would not arise. So we know the veils are none other than the nature of reality; when the veils arise, the nature of reality arises, and when the veils cease, the nature of reality ceases.

The *Scripture on Absence of Conformations* says, "Desire is the Path, and so are anger and folly. All Buddhist teachings are in these three things. If people seek enlightenment apart from desire, they are as far from it as sky from earth. Desire is none other than enlightenment."

The *Pure Name Scripture* says, "One realizes the path of Buddhas while traveling on false paths. All beings are the appearance of enlightenment, and it cannot be further attained; all beings are the appearance of nirvana, and it cannot be further extinguished. For the conceited, detachment from lust, anger, and folly is called liberation; for those without conceit, it is said that the essence of lust, anger, and folly is itself liberation." All passions are seeds of buddhahood; the mountains and seas, form and flavor, are none other. This is the inconceivable principle of *seeing* evils.

Constantly cultivating wisdom by *seeing,* uniting with the noumenon of the veils like form and shadow, is called the stage of contemplative practice. Being able to not deviate from true contemplation in the midst of all bad things and worldly occupations is the stage of conformity. Advancing into the realm of the bronze wheel [partial realization], breaking the root of the veils (the root is ignorance, and when the root is broken down the branches snap), and revealing the buddha nature is the stage of partial realization of reality. Finally, when Buddhas exhaust the source of the veils, that is called the ultimate stage.

Next observe the veil of anger. If people have a lot of anger, depression and excitement successively arise all the time. When they try to stop it, they cannot do so, and when they try to suppress it they cannot do that either. They should let it arise as it will and view it by *stopping and seeing.* Observe the four aspects: where does anger come from? If you cannot grasp its origin, you cannot grasp its passing away either. Who is angry? Who is the object of anger? When you *see* in this way, you cannot grasp anger; its traces of coming and going, and its appearances, are empty and quiescent. Seeing all states of being in anger and the qualities of enlightenment in anger are as explained above. This is realizing the path of Buddhas while on the wrong path of anger.

Seeing the veils of misconduct, laziness, distraction, error, and folly, as well as all other bad things, is done in the same way.

from *MUSINGS ON THE FLOWER ORNAMENT COSMOS*

[on flower ornament absorption]

The flowers stand for the myriad practices of enlightening beings. This is because flowers have the function of producing fruits, and practices have the capacity to effect results: although they are different in terms of inside and outside, nevertheless there is a resemblance in the powers of production and effect.

The ornament stands for the mutual accord of the completion of the practices and the fulfillment of their effects. Obstructions caused by defilements permanently dissolved, realization of noumenon is complete and pure.

Absorption means that noumenon and knowledge are indivisibly merged, with "that" and "this" both disappeared, subject and object obliterated. This is why it is called absorption.

Also, it is possible to regard the flowers as identical to the ornament, because there is no barrier between noumenon and knowledge. The flower ornament is itself absorption, because practice merges with detachment from conceptions.

It is also possible to regard the flowers as identical to the ornament because all practices are carried out at once through the medium of one practice. The flower ornament is itself absorption, because one practice is multifold, without interfering with either its unity or its multiplicity.

It is also possible to regard the flower ornament as itself absorption because concentration and distraction merge. It is also possible to regard absorption as itself the flower ornament, because noumenon and knowledge are suchness as is.

THE FIVE RANKS OF ZEN

explained by Zen Master Caoshan (Sōzan)

Coming within the Absolute

The whole being is revealed alone, the root source of myriad phenomena, without blame or praise.

Arriving within the Relative

Going along with things without being inhibited, like an empty boat, getting through by openness, independent and free.

The Relative within the Absolute

A fragment of space pervading everywhere, senses and objects silent.

The Absolute within the Relative

The moon reflected in the water, or an image reflected in a mirror, basically has no origin or extinction; how could there be any traces?

Arrival within Both at Once

The absolute is not necessarily empty, the relative is not necessarily substantial; there is neither rejection nor inclination.

SAYINGS OF BAIZHANG

It is said, "Reality has no comparison, because there is nothing to which it may be likened; the body of reality is not constructed and does not fall within the scope of any classification."

This is why it is said, "The substance of the sage is nameless and unspoken; it is impossible to linger in the empty door of truth as it really is."

Just as insects can alight anywhere but in the flames of a fire, in the same way conditioned minds can form relations to anything except transcendent wisdom.

The teaching that the present mirroring awareness is your own Buddha is the elementary stage of good. Not to keep dwelling in the immediate mirroring awareness is the intermediate stage of good. Furthermore, not to make an understanding of nondwelling is the final stage of good.

It is like the water of the ocean: without wind there are waves all around. Suddenly knowing of the waves all around is the gross within the subtle; letting go of knowledge in the midst of knowing is like the subtle within the subtle.

This is the sphere of the enlightened ones, whence you really come to know. This is called the pinnacle of meditation, the monarch of meditation. It is also called knowledge of what is knowable: it produces all the various meditational states and anoints the heads of all heirs to complete enlightenment.

In all fields of form, sound, fragrance, flavor, feeling, and phenomena, you realize complete perfect enlightenment. Inside and outside are in complete communion, without any obstruction whatsoever.

One form, one atom, is one Buddha; one form is all Buddhas; all forms, all atoms, are all Buddhas. All forms, sounds, smells, feelings, and phenomena are also like this, each filling all fields. This is the coarse within the fine; this is a good state.

This is the knowledge, discernment, seeing, and hearing of all those in progress; this is all those in progress going out in life and entering death, crossing over everything existent, nonexistent, or whatever. This is that of which those in progress speak; this is the nirvana of those in progress. This is the unexcelled Way, this is the spell that is peer to the peerless.

This is the foremost teaching, considered the most exceedingly profound of all teachings. No human being can reach it, but all the enlightened keep it in mind, like pure waves able to speak of the purity and pollution of all waters, their deep flow and expansive function. All enlightened ones keep this in mind: if you can be like this all the time, whatever you are doing, then the body of pure clear light will be revealed to you.

You are inherently equal, your words are equal, and I am also the same: a buddha-field of sound, a buddha-field of smell, a buddha-field of taste, a buddha-field of feeling, a buddha-field of phenomena—all are *thus*. From here all the way throughout the universe, in every direction, all is *thus*. If you hold on to elementary knowledge as your understanding, this is called bondage at the pinnacle, or falling into bondage at the pinnacle. This is the basis of all mundane troubles; giving rise to subjective knowledge and opinion, you bind yourself without rope.

The discipline of doing is to cut off the things of the world. Just do not do anything yourself, and there is no fault; this is called the discipline of nondoing. It is also called unmanifested discipline, and it is also called the discipline of nonindulgence. As long as there is arousal of mind and movement of thoughts, this is all called breaking discipline.

For now, just do not be confused or disturbed by anything at all, existent or nonexistent. Then do not stop and abide in disillusion; and yet have no understanding of nonabiding. This is called all-embracing study.

All the verbal teachings are just to cure illnesses. Because the illnesses are not the same, the remedies are also not the same. That is why it is sometimes said that there is Buddha, sometimes that there is no Buddha.

True words are those that cure illness. If the cure works, the words are true; if they don't cure the illness, the words are false.

True words are false if they give rise to opinionated views. False words are true if they cut off delusions. Because illnesses are unreal, there are only unreal remedies for them.

Cultivating ordinary causes while in the sanctified state, Buddhas enter the company of ordinary people, becoming like them in kind to lead, teach, and guide them. In the company of greedy people, their limbs afire, Buddhas expound transcendent wisdom to them, inspiring them with the will for enlightenment.

If Buddhas only stayed in the sanctified state, how could they go talk to ordinary people? Buddhas enter into various classes to make a way out for people; like the people, Buddhas feel pain, toil, and stress. When Buddhas enter painful places, they too feel pain, just like ordinary people do; Buddhas are different from ordinary people only in that they are free to go or to stay.

Most importantly, it is necessary to have two eyes, to shine through the affairs of both sides [relative and absolute]. Do not just wear one eye and go on one side, for then you will still have to attain the other side.

TEACHINGS OF MASTERS OF THE DONGSHAN ZEN SUCCESSION

First Generation
DONGSHAN: I don't ask about the realm of Buddha or the realm of the Way: who is it that speaks of the realm of Buddha and the Way?

Second Generation
YUNJU: A general asked Yunju, "When will the world be at peace?" Yunju replied, "When the generals' hearts are satisfied."

CAOSHAN: Someone asked Caoshan, "What is the great meaning of Buddhism?" Caoshan replied, "It is everywhere."

DAOQUAN: Someone asked, "If the Buddha was inherently enlightened, why did he still practice austerities for six years?"
Daoquan replied, "A phantom presenting an illusion."

LANGYA: Just think of the trees: they let the birds perch and fly, with no intention to call them when they come and no longing for their return when they fly away. If people's hearts can be like the trees, they will not be off the Way.

XIUJING: Heaven sends rain and dew without choosing between the thriving and the withering.

PUMAN: Someone asked, "What is your Way?"
Puman said, "What is right now?

DAOYUN: Someone asked, "Where are you going to go after you die?"
Daoyun said, "It's all settled."

SHIJIAN: Someone asked, "The treasury of the eye of truth has been witnessed alike by all the enlightened: to whom will you transmit it?"
Shijian replied, "Spiritual sprouts grow where there is ground; great enlightenment doesn't maintain a teacher."

DUNRU: Someone asked, "I heard of you from afar: now that I'm here, why don't I see you?"
Dunru said, "It's your not seeing; what's it got to do with me?"

XIANGQI: Someone asked, "What is original nothing?"
Xiangqi answered, "The stone is lustrous but has no gem inside; the ore is different, but from it comes gold."

BAOGAI: Someone asked, "Is there any target?"
Baogai said, "I don't set up a standard rule."

BEIYUAN: Someone asked, "What is no mind?"
Beiyuan replied, "Not being tied up."

BENREN: You people want instructions, but to whom would you have me entrust them?

GUANGREN: My path is beyond the sky.

WENSUI: Someone asked, "It is said, 'All Buddhas' teachings come from *this* scripture.' What is *this* scripture?"

Wensui answered, "It is always being recited."

TONGXUAN: Someone asked, "Can one's own mind and the mind of another see each other?"

Tongxuan replied, "If you can't even see yourself, how can you see others?"

Third Generation

DAOYAN: Someone requested, "Please intimate the real mind."

Daoyan said, "Why do you pretend there's no one here?"

XUANMING: If I mention anything, people will criticize: but if I don't, they'll ridicule. Between the two, what should I do?

CHUZHEN: One single still light shines bright: if you intentionally pursue it, after all it's hard to see. Suddenly encountering it, people's hearts are opened up, and the great matter is clear and done. This is really living, without any fetters—no amount of money could replace it. Even if a thousand sages should come, they would all appear in its shadow.

FAYI: Someone asked, "Wherein lies your power?"

Fayi replied, "In being as though blind and deaf."

ZHIQU: When you're deluded, every statement is an ulcer; when you're enlightened, every word is wisdom.

GUANGFAN: Someone asked, "What am I?"

Guangfan answered, "There is nothing in the whole universe that is not you."

GUANGLI: Someone asked, "How is it when a thousand roads end and neither speech nor thought can get through?"

Guangli replied, "You're still at the bottom of the stairs."

SHUIYAN: Someone asked, "How is the sword of wisdom before it is whetted?"

Shuiyan said, "Can't be used."

The questioner continued, "How is it after it is whetted?"

Shuiyan said, "Can't be touched."

TONGAN PI: Someone asked, "How is it when one mistakes one's reflection for one's head?"

Tongan replied, "To whom are you speaking?"

The questioner now asked, "What should I do?"

Tongan said, "If you seek from another, you go further afield."

The questioner said, "How is it when one doesn't seek from another?"

Tongan responded, "Where is your head?"

HUAIYUE: Someone asked, "What is the medicine such that one pill will cure myriad ills?"

Huaiyue said, "What's your trouble?"

BENKONG: Even myself is my enemy; how could I take anything from others?

YONGGUANG: You should let go over a cliff, give in and accept it, then revive after annihilation.

DANJIAN: Someone asked, "How is it when one makes an offering of one's whole being?"

Danjian said, "What have you brought?"

NANTAI: Someone asked, "What did the succession of Zen masters transmit?"

Nantai said, "If you hadn't asked, I wouldn't know either."

DAOJIAN: Someone asked, "What is your way?"

Daojian answered, "To be free wherever I am."

FENGHUA: Someone asked, "How is it when one has no gain or loss?"

Fenghua replied, "What are you saying?"

GUANGJI: Someone asked, "What is talk beyond convention?"

Guangji answered, "What do you say?"

ZHUXI: Looking at a newly completed buddha shrine, Zhuxi said, "What Buddha will be put in here?"

HUIHAI: Someone asked, "What is the meaning of Zen?"

Huihai said, "The world levels off."

RESHAN: Someone asked, "It is said, 'When you meet Zen masters on the road, don't face them with speech or silence'—how can one face them?"

Reshan said, "Just *thus.*"

GUIREN: Someone asked, "Can lay people understand Buddhism?"

Guiren answered, "On which terrace is there no moonlight? At whose house do the trees not bloom?"

SUSHAN ZHENG: Someone asked, "What is study of phenomena?"

Sushan replied, "Dressing and eating."

HUANGBO HUI: Space doesn't need to be worked with a gold hammer; when have the sun and moon ever waited to shine on people?

FENGLIN: Someone asked, "Do you like money and sex?"

Fenglin answered, "Yes."

The questioner continued, "If you're a spiritual teacher, why do you like money and sex?"

Fenglin said, "Few people are grateful."

DA-AN SHENG: I don't push someone who's standing at the edge of a pit.

ZHENGQIN: Someone asked, "How does one arrive at the road of right effort?"

Zhengqin said, "Where are you coming from?"

XIANGYUN: Someone asked, "What is your way?"

Xiangyun replied, "Without form, not dwelling in ordinary or holy states, traversing the bird's path, without tracks."

GUANGYAN: It's the same moon in a thousand rivers; myriad families all meet the spring.

BAQIAO: Someone asked, "What are people of the Path like?"

Baqiao answered, "They stop mentioning news of the clouds; the sun shines at midnight."

HUIQU: Someone asked, "What is a sanctuary?"

Huiqu said, "Just *this*."

The questioner went on, "What is a person in the sanctuary?"

Huiqu said, "What? What?"

ZHIHUI: Someone asked, "What is 'pursuing perceptions and losing the source'?"

Zhihui replied, "The house is robbed."

YAOZHANG: Superficial literalists don't look into themselves and realize their mistakes. They just want to pick flowers in the sky and scoop the moon from the water.

RUGUAN: Someone asked, "What is your way?"

Ruguan answered, "Picking up fresh vegetables with a bottomless basket."

GUANGHUA: Someone asked, "What is the realm of true seeing?"

Guanghua said, "Nothing at all interposed.

SHENZHE: What is your original name?

DINGJIAO: Someone asked, "How is it when the road of knowing is ended and thought is forgotten?"

Dingjiao replied, "While imprisoned one may increase in wisdom; while nursing sickness one may perish."

Fourth Generation

HUIZHONG: Though one's appearance may change, the Way is always there; though one mix with the ordinary world, the source of mind isn't obscured. Just shed emotional views and the Way is clear of itself. Just clearly see your own mind and emotional views will be broken through.

TONGAN ZHI: Someone asked, "What is the transcendental?"

Tongan answered, "It is transcendent, unchanging; if you point to a target you are turning away from it."

YANGSHAN: When it's cold I sit by the fire, when it's hot I walk by the stream.

DAOJIAN: Someone asked, "What is a person on the Way like?"

Daojian replied, "Without other thoughts."

ZHONGCAN: Someone asked, "Isn't *this* the meaning of the appearance of reality?"

Zhongcan said, "What is *this*?"

LONGQUAN: Someone asked, "What is the meaning of Zen?"

Longquan answered, "None of your business."

YANHUA: Someone asked, "How is it when one doesn't keep one's mind on the world?"

Yanhua said, "Everything gained in war is ruined by singing and dancing."

YUANZHAO: Someone asked, "What is your way?"

Yuanzhao said, "I don't stick a sign on my forehead."

YUANMING: Someone asked, "What is the source of all things?"

Yuanming said, "Even space cannot contain it; how can I comprehend it?"

WUFENG SHAO: If you haven't the flexibility and perceptivity to see meaning according to the circumstances, you're far away from truth.

GUANGDE YI: Someone asked, "What is the ocean of great tranquillity?"

Guangde replied, "Galloping on a horse down a busy street without bumping into anyone."

HUICHE: How do you sing the song of peace? And can anyone harmonize?

DALANG: Only when you go along with the stream do you find the wonder; if you stay on the shore you wind up deluded.

Fifth Generation

YUANGUAN: Someone asked, "What is my self?"

Yuanguan answered, "In the heartland, the emperor; beyond the borders, the general."

CHANGJIAO: Just see to it that the door of wisdom is not blocked; then how could virtue stagnate?

QINIAN: Myriad streams cannot mix up the source of the Great Way.

HUAIGAN: Someone asked, "What is the saying of the sages for the benefit of humanity?"

Huaigan replied, "The crimson orb reaches all houses, the light originally has no mind."

SHOUCHEN: Someone asked, "How is it when delusion and enlightenment do not enter into objects?"

Shouchen said, "Where do objects come from?"

Sixth Generation

JINGXUAN: You should understand the nonorigination of the ordinary, the impersonality of the mysterious, and the inexhaustibility of complete understanding.

LIYU: The mountains, rivers, earth, sun, moon, stars, and planets are born together with you; the Buddhas of past, present, and future study together with you; the sacred teachings are simultaneous with you.

YONGDING JIAN: Someone asked, "What can be done about right now?"

Yongding said, "You're still complaining of lack."

QINGJU SHENG: Someone asked, "Whose successor are you?"

Qingju replied, "I appreciate your coming here to rebuke me."

NANCHAN CONG: Someone asked, "What is the meaning of Zen?"

Nanchan answered, "Rain deep in the forest in winter, wind on the plains in spring."

Seventh Generation

TOUZI YIQING: When you don't fall into vacant stillness, the way back is the more marvelous.

QINGFOU: The living meaning of Zen is beyond all notions. To realize it in a phrase is completely contrary to the subtle essence; we cannot avoid using words as expedients, though, but this has limitations. Needless to say, of course, random talk is useless. Nonetheless, the matter is not one-sided, so we temporarily set forth a path in the way of teaching, to deal with people.

XIANRU: The mind of sages is ungraspable; how could their meditation be named?

GUIXI: Someone asked, "What is the door of silence?"

Guixi answered, "Don't make noise."

DAYANG HUI: Someone asked, "What is your way?"

Dayang said, "I patch my simple garment of coarse cloth over and over; I go out and hoe in the fields every day."

BAOYIN: Last night the clouds and rain dispersed in the eternal sky; the moon is in myriad forms. In the myriad forms and spiritual light there is no inside or outside; how can one convey an expression approximating illumination?

JICONG: Someone asked, "What is the main meaning of Buddhism?"

Jicong replied, "This question is not useless."

SHANXI: Someone asked, "How is it when one gets rid of the dust to see Buddha?"

Shanxi said, "Don't hallucinate."

Eighth Generation

DAOKAI: I don't ask you about before the last day; what about the matter of the last day? When you get here, the Buddha can't do anything for you, the Dharma can't do anything for you, the founding teachers can't do anything for you, the Zen masters all over the world can't do anything for you, I can't do anything for you, and the king of the underworld can't do anything for you.

You simply must use the present to the full. If you use the present to the full, then even the Buddha can't do anything to you, the Dharma can't do anything to you, the founding teachers can't do anything to you, the Zen masters all over the world can't do anything to you, I can't do anything to you, and the king of the underworld can't do anything to you.

But tell me, what is the principle of using the present to the full? Do you understand?

Next year there will be yet another new condition, disturbing the spring wind with never an end.

DONGSHAN YUN: The autumn breeze enwraps the earth, the night rain whirls in the sky: herein there is a special clear coolness, there is no burning affliction. Whose livelihood is this?

Those who arrive here will then know that as soon as you fall into seeing and hearing you are resting halfway along.

But how is it after reaching home?

Going alone, come what may, without any companions; not dwelling in the absolute state, and not dwelling in the relative.

YINGWEN: Clear in everything, clear, the meaning of Zen: but if you immediately take it at that, you are mistaking the bow for the arrow. Those who are alert bump into it everywhere; those who are befuddled slog in the mire.

Ninth Generation

ZIQUN: The jewel-like moon streams with light, the clear pond sets forth the reflection: the water has no intention of reflecting the moon, and the moon has no intention of distributing its light. Once water and moon are both forgotten, only then can it be called cessation.

That is why it is said that even ascent to heaven should be blown away, and even completion should be removed; one should not turn one's head at the sound of gold tossed on the ground. If you can be like this, only then can you act among different kinds.

FACHENG: When you return to the original essence, there is no duality; but as far as method is concerned, there are many approaches. If you just get back to the original essence, why worry about expedient methods?

WEIZHAO: Ordinary people and sages are fundamentally one; it is because of habits that they differ.

YUANYI: How do you explain the principle of emptiness of mind?

Is it not "seeing without seeing, hearing without hearing?"

Wrong!

Is it not "ceasing thought so that all things vanish, merging subject and object to enter the mysterious source, effacing nature and characteristics to return to the realm of reality"?

Wrong!

"This way" won't do, "not this way" won't do, "this way and not this way" won't do at all. So after all how do you understand?

JILIAN: All Buddhas and Zen masters alike return to the principle of pure emptiness. Ultimately there is no body; sages and ordinary people are one substance.

The principle is like this; how about the myriad forms filling the eyes?

Tenth Generation

QINGLIAO: Even if upon hearing you immediately return, how can that compare to never having left?

HONGZHI: Walking in the void, one forgets objects; penetration illumination goes beyond images. One point of spiritual energy shines clearly, unobscured. The consciousness of past, present, and future dies out, and focus on physical elements ends. An empty, clear, subtle brightness shines alone through eternity. If you can practice like this, you will not be bound by life and death.

QINGYU: If you take a step forward, you step on the water plants of the king of another country; if you take a step back you tread on another's ancestral field. If you neither advance nor retreat you are right in stagnant water. Is there any way out?

PUYUE: Even if you realize the "other side," you haven't yet escaped dualism; even if you practice on "this side," you will still not yet attain full completeness.

DAOHUI: When you willingly undertake the business of the empty eon, it is fully apparent in your daily affairs, without any leak. This is just the time to return home and sit in peace; let the snow cover the green mountain. Not keeping a single letter on the mind, who minds the waves churning on the surface of the water? Now tell me, how do you express "not setting up mystery in the absolute, not sticking to things in the relative"?

QINGYUAN JI: Preaching is not as close as *this*. The galaxies of the ten directions are one minute particle.

FACONG: A cold lamp needn't be fetched in a dark room; the bright moon in the sky pierces the cloudy night. If you want to know continuity in daily affairs, "unusual sprouts emerge in the light of fierce flames."

Eleventh Generation

HUIWU: The whole world is a door of liberation, but people are unwilling to enter it.

FATONG: Why can't you open your mouth when you have swallowed past, present, and future? Why can't you open your eyes when you see through the world?

ZIDE: When you shed your skin, there are no sides or corners; when you clearly understand body and mind, there's not a single thing.

FAGONG: Return home without taking a step, and the oozing of habits will dry up at once.

FAZHEN: Although there is a method of hiding the body in the dust, how can that compare to entering the imperial precincts with the whole body?

SICHE: The Way has no North or South, no East or West.

FAWEI: The pure spiritual body has no characteristics; it cannot be sought through sound. The marvelous path has no words; it cannot be understood through writings. Even if you transcend Buddhas and Zen masters, you still fall into gradation. Even if you speak of the marvelous and mysterious, after all it sticks to your teeth.

You should be unaffected by training, not leaving a trace of form, a withered tree on a frigid cliff, without any moisture left, a phantom, a wooden horse, all emotional consciousness empty: only then can you enter the marketplace with open hands, operating freely in the midst of all different kinds of people and situations. Have you not read the saying, "Not staying in the land of noncontamination, come back instead to the misty bank, lie on the cold sand"?

CHANGLU LIN: The school is apart from conscious thought and perception; the message transcends past, future, and present.

Being apart from conscious thought and perception, in classifying myriad species no difference is seen; transcending time, throughout the ten directions there's no more contamination.

Immediately not transgressing, ultimately not depending, awakening is before the appearance of signs, its function is where training doesn't reach.

In daily life one shouldn't hesitate; in the interval of hesitation one loses control.

LIWU: All sounds are the voice of Buddha: the sound of raindrops dripping from the eaves is cool. All forms are the form of Buddha: presented face to face, one cannot turn away.

Being this way, how is it made clear?

Beyond the clouds in the blue sky the moonlight is clear.

Twelfth Generation

DAOQIN: With what do I entertain guests? In a bottomless basket I heap bright moonlight, in the bowl of nonminding I store the clear breeze.

Thirteenth Generation

RUJING: If you get near my fireplace, you'll burn to death; if you withdraw, you'll freeze to death.

[Rujing was the Zen teacher under whose tutelage Dōgen realized great enlightenment.]